One Bake Two Ways

Pavilion
An imprint of HarperCollins*Publishers* Ltd
1 London Bridge Street
London SE1 9GF

www.harpercollins.co.uk

HarperCollins*Publishers*
Macken House
39/40 Mayor Street Upper
Dublin 1
D01 C9W8
Ireland

10 9 8 7 6 5 4 3 2 1

First published in Great Britain by Pavilion
An imprint of HarperCollinsPublishers 2024

ISBN 978-0-00-860382-3

Publishing Director: Stephanie Milner
Commissioning Editor: Lucy Smith
Editor: Ellen Simmons
Copyeditor: Kate Reeves-Brown
Proofreader: Vicky Orchard
Indexer: Ruth Ellis
Senior Designer: Alice Kennedy-Owen
Creative Direction and Design: Bell Blood Studio
Artworking: maru studio G.K.
Photography: Matt Russell
Prop Styling: Rachel Vere
Food Styling: Joss Herd, El Kemp
Production Controller: Grace O'Byrne

Printed in Malaysia by Papercraft

WHEN USING KITCHEN APPLIANCES PLEASE ALWAYS
FOLLOW THE MANUFACTURER'S INSTRUCTIONS

COOK'S NOTE:
Recipe key throughout refers to:
EF = egg free
GF = gluten free

Fifty bakes with
an all-plant option
every time

One
Bake
Two
Ways

Ruby Bhogal

PAVILION

The
Concept

If I bake for you, just know you ain't special, as I do it, quite *literally*, at the drop of a hat.

But DO KNOW that we're about to *demolish* a slice, share a few knowing, *goofy-smiled glances* and be bonded by warm, fuzzy feelings *of happiness* that cake will always bring. Now that, for me, *is* special.

I'm Rubes and I was a finalist on *The Great British Bake Off* in 2018. I can just hear you thinking right now, 'How the bleeding heck did that happen?!' Trust me, I asked myself this every single week I stayed in the competition. There's no doubt about it, I truly was the cat with nine lives, so THANK GOD the show lasted only ten weeks.

I found baking during a time where I hadn't expected life to take me. A time of unemployment. Which, sure, doesn't sound totally horrendous, but after studying for what seemed like an eternity getting my master's degree in architecture – I thought I'd land a job immediately after. That's why we were all sold that big uni dream, wasn't it? I studied hard, worked hard, moved back from Liverpool to London after ten years and just thought I would land on my feet. Sounds naive, but that's how 27-year-old Rubes was.

Turns out, that series of events I had pre-planned in my head didn't quite go to schedule and it took ten months of living at my parents' house, staying in my pajamas until midday, applying for every job under the sun, and watching far too many episodes of *Bargain Hunt*, for my life to regain some order. One day, in amongst redrafting my CV for the millionth time, I found a baking book gathering dust on my parents' shelves, written by none other than the steely blue-eyed Paul Hollywood. Lord knows why that book was even there. Baking was never a thing when I was growing up – sure Mum would make a few fairy cakes here and there, but let me tell you, I have seen pancakes with more rise than those bad boys. I would look for recipes that would take hours to make, just so whenever anyone asked me what I was doing with my day, I FINALLY had a productive answer. Now my days were filled with sourdough starters and carby, buttery delights. During a dark period of time, I found baking. I found happiness: for my soul, for those around me. *I found me.*

Two words: Vegan Week. Let's take a little trip down memory lane to week seven on *Bake Off*, which was the very first vegan week they have ever had on the show. Sure, doesn't sound like a big deal, but plant-based food has come on a LONG WAY since 2018. Now we are spoilt for choice when it comes to like-for-like substitutes, but back then it was xanthan gum what? Agar agar who? Aquafaba, huh?

I've grown up in an Indian household, where we really only ate meat on a Saturday. Eating a mostly vegetarian diet is so easy when you're growing up with Indian food. Spices can transform any basic vegetable and before you know it, garam masala has given an aubergine the glow up of its life. The one thing that Indian food doesn't do too well is desserts. It's all about sugar and it's all about overload. What I am trying to say is, I had to learn all about plant-based baking literally days before we filmed vegan week. Mad googling, crazy amounts of skim-reading, and all I had really nailed was understanding that if you whisk the hell out of chickpea water, you can make meringue – *MIND BLOWN*.

The long and short of it was this: my vegan week showstopper cake, which I toiled over for four hours, toppled over right as I walked out of the tent as the challenge finished. I mean the audacity of that cake – to wait for everyone to leave the tent and steal the limelight – is quite outrageous really. The slow-mo fall of that cake still haunts me. Millions of people watched it. A sh*t ton of people tweeted about it. It got made into a GIF and I still get tagged in it often. The most common meme to go alongside it is: 'How my week is going'. And honestly, I can't be mad about it.

Since my almighty baking collapse, I thought vegan baking would never be my thing, but over time, I've gradually veered back towards the diet I grew up with. A conscious and unconscious choice. I've started to pay more attention to understanding the impact of our food choices on not just the planet, but on ourselves, too. I am not someone who identifies as plant-based. Nor do I identify as a meat-eater. Both feel too extreme for my liking, so here I am, sitting on the fence in between the two, like the true Libra I am.

This book, my friends, is a book in the middle ground. A book for those who don't like to be cornered and who like to dip their toes in plant-based food, but also still enjoy the comforts of their familiar diet. I'm sure I am not the only flexi-queen out here trying to live my best life. Maybe you're a parent who enjoys nothing more than a full-trimmings, slap-up Sunday roast, but has a kid who has just gone vegan? Or maybe you are someone who wants to make a birthday cake for their plant-based best bud, but has no clue where to start? Or maybe you are just someone who wants to enjoy a bit of both. This book finds that sweet-spot middle ground for those looking to make changes in their diet, but who also don't quite want to go the whole hog just yet. *I mean this just screams of commitment issues doesn't it?*

This book gives you like-for-like recipes, offering fifty mouthwatering, drool-worthy bakes with a plant-based and non-plant based version. This isn't a book where the vegan recipes are shoved at the back or added last-minute for tokenism, or, more often than not, where plant-based = boring. I am SO over those books. This is a book where both sides of the diet are celebrated and not one where anyone misses out – the choice of what to delight your belly with is abundant. No one misses out, not on my watch. You get a cake, they get a cake, EVERYONE GETS CAKE!

I often diminish the achievement of making it to the *Bake Off* final by saying I winged it. 'Ohhhh you know, it was pure luck. I was kept in as the class clown who clearly didn't know what she was doing.' I think that us Brits are pretty terrible at championing our successes. Was I ever going to let myself be defeated by a toppling cake? Yeah, sure, for a few years, but now I am ready to make plant-based baking my b*tch. And now, yours too.

As much as I have made this book for me, make this book YOURS. I want this baking book to be super efficient and easy for you to navigate, so I've put the plant-based recipes on green pages and the classic versions on orange. Write down your scribbles, doodle, add preferences – whatever ya wanna do. Be bold, be brave, get adventurous, mix and match different parts of each recipe, and muddle your way through the deliciousness. The most important part of baking (eating aside, obvs) is the learning. Treat each mistake as a blessing and just know you're a step closer to perfection. Devour and savour every page, share the good stuff and fall in love with the power of baking. It changed my life, and I hope it does the same for you, too.

Remember: If they let this mug into the tent with very little experience but a huge hunger to learn, then you're gonna do just fine.

I *secretly* used to LOVE IT when someone would quit work because it meant cake in the office.

Heartbreak? *Cake.*
Bad news? *Cup of tea and cake.*
Drama at a family event?
Slice of cake and a good seat.
Every cloud has a plate of cake,
I am telling you.

Oh Crumbs

Your basic cakes, everyday cakes, celebration cakes,
and all the different sorts of cakes in between.

Coconut Cake with Whipped Ricotta and Mango Cream

This cake tastes of summer, looks like a dream and goes down a treat. You've got a coconut sponge drenched in coconut syrup and sandwiched between whipped ricotta and mango cream and layers of mango purée. A holiday for your mouth. Does that sound weird? It feels weird. It's gotten awkward now hasn't it? Sorry.

Moving on, this sponge is a great one as a stacker for a tiered number if you are going all out. I've added an alternative recipe for a more stable cream, which is the only buttercream I will ever use when it comes to cake. Swiss meringue buttercream is a dream to work with; it's sturdy, takes on colour and flavour well, and is super reliable. Once you have nailed how to make the base of the recipe, you can add whatever flavourings you wish and use with any of the sponges in this chapter.

The quantity listed below will make a little more than needed for this recipe, however, it stores well in the freezer. Just transfer it into an airtight container, pop it in the freezer and you're good for up to 4 months.

Coconut Cake with Whipped Ricotta and Mango Cream

Serves: 12

For the Coconut Sponge
325 g unsalted butter or baking margarine, room temp
325 g light soft brown sugar
1½ tsp vanilla bean paste
5 large eggs, room temp
300 g self-raising flour
100 g desiccated coconut
70 g crème fraîche

For the Coconut Syrup
200 ml water
150 g caster sugar
25 g desiccated coconut

For the Mango Whipped Cream
375 g ricotta
1½ tsp vanilla bean paste
45 g caster sugar
525 ml double cream
120 ml mango purée or pulp

For the Mango Swiss Meringue Buttercream
250 ml egg whites, room temp (don't use the sort in a carton)
550 g caster sugar
500 g unsalted butter, cold and diced
500 g unsalted butter, room temp and diced
1 tsp vanilla bean paste
100 ml mango purée or pulp

For the Filling
90 g mango purée or pulp

To Decorate
dried flowers and fruits of your choice

3 x 18-cm/7-in. cake tins, greased and lined (base and sides)

Preheat the oven to 150°C fan/170°C/gas mark 3.

Place the butter, sugar, and vanilla bean paste into the bowl and mix until light and fluffy. Next, add the eggs, mixing well between each addition. Make sure you give each addition sufficient time to emulsify and combine with the mixture.

Sift one-third of the flour into the bowl, before mixing. Sift in the remaining flour and desiccated coconut and fold in with a rubber spatula.

Finish the batter by adding the crème fraîche, lightly folding through to help loosen the mix. Divide the batter amongst the three tins and smooth using the back of the spoon, tapping the tins lightly on the work surface to remove any large air bubbles. Bake for 32–34 minutes until the sponge starts coming away from the edges.

Remove the tins from the oven and leave to sit for 5 minutes before turning out onto a cooling rack. Once the sponges have cooled for 30 minutes at room temp, wrap the sponges in clingfilm and leave to cool completely. If you are making these the day before, layer the wrapped sponges on top of each other and let gravity do its thing. Remember to change the sponges around every so often so the top isn't the only domed loser. Doing this should save you from having to cut off any unlevelled tops.

Meanwhile, make the coconut syrup by adding all the ingredients to a pan. Gently stir before bringing to the boil over a medium heat for 15 minutes until reduced and thickened.

Once you are ready to construct, make your cream of choice. If you are making the easier whipped cream, make it just before needed to keep fresh and stable. Add the ricotta, vanilla bean paste and sugar to a bowl and mix until smooth. Add the cream and mix until it begins to thicken to medium peaks, before pouring in the mango purée. Keep mixing until you have a thickened, spreadable consistency.

If you are making the Swiss meringue buttercream, you can make this a day or two in advance. Just mix it well before using. First, add the egg whites and caster sugar to a bowl. Whisk the two together until the sugar begins to dissolve and the mixture begins to thicken slightly. Place the bowl on top of a pan of simmering water. Cook out the whites and ensure the sugar has dissolved, so keep the heat low–medium and stir using a balloon whisk to avoid any sugar crystals forming. It should take about 10 minutes for the whites to come up to temperature – you want this to be at least 65–67°C before removing from the heat. Patiently whisk until stiff peaks form.

Gently mix once again. Begin to add the cold butter to the bowl, bit by bit, to help lower the meringue's temperature. Next, go in with the room temp butter. It may begin to look curdled or too loose, but whisk quicker and it will begin to come together. Add the vanilla bean paste and mango purée and mix well.

Before you construct, cut off any domed tops on the sponges using a serrated knife, before liberally brushing over the coconut syrup. We want them generously coated – but not drowning in syrup, as we don't want to compromise the sponges' stability. Spread or pipe a generous layer of mango cream onto one sponge. Make a dip in the cream in the middle using the back of a spoon, leaving a dam around the outside, before adding one-third of the mango purée to it. Stack and repeat for all sponges. Use the remaining cream to crumb-coat, then place in the fridge for 30 minutes. Add the final coat of cream and decorate as you wish. I used dried petals and physalis (which, I'll be honest, tastes weird, but looks pretty).

Make sure you refrigerate this baby to set completely before serving.

Plant-Based Coconut Cake with Whipped Ricotta and Mango Cream

Serves: 12

For the Coconut Sponge
300 ml coconut milk
1 tsp apple cider vinegar
325 g self-raising flour, sifted
150 g desiccated coconut
½ tsp bicarbonate of soda, sifted
½ tsp baking powder, sifted
285 g golden caster sugar
115 ml vegetable oil
35 g plant-based unsalted butter, melted
2 tsp vanilla bean paste

For the Coconut Syrup
200 ml water
150 g caster sugar
25 g desiccated coconut

For the Mango Cream
100 g plant-based cream cheese
1½ tsp vanilla bean paste
45 g icing sugar, sifted
650 ml plant-based double cream
120 ml mango purée or pulp

For the Filling
90 g mango purée or pulp

To Decorate
dried flowers and fruits of your choice

3 x 18-cm/7-in. cake tins, greased with
    coconut oil and lined (base and sides)

Let's start by preheating the oven to 150°C Fan/170°C/gas mark 3.

Let's get cracking with a super easy cake batter, which is like music to your ears, I know. Get the coconut milk and apple cider vinegar into a bowl and give it a mix. Let it sit on the side for 10 minutes to lightly curdle.

In the meantime, add all the dry ingredients to a bowl and give it a good stir to combine.

Once the coconut milk has lightly curdled, add all the remaining wet ingredients. Mix well before pouring into the dry ingredients. Use a balloon whisk to combine until smooth (don't go nuts on the overmixing here – stop once there are no visible streaks of flour).

Now evenly divide the batter amongst the three tins. Being pedantic and weighing each tin to make sure they hold the same batter is worth it – this way you know all three sponges will bake and cook all at the same time.

Smooth out the cake batter using the back of the spoon, tapping the tin lightly on the work surface to remove any large air bubbles. Pop in the oven and bake for 28–30 minutes until the sides of the sponge have started coming away from the tins and a cocktail stick poked into the middle comes out clean.

Remove cakes from the oven and leave the sponges to sit in the tins for about 5 minutes before turning out onto a cooling rack. Leaving them will a) continue heating the sponge slightly and most importantly b) make sure you don't burn the living crap out of your fingertips.

Once the sponges have cooled for about 30 minutes at room temp, wrap the sponges in clingfilm and leave to completely cool. If you are making these the day before, a nice trick to even out any lightly domed sponges is layering the wrapped sponges on top of each other and letting gravity do its thing. Remember to change the sponges around so the top isn't the only domed loser, but this should save you from having to cut away any sponge to level out.

While the sponges are cooling, you can get on with making the coconut syrup by adding all the ingredients to a pan. Gently stir before bringing to the boil over a medium heat. We want this syrup to have reduced and thickened – about 15 minutes should do the trick.

Once you are ready to construct, then make the mango cream to keep it fresh and stable. Add the cream cheese, vanilla bean paste and icing sugar to the stand mixer bowl and mix until smooth using the whisk attachment.

Add the double cream and mix until it begins to thicken to medium peaks before pouring in the mango purée. This will take the cream from a white to a gloriously golden colour. Keep mixing until you have a thickened, spreadable consistency. Remember this will be used to stack the cakes, so you will have to take this quite far and give it time to do its thing.

Cut off any domed tops on the sponges using a serrated knife before liberally brushing the cocunut syrup over each sponge. We want them generously coated – but not drowning in syrup, as that would compromise the sponges' stability. Spread or pipe a generous layer of mango cream onto one sponge. Make a dip in the cream in the middle using the back of a spoon, leaving a dam around the outside, before adding one-third of the mango purée to it. Stack and repeat for all sponges. Use the remaining cream to crumb-coat, then place in the fridge for 30 minutes. Add the final coat of cream and decorate as you wish. I used dried petals and physalis. Chill the cake before serving.

Victoria Sponge Loaf with Roasted Strawberries and Mint

I couldn't not include a recipe for a classic like this, could I? Not everyone wants a stack of 3 sponges to plough through – which is why we have sacked off the layered sponge and turned it into a loaf instead.

To top it all off, the crumb on this cake is giving real madeira sponge vibes – think denser texture, but with an almond hint. It is crazy how moist this sponge stays, even days after it is made. We aren't sandwiching the cream and strawberries in this, instead we are topping the loaf with a vanilla-laden whipped clotted cream and copious amounts of roasted strawberries. It's a real classic, but all glowed up.

Victoria Sponge Loaf with Roasted Strawberries and Mint

Serves: 6

For the Sponge
160 g unsalted butter or baking margarine, room temp
170 g caster sugar
2 tsp vanilla bean paste
2 large eggs, room temp
40 ml vegetable oil
150 g self-raising flour, sifted
115 g ground almonds
½ tsp baking powder, sifted
55 g natural yoghurt

For the Roasted Strawberry Topping
300 g strawberries, hulled and halved
15 ml maple syrup
5–6 mint leaves, finely chopped

For the Whipped Clotted Cream
300 ml double cream
125 g clotted cream
40 g icing sugar
1½ tsp vanilla bean paste

For the Sugar Syrup
1 quantity simple vanilla syrup (see page 303)

To Decorate
micro mint shoots or chopped mint leaves

deep 2-kg/900-g loaf tin, greased and lined (allow the paper to come up over the sides)

Preheat the oven to 150°C fan/170°C/gas mark 3.

Add the butter, sugar and vanilla bean paste to the bowl of a stand mixer and mix using the paddle attachment on a medium speed until light and fluffy; this will take about 5 minutes. Alternatively, feel free to do this step with an electric hand whisk – you'll get the same results, it will just take a bit more time and a little more effort from you. Next, add the eggs, one by one, mixing well for a minute or two between each addition to ensure they are fully incorporated. Add the oil and mix well. You want to make sure all the fats have emulsified before moving on. Add the flour, ground almonds and baking powder and give this a quick mix until the dry ingredients have mostly incorporated to the wet. Before fully mixing, go in with the yoghurt and give it a good mix to help loosen the batter. Now mix it all well. Pour or scoop the batter into your lined loaf tin and pop it in the oven to bake for 60–65 minutes. I always tend to go lower on timings to keep the sponge super moist, even if slightly under-baked in the middle, as that mildly gooey softness is just a *dream*.

Once the loaf has baked, remove it from the oven and leave to sit in the tin for a few minutes before lifting out. Allow to cool at room temperature for about 30 minutes, then wrap in clingfilm until fully cooled. This will keep the sponge super-fresh, even if you're using it the next day.

Crank that oven temp up to 180°C fan/200°C/gas mark 6 to get it nice and toasty to roast our strawberries.

Place the strawberries into an ovenproof dish. Pour over the maple syrup and use a spoon to mix, ensuring all the strawberries are coated before popping in the oven for 10 minutes. Give them a quick stir and then roast again for a further 10 minutes. Leave the strawbs to cool completely, then mix in the chopped mint.

Make the whipped clotted cream once everything is cool, and about an hour before you are ready to serve. This will keep it fresh and stable. Add all the cream ingredients to a bowl and whisk to medium peaks. We want a spreadable but firm consistency, so if the cream is still a little too loose, I would recommend finishing it by hand to judge the consistency. Trust me, you blink and a stand mixer has taken it waaaayyy too far. Don't live with that disappointment. Once done, leave to one side.

Let's get this loaf cake made up and eaten. Use a pastry brush to liberally brush over the sugar syrup on the loaf top and sides, so it's glistening and looks glorious. Dollop the whipped clotted cream on top and use the back of a spoon or a small palette knife to swirl (not imperative but feels and looks satisfying).

Strain the strawberries (but keep the juice to drizzle on top) and add a generous layer of the roasted strawberries on top. Let the juice trickle down, let the strawbs overflow, let the magic just be magic. Drizzle a little bit of the strained juice on top and finish with a few micro mint shoots or chopped mint leaves for a bit of jazz. Keep in the fridge until serving.

Plant-Based Victoria Sponge Loaf with Roasted Strawberries and Mint

Serves: 6

For the Sponge
275 g self-raising flour, sifted
75 g ground almonds
1 tsp bicarbonate of soda, sifted
½ tsp baking powder, sifted
235 g caster sugar
300 ml almond milk
115 ml sunflower oil
35 g golden syrup
1½ tsp vanilla bean paste
1 tsp apple cider vinegar

For the Roasted Strawberry Topping
300 g strawberries, hulled and halved
15 ml maple syrup
5–6 mint leaves

For the Cream
60 g plant-based cream cheese
20 g icing sugar, sifted
150 ml plant-based double cream
1 tsp vanilla bean paste

For the Sugar Syrup
1 quantity simple vanilla syrup (see page 303)

To Decorate
micro mint shoots or chopped mint leaves

deep 2-kg/900-g loaf tin, greased with
    coconut oil and lined (allow the paper to
    come up over the sides)

Preheat the oven to 160°C fan/180°C/gas mark 4.

The good news is: the mix for this cake is super easy. In a large bowl, add all the dry ingredients and use a balloon whisk to mix. In another bowl, add all the wet ingredients, leaving the apple cider vinegar until last. Add the wet mix into the dry, and use a balloon whisk to mix until smooth.

Pour the batter into the prepared loaf tin and pop it in the oven to bake for 58–60 minutes. I always tend to go lower on timings to keep the sponge moist.

Leave it to sit in the tin for a few minutes before lifting out. After allowing to cool at room temperature for about 30 minutes, wrap in clingfilm until fully cooled. This will keep the sponge super fresh, even if you're using it the next day.

Crank that oven temp up to 180°C fan/200°C/gas mark 6 to get it nice and toasty to roast our strawberries.

Place the strawberries into an ovenproof dish. Pour over the maple syrup and use a spoon to mix, ensuring all the strawberries are coated before popping in the oven for 10 minutes. Give them a quick stir and then roast again for a further 10 minutes. Leave the strawbs to cool completely, then mix in the chopped mint.

Make the cream once everything is cool, and about an hour before you are ready to serve. This will keep it fresh and stable. Add the cream cheese and icing sugar to a bowl and mix until smooth. Go in with the double cream and vanilla bean paste and whisk to medium peaks. We want a spreadable but firm consistency, so if the cream is still a little too loose, I would recommend finishing it by hand to judge the consistency. Once done, leave to one side.

Use a pastry brush to brush the sugar syrup liberally over the loaf top and sides of the cake, so it's glistening and looks glorious. Dollop the whipped cream on top and use the back of a spoon or a small palette knife to swirl (not imperative but feels and looks satisfying).

Strain the strawberries (but keep the juice to drizzle on top) and add a generous layer of the roasted strawberries on top. Let the juice trickle down, let the strawbs overflow, it's all magic. Drizzle a little bit of the strained juice on top and finish with a few micro mint shoots or chopped mint leaves. Keep in the fridge until serving.

Sticky Jamaican Ginger Cake with Butterscotch Sauce and Orange Cream

I made a similar version to this cake while on the show. One judge said it was a little too boozy and the other said it was a little too un-gingery, but the only feedback I could see was that they couldn't stop eating it – and that, for me, is the best feedback anyone can get. Since then, I've tweaked and played around to make this the best it can be. Sticky and spicy, the right amount of sweetness, gloriously indulgent, an unexpected hit of zing from the orange – and no booze.

This truly is an ideal cake for anyone who's not mad on chocolate (crazy talk, I know) but still wants their sugary taste buds screaming with joy.

If a stacked cake is too much of a task, go ahead and convert this into a traybake. Timings will need to be increased ever so slightly, but it turns something quite fancy into a little more relaxed affair, which makes it my idea of a perfect Sunday lunch pud.

Sticky Jamaican Ginger Cake with Butterscotch Sauce and Orange Cream

Serves: 10–12

For the Sponge
260 g unsalted butter or baking margarine, room temp
210 g dark brown sugar
100 g golden syrup
75 g black treacle
4 large eggs, room temp
260 g self-raising flour, sifted
1½ tbsp ground cinnamon
2½ tbsp ground ginger
1½ tsp vanilla bean paste
45 g soured cream, room temp
5 pieces preserved stem ginger, finely diced, plus some syrup from the jar for brushing

For the Butterscotch Filling
150 ml double cream
75 g light soft brown sugar
40 g salted butter, room temp and diced
pinch of sea salt

For the Whipped Cream Cheese Frosting
200 g mascarpone cheese
100 g cream cheese
1½ tsp vanilla bean paste
50 g caster sugar
grated zest of 3 large oranges
400 ml double cream

3 x 18-cm/7-in. cake tins, greased and lined (base and sides)

Preheat the oven to 150°C fan/170°C/gas mark 3.

Add the butter, sugar, golden syrup and treacle to a stand mixer bowl and mix on a medium speed using the paddle attachment until light and fluffy. Make sure you give this a few minutes to really work some air into the mixture. Add the eggs one by one (you want each egg to emulsify fully before adding the next).

In a separate bowl, combine the flour, cinnamon and ground ginger with a fork or balloon whisk before adding one-third to the stand mixer bowl. Mix well before removing the mixer bowl.

Use a rubber spatula or large metal spoon to fold in another one-third of dry ingredients with the vanilla bean paste, before adding the remaining dry mixture alongside the soured cream and finely diced stem ginger. Keep the folding light to make sure you keep as much air in the batter as possible.

Divide the cake batter evenly amongst the three prepared tins. Pop in the oven and bake for 32–35 minutes until the sponge is coming away from the sides of the tins and a cocktail stick poked into the middle comes out clean.

Leave in the tins for 5 minutes before turning out onto a cooling rack. Leave to cool for 30 minutes before wrapping in clingfilm to cool completely.

While the cakes are cooling, make the butterscotch filling. In a saucepan, add the cream, light brown sugar and butter. Cook over a gentle medium heat until the sugar has dissolved, the butter has melted, and the liquid begins to bubble. Take off the heat, add the sea salt (just a tiny pinch!) and give it a mix before transferring to a bowl to cool. Once cooled, pop the bowl into the fridge to firm up, which makes it easier when stacking the sponges.

Let's get the frosting made. Into the bowl of a stand mixer, add the mascarpone, cream cheese, vanilla bean paste, sugar and orange zest. Mix using the whisk attachment until smooth. Pour in the double cream and mix on a slow–medium speed until the cream nearly hits stiff peaks – don't go over, as you don't want your mix to curdle. If in doubt, stop mixing early and work the rest of the mixture by hand to achieve that firm-but-pipeable consistency. Transfer to a piping bag.

Once the sponges have cooled, use a serrated knife to trim off any domed tops, before using a pastry brush to brush the top of each sponge with the syrup from the stem ginger jar.

When you are ready to construct the cake, place one sponge onto your serving board (you can use some cream here to glue the sponge to your serving plate). Pipe an even layer of cream over the sponge before using the back of a spoon to create a dip in the middle to add a generous slathering of the butterscotch filling. Repeat with the remaining sponges before covering the entire cake with the remaining cream. You can go as fancy as you like with the decoration, or opt for a naked finish.

I'd recommend serving up a slice alongside a cup of tea and a good drizzle of any remaining butterscotch sauce. Unbuckle your belt and then go and help yourself to another serving.

Plant-Based Sticky Jamaican Ginger Cake with Butterscotch Sauce and Orange Cream

The major change in this recipe is the egg replacement (shocking news, there is none) and substituting the soured cream. For that, I have offered up a suggestion that will give you that dense, incredibly moist and tender crumb. The best thing about this sponge is you still get that same sticky texture and spiced flavour, but without all the faff of having to work the air into the butter and sugar. Work smarter, not harder.

Serves: 10–12

For the Sponge
200 ml soy milk
1 tbsp cider vinegar
260 g plant-based unsalted butter
210 g dark soft brown sugar
100 g golden syrup
100 g black treacle
1½ tsp vanilla bean paste
4 pieces preserved stem ginger, finely diced,
    plus some syrup from the jar for brushing
400 g self-raising flour, sifted
¼ tsp bicarbonate of soda
2 tbsp ground ginger
1½ tbsp ground cinnamon

For the Butterscotch Filling
150 ml plant-based double cream
75 g light soft brown sugar
40 g plant-based salted butter, cubed
1 tsp cornflour, sifted
pinch of sea salt

For the Whipped Cream Cheese Frosting
250 g plant-based cream cheese
50 g caster sugar
1½ tsp vanilla bean paste
grated zest of 3 large oranges
400 ml plant-based double cream

3 x 18-cm/7-in. cake tins, greased with
    coconut oil and lined (base and sides)

Preheat the oven to 150°C fan/170°C/gas mark 3.

Add the soy milk and cider vinegar to a bowl and leave to sit for 10 minutes until lightly curdled.

In the meantime, add the butter, sugar, golden syrup, treacle and vanilla bean paste to a saucepan and gently heat until the butter has melted and the sugar has dissolved. We don't want this boiled, so take it low and slow. Remove from the heat and add the stem ginger. Give it all a good mix and set aside to cool.

In a large bowl, combine the dry ingredients with a balloon whisk. Pour in the cooled butter mix and the curdled soy milk, and mix until smooth.

Divide the cake batter evenly amongst the three prepared tins. Pop in the oven and bake for 26–28 minutes until the sponge is coming away from the sides of the tins and a cocktail stick poked into the middle comes out clean.

Leave in the tins for 5 minutes before turning out onto a cooling rack. Leave to cool for 30 minutes before wrapping in clingfilm to cool completely.

While the cakes are cooling, make the butterscotch filling. In a saucepan, add the cream, light brown sugar, butter and cornflour. Cook over a gentle medium heat until the sugar has dissolved, the butter has melted, and the liquid begins to bubble. Take off the heat, add the sea salt (just a tiny pinch!) and give it a mix before transferring to a bowl to cool. Once cooled, pop the bowl into the fridge to firm up, which makes it easier when stacking the sponges.

Let's get the frosting made. Into the bowl of a stand mixer, add the cream cheese, vanilla bean paste, sugar and orange zest. Mix using the whisk attachment until smooth. Pour in the double cream and mix on a slow–medium speed until the cream nearly hits stiff peaks. Transfer to a piping bag and place in the fridge for at least 30–45 minutes before using.

Once the sponges are cool, trim off any domed tops with a serrated knife before using a pastry brush to brush the tops of each sponge with syrup from the stem ginger jar.

Now it's time to construct the cake by placing one sponge onto your serving board (you can use some cream here to glue the sponge to your serving plate). Pipe an even layer of cream over the sponge before using the back of a spoon to create a dip in the middle to add a generous slathering of the butterscotch filling. Repeat with the remaining sponges before covering the entire cake with the remaining cream. You can go as fancy as you like with the decoration or opt for a naked finish.

Place the cake in the fridge to set for at least an hour before slicing and serving with a good drizzle of any remaining butterscotch sauce.

Chocolate Fudge Sponge with Milk Chocolate Fudge Frosting

Everyone needs a killer chocolate cake recipe in their back pocket.

This cake pays homage to the Bruce Bogtrotter Cake, inspired by the fictional dessert from Roald Dahl's *Matilda*. In the story, Bruce Bogtrotter defies the tyrannical headmistress, Miss Trunchbull, by consuming an entire chocolate cake meant for the school assembly. The cake itself is described as enormous, rich and decadent – a formidable challenge to eat due to its size and indulgent nature. Despite Miss Trunchbull's attempts to humiliate Bruce, he successfully finishes the WHOLE cake, defying her authority and becoming a hero in the eyes of his classmates.

The Bruce Bogtrotter cake symbolises indulgence, rebellion and triumph – and made me so envious that I have worked on this chocolate cake recipe for YEARS. It's rich, smooth, moist, deep, intense and incredibly moreish – all those yummy, scrummy adjectives that you know for certain will make this the best chocolate cake you'll *ever* eat. Purposefully under-baked, but perfectly set.

Chocolate Fudge Sponge with Milk Chocolate Fudge Frosting

Serves: 1 Bruce Bogtrotter or 10–12 normal people

For the Sponge
300 g self-raising flour, sifted
180 g cocoa powder, sifted
180 g ground almonds
660 g light soft brown sugar
   (don't panic, this is correct)
pinch of sea salt
3 eggs, large
2 tsp vanilla bean paste
400 g natural yoghurt
50 ml full-fat milk
150 ml sunflower oil
300 ml hot water

For the Chocolate Fudge Frosting
450 g milk chocolate, chips or callets
300 ml double cream
110 g icing sugar, sifted
100 g unsalted butter, room temp

For the Sugar Syrup
½ quantity of simple vanilla syrup
   (see page 303)

2 x 20-cm/8-in. cake tins, greased and lined
   (base and sides)

Preheat the oven to 150°C fan/170°C/gas mark 3.

Sponges don't get much simpler than a wet and dry cake mix. In one bowl, combine all the dry ingredients. Break up any large lumps and make sure everything is evenly mixed. In another bowl, combine the wet ingredients, leaving the hot water until last and mixing together lightly with a balloon whisk.

Pour the wet into the dry and work the ingredients well using a balloon whisk. Scrape down the sides of the bowl with a rubber spatula to ensure everything is well combined.

Evenly divide the batter between the two tins before baking in the oven for 36–38 minutes. Go lower on the timings because a gooey, fudgy middle is exactly what we are after – even if this does mean the top may sink a little.

You wanna leave the sponges to cool for at least 45 minutes; we are after a fondant-esque inside and don't want to risk any major collapses, so let them sit in the tins.

Once the sponges have firmed up a little, remove from the tins, wrap in clingfilm and leave to cool completely.

Next, let's get the chocolate fudge frosting made. Add the chocolate chunks to a large heatproof bowl. To a saucepan, add the double cream and place over a medium heat. Heat the cream gently until it is near boiling before removing from the heat. Pour the hot cream on top of the chocolate chunks and leave to sit for a minute.

Use a balloon whisk or rubber spatula to mix the chocolate and cream together. You are after a smooth and glossy consistency – so if your cream isn't hot enough, the chunks won't melt. If this is the case, fill a saucepan with cold water and gently heat until simmering, then place the bowl on top, making sure the bottom of the bowl doesn't touch the water. The indirect heat from the steam will melt the chocolate.

Once smooth, leave the ganache to sit and cool. When the ganache is lukewarm, add the icing sugar and mix until whipped – you will know when this has happened as it will have turned lighter in colour and in texture. Add the butter and mix well until thickened and fully incorporated.

If your cake sponges have domed a little, trim off the tops with a serrated knife and keep as little chef snacks.

Generously glaze both sponge tops and sides with the vanilla sugar syrup using a pastry brush. Once the syrup has soaked through, glaze the sponges once more.

Place a sponge onto your serving plate. Top with one-third of the frosting. Place the second sponge on top, bottom-side up for a super-flat top, before using the remaining two-thirds of the frosting to smother the top and the sides. You can either keep the outside rustic by swirling with the back of a spoon or you can smooth down the sides and top with a cake scraper.

Leave in the fridge until serving. To serve, slice with a hot knife or go in big Brucey-style with your hands.

Plant-Based Chocolate Fudge Sponge with Milk Chocolate Fudge Frosting

(EF)

Serves: 1 Bruce Bogtrotter or 10–12 normal people

For the Chocolate Fudge Frosting
350 g tinned coconut cream, chilled overnight
380 g plant-based milk or dark chocolate, chunks or callets
110 g icing sugar, sifted
100 g plant-based unsalted butter, room temp
1 tbsp golden syrup

For the Sponge
345 g self-raising flour, sifted
150 g cocoa powder, sifted
390 g light soft brown sugar
1¼ tsp baking powder, sifted
540 ml almond or soy milk
225 ml sunflower or vegetable oil, plus extra for greasing
2 tsp vanilla bean paste
2¼ tsp apple cider vinegar

For the Sugar Syrup
½ quantity simple vanilla syrup (see page 303)

2 x 20-cm/8-in. cake tins, greased with coconut oil and lined (base and sides)

Let's start by making the ganache base for the fudge frosting. Scoop out the solids from a coconut cream tin – if you are a bit short on the milk solids making up the final quantity, use some of the clear coconut water. Place into a pan and gently heat over a medium heat. Once near boiling, remove from the heat and add the chocolate. Place a lid or cloth over the top and leave to sit for 1 minute. Use a balloon whisk or rubber spatula to mix until smooth. Leave to cool in the fridge until lightly firm but spreadable; about 1–2 hours.

Preheat the oven to 150°C fan/170°C/gas mark 3.

In a large bowl, combine all the dry ingredients for the sponge and mix well using a balloon whisk.

In another bowl, mix all the wet ingredients, adding the apple cider vinegar last. Pour the wet mix into the dry and mix well with a balloon whisk until smooth. Scrape down the sides of the bowl with a spatula and ensure no streaks of flour remain.

Divide the batter evenly between the two cake tins and bake in the oven for 29–32 minutes. I always like to go less on a fudge sponge, just to keep the texture of the sponge almost jammy. This will firm up once cooled, but you do whatever floats your boat.

Remove the sponges from the oven and leave to cool in the tins for 15 minutes. If you are opting for a squidgier middle and going for the shorter cooking time, leave the sponges in the tins to cool completely. If you opted for a more thoroughly baked sponge and left the cakes in the oven for longer, carefully turn out before wrapping the sponges in clingfilm and leaving to cool.

When the ganache has thickened, add the icing sugar and mix until whipped – you will know when this has happened as the ganache will have turned lighter in colour and in texture. Add the butter and golden syrup and mix well until combined. You should now have a fudgy choccy frosting. If you are after something a little looser, add more golden syrup; if you are after something a little thicker, add more icing sugar and butter.

Once the sponges have cooled, level out any domed sponge tops with a serrated knife. (Note: These offcuts can be kept to make vegan truffles with any leftover chocolate ganache, or you can just gobble them ... the chef always deserves a snack.)

Use a pastry brush to glaze the sponge tops and sides generously with the vanilla sugar syrup. Give it a few minutes for the syrup to soak through before glazing one more time.

Place one of the sponges, glazed-side up onto your serving plate. Smother the top with one-third of the frosting. Top with the second sponge, bottom-side up for a super-flat top, before using the remaining two-thirds of the frosting to cover the tops and the sides. You can either keep the outside rustic by swirling with the back of a spoon or you can smooth down the sides and top with a cake scraper.

Leave in the fridge until serving. To serve, slice with a hot knife.

Lemon and Thyme Drizzle Loaf with Lemon Custard Cream

Hear me out before you turn the page in bewilderment at the addition of thyme. IT WORKS. I promise. I wouldn't do you dirty like that. I love the addition of herbs in baking. They are underused in my eyes, but they really can add a new depth and flavour profile when included. Now I'm not talking about chucking in a whole bunch – just a light, delicate sprinkling to bring out that sherbetty, lemony zestyness. Baking for me is about being playful and bold all at the same time. We are here to create moments with our bakes, not something someone is going to forget about as soon as they put their fork down.

This recipe doubles up really well, meaning you can take this from a loaf tin to a stacked double or triple sponge, depending on how many hungry hippos you gotta feed.

Lemon and Thyme Drizzle Loaf with Lemon Custard Cream

Serves: 6

For the Sponge
175 g caster sugar
grated zest of 3 large lemons
160 g unsalted butter or baking margarine,
   room temp, plus extra for piping
1½ tsp vanilla bean paste
3 large eggs, room temp
50 g crème fraîche, room temp
50 ml olive oil
1½ tbsp lemon curd (see page 300 or use
   store-bought, I won't judge)
115 g ground almonds
130 g self-raising flour, sifted
½ tsp baking powder, sifted

For the Thyme Drizzle
80 g icing sugar, sifted
40 g caster sugar
freshly squeezed juice of 2 lemons
20 ml water

50 g lemon curd, plus 1 tbsp to glaze
   (see page 300 or use store-bought)
1 sprig of thyme, leaves only

For the Lemon Custard Cream
125 ml full-fat milk
1 tsp vanilla bean paste
grated zest of 2 lemons
2 egg yolks
35 g caster sugar
10 g cornflour, sifted
5 g plain flour, sifted
250 ml double cream

To Finish
1 sprig of lemon thyme, leaves only

deep 2-kg/900-g loaf tin, greased and lined
   (allow the paper to come up over the sides)

Preheat the oven to 150°C fan/170°C/gas mark 3.

In a stand mixer bowl, add the caster sugar and lemon zest. Using the paddle attachment, mix on a medium speed for a few minutes to allow the oil from the zest to be released and until the sugar smells sherbetty.

Add the room temp butter and vanilla bean paste to the bowl and cream together on a medium speed for 5 minutes until light and fluffy.

Next in are the eggs – add these one at a time, mixing well between each addition. Make sure the mixture is emulsified and do not stress if it looks a little curdled, we will sort that out in the next few steps. Add the crème fraîche, oil and lemon curd to the bowl and mix.

Add the ground almonds, baking powder and flour to the bowl and mix on a medium speed until everything has just combined. Before you scoop the batter into the prepared tin, work the mixture with a rubber spatula, making sure everything at the bottom has been mixed well.

Scoop the batter into the lined tin and level out with the back of a spoon. A nifty tip here is to pipe a thin line of softened butter down the middle – to control where the sponge will crack – for that nice flat top. Pop the tin into the oven for 60 minutes, or until the sponge is baked through.

Leave the sponge to sit in the tin while you mix all the ingredients for the thyme drizzle in a bowl. Set aside for 10 minutes.

After 10 minutes, carefully pour one-quarter of the drizzle on top of the sponge and brush over with a pastry brush. Leave to sit for 5 minutes before repeating with another quarter of the drizzle. Allow the sponge to cool completely in the tin, then transfer to a cooling rack with a tray underneath. Pour over the remaining drizzle to drench it completely. I like to use a pastry brush to ensure the sides of the sponge are also well coated – not a dry crumb in this house, please!

Finish by smothering the extra 1 tbsp lemon curd all over to glaze, before wrapping the sponge tightly in clingfilm. Pop in the fridge until serving.

To make the lemon custard cream, pour the milk into a saucepan with the vanilla bean paste and lemon zest. Place this over a medium heat to bring to near boiling. In the meantime, whisk together the egg yolks, caster sugar and both flours until smooth. This will take a minute or two to work through the stage where the yolks go clumpy. Persevere and whisk like mad and it will go from gritty to smooth in no time. When the milk is near boiling, pour one-third over the egg yolks and mix until smooth. Pour the mixture back into the saucepan and stir immediately. You want to keep stirring this until it thickens – we are after a consistency where it's gone past pourable and generously coats the back of a spoon. Take the pan off the heat and transfer the custard to a shallow tray to cool. Cover with clingfilm or greaseproof paper to prevent a skin from forming.

Once the custard has cooled, transfer this to the bowl of a stand mixer. If it has gone a little lumpy, pass through a sieve to bring it back to glossy glory. Pour in the double cream and whisk until mixed. Give the cream a quick taste test and, if you think it needs a touch more sweetness, now is the time (sift in another 5 g of icing sugar, taste, and adjust accordingly if needs be). When you are happy, whack the speed back up until the cream hits a medium peak – we want a spreadable but firm consistency. If it feels a little loose, you can work the mixture by hand to avoid over-mixing.

Generously dollop the cream on top of the loaf and smush around with the back of a spoon or pipe for a more finessed finish. Finish it all off by adding a few thyme leaves on top. Pop in the fridge until serving before slicing with a hot knife. Enjoy that very first slice slap – it is like music to my ears.

Plant-Based Lemon and Thyme Drizzle Loaf with Lemon Curd Cream

I KNOW the other version has a custard cream and you guys have been lumped with a curd cream, but this version is just as delicious. If not more so, because it's easier and quicker to make which means it will be in your belly sooner. I tried this recipe with a lemon custard and it tasted... nice. Nice is a place in France as far as I'm concerned, and should never be used as a positive adjective. You my friends, deserve way more than just nice, which is why this version uses a curd cream instead.

Serves: 6

For the Sponge
200 ml coconut milk
20 ml freshly squeezed lemon juice
100 g plant-based unsalted butter
2½ tbsp golden syrup
1½ tbsp plant-based lemon curd (see page 301 or use store-bought, I won't judge)
115 g caster sugar
grated zest of 2 large lemons
125 g self-raising flour, sifted
90 g ground almonds
20 g cornflour, sifted
½ tsp bicarbonate of soda, sifted
¼ tsp baking powder, sifted

For the Thyme Drizzle
40 g icing sugar, sifted

20 g caster sugar
freshly squeezed juice of 1 lemon
10 ml water
25 g plant-based lemon curd, plus 1 tbsp to glaze (see page 301 or use store-bought)
1 sprig of thyme, leaves only

For the Lemon Curd Cream
100 g plant-based cream cheese
75 g plant-based lemon curd (see page 301 or use store-bought)
10 g icing sugar, sifted
250 ml plant-based double cream

deep 2-kg/900-g loaf tin, greased with coconut oil and lined (allow the paper to come up over the sides)

Preheat the oven to 150°C fan/170°C/gas mark 3.

For the sponge, pour the coconut milk into a bowl and add half the lemon juice. Give it a good stir and let that sit for 10 minutes until the milk begins to curdle.

Meanwhile, add the butter, golden syrup and lemon curd to a saucepan and place over a medium heat. Once the butter has melted, take off heat and set aside to cool.

Add the caster sugar and lemon zest to a bowl. Either mix the two together with your fingertips to help release the oils or give it a quick whizz with an electric hand whisk. Add the flour, ground almonds, cornflour, bicarbonate of soda and baking powder and mix well with a balloon whisk. Add the curdled milk, cooled butter and remaining 10 ml of lemon juice and whisk until smooth.

Pour the batter into the prepared tin and bake for 42–44 minutes, or until the top of the sponge has a little bounce and a toothpick returns no wet batter. Leave the sponge to sit in the tin while you mix all the ingredients for the thyme drizzle in a bowl. Set aside for 10 minutes.

After 10 minutes, carefully pour one-quarter of the drizzle on top of the sponge and brush over with a pastry brush. Leave to sit for 5 minutes before repeating with another quarter of the drizzle. Allow the sponge to cool in the tin, then transfer to a cooling rack with a tray underneath. Pour over the remaining drizzle to drench it completely. I like to use a pastry brush to ensure the sides of the sponge are also well coated.

Glaze the sponge with the extra 1 tbsp lemon curd before wrapping it tightly in clingfilm and popping in the fridge until later.

Make the lemon curd cream by adding the cream cheese, lemon curd and icing sugar to a bowl and mixing until smooth. Pour in the double cream and mix until the cream hits a medium–stiff peak – we want a spreadable but firm consistency. If it feels a little loose, you can work the mixture by hand to avoid overmixing.

Generously dollop the cream on top of the loaf and smush around with the back of a spoon or pipe for a more finessed finish. Pop in the fridge until serving. To serve, slice with a hot knife.

Spiced Carrot Cake with Orange Cream Cheese Frosting

Carrot Cake is the sort of cake that is an all-round crowd pleaser. Everyone from your nan to your uncle (even the kids who swore they'll never eat a vegetable) seem to like it.

The subtle spicing from the blend of cardamom and cinnamon against the zesty cream cheese frosting is a total dream. I love the sour coolness you get from the cream cheese frosting against the depth of spice in the cake. However, if you are after a cream with more stability, opt for a Swiss meringue buttercream spiked with orange zest instead.

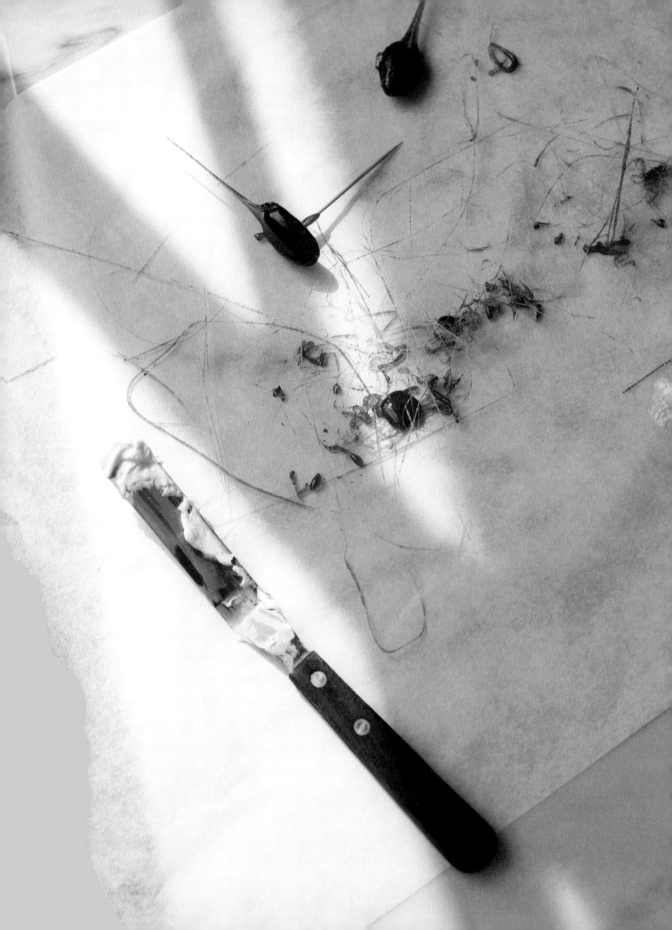

Spiced Carrot Cake with Orange Cream Cheese Frosting

Serves: 12

For the Sponge
300 g carrots, peeled and finely grated
115 g pecans, finely chopped
300 ml vegetable oil
300 g light soft brown sugar
5 large eggs
2 tsp vanilla bean paste
125 g tinned pineapple, blitzed to a purée
1 tbsp pineapple juice from tin, plus 2 tbsp
   for brushing
350 g self-raising flour, sifted
1 tsp baking powder, sifted
2 tbsp ground cinnamon
2 tsp ground cardamom

For the Cream Cheese Frosting
500 g full-fat cream cheese
60 g icing sugar, sifted
grated zest of 2 large oranges
2 tsp vanilla bean paste
250 ml double cream

To Decorate
150 g caster sugar
handful of pecans

3 x 18-cm/7-in. cake tins, greased and lined
   (base and sides)

Get that oven preheated to 150°C fan/170°C/ gas mark 3.

In a large mixing bowl, mix together the grated carrots and chopped pecans with a wooden spoon. Go in with the oil, sugar, eggs, vanilla bean paste and blitzed pineapple, plus the 1 tbsp pineapple juice. Give this all a real good mixy mix with a balloon whisk until smooth.

Sift all the dry ingredients into another mixing bowl and mix well. You really want to get the spices distributed well within the flour. Add the dry ingredients to the wet and mix with a spatula until just mixed, scraping down the sides and bottom of the bowl to ensure everything is incorporated.

Divide the batter amongst the three tins and bake in the oven for 30–32 minutes until a toothpick poked into the cake comes out clean (give it an extra 5 minutes if needed). Leave in the tins for 5 minutes before turning out onto a cooling rack. Leave to cool for 30 minutes before wrapping in clingfilm to cool completely.

Once cooled, use a serrated knife to even out the top of the sponges. Use a pastry brush to brush the extra 2 tbsp pineapple juice over the tops of the sponges.

When ready to construct the cake, add all the ingredients for the frosting, except the double cream, into the bowl of a stand mixer fitted with the whisk attachment and mix until smooth. Scrape down the sides before adding the double cream and whisking until thickened.

Transfer to a piping bag or use a palette knife to generously pipe or spread a layer of cream cheese frosting onto the first sponge. Place the next sponge on top and repeat, then finish with the third sponge and repeat once more. Use a palette knife to crumb coat the outside of the cake, pop in the fridge to set for about 30 minutes before using the remaining frosting to decorate. Smooth down the sides with a cake scraper or keep it slightly rustic by using a tilted palette knife to smooth down.

I like to top the cake with some caramelised chopped pecan spikes. To make these, place a large saucepan over a medium heat to begin to warm. Add the caster sugar and continue heating until the sugar has dissolved. While waiting for the sugar to melt, occasionally tilt and turn the pan, but do not stir. Not even if you are tempted. Once the sugar has all melted and turned a deep amber colour, remove the pan from the heat to slightly cool until it begins to thicken.

Use a cocktail stick to push into each pecan part. Prep the floor by the pan with a sheet of baking paper or a silicone mat to catch any drips of caramel. Get some tape at the ready. Dip each pecan into the caramel, making sure it is generously coated before removing from the pan and taping the end of the cocktail stick to your worktop. This allows the pecan and caramel to hang off the edge to create a drip. Repeat for all the pecans and leave to set and harden.

Arrange the pecan shards on top of the cake to complete. Dramatic yet elegant, but god damn dirtily delicious.

55

Plant-Based Spiced Carrot Cake with Orange Cream Cheese Frosting

While I always say, don't play with the recipe quantities and ingredients, I totally get that nut allergies are a thing, so feel free to swap these out for walnuts, macadamia nuts, hazelnuts, or even pistachios. Similarly if you can't find any plant-based double cream, sub for an American buttercream, adding the same orange zest spike, for an easy, stress-free alternative.

Now, who said I can't compromise?

Serves: 12

For the Sponge
150 ml vegetable oil
150 g plant-based unsalted butter
300 g light soft brown sugar
395 g self-raising flour, sifted
1 tsp baking powder, sifted
2 tbsp ground cinnamon
2 tsp ground cardamom
115 g pecans, finely chopped
125 g tinned pineapple, blitzed to a purée
1 tbsp pineapple juice from tin, plus 2 tbsp for brushing
2 tsp vanilla bean paste
300 g carrot, peeled and finely grated

For the Egg Replacer
10 tbsp water
10 tsp baking powder
5 tsp vegetable oil

For the Cream Cheese Frosting
500 g plant-based cream cheese
80 g icing sugar, sifted
grated zest of 2 large oranges
2 tsp vanilla bean paste
250 ml plant-based double cream

To Decorate
150 g caster sugar
handful of pecans

3 x 18-cm/7-in. cake tins, greased with coconut oil and lined (base and sides)

Get that oven preheated to 150°C fan/170°C/ gas mark 3.

In a saucepan, add the oil, butter and sugar. Place over a medium heat to melt the butter and sugar gently.

Meanwhile, add all the dry ingredients, including the pecans, to a large bowl and use a balloon whisk to combine. Combine the egg replacer ingredients in a small bowl.

Once the butter has melted, remove the pan from the heat. Next in is the blitzed pineapple, 1 tbsp juice, and the vanilla bean paste. Give it all a good mix together before adding the egg replacer and grated carrot. Stir this all really well before pouring it into the dry ingredients.

You want to make sure this is mixed well without overmixing... if that makes any sense. As soon as there are no visible streaks of flour left, stop!

Divide the batter amongst the three tins and place into the oven for 30–32 minutes until a toothpick poked into the cake comes out clean (give it an extra 5 minutes if needed). Leave in the tins for 5 minutes before turning out onto a cooling rack. Leave to cool for 30 minutes before wrapping in clingfilm to cool completely.

Once cooled, use a serrated knife to even out the top of the sponges (although these should be pretty flat) and use a pastry brush to brush the extra 2 tbsp pineapple juice over of the sponges.

When ready to construct the cake, add all the ingredients for the frosting, except the double cream, into the bowl of a stand mixer fitted with the whisk attachment and mix until everything has combined. Scrape down the sides before adding the cream and whisking until thickened. Pop this into the fridge for about 30 minutes to begin to solidify.

Transfer to a piping bag or use a palette knife to generously pipe or spread a layer of cream cheese frosting onto the first sponge. Place the next sponge on top and repeat, then finish with the third sponge and repeat once more. Use a palette knife to crumb coat the outside of the cake, pop in the fridge to set for about 30 minutes before using the remaining frosting to decorate. Smooth down the sides with a cake scraper or keep it slightly rustic by using a tilted palette knife to smooth down.

I like to top the cake with some caramelised chopped pecan spikes. To make these, place a large saucepan over a medium heat to begin to warm. Add the caster sugar and continue heating until the sugar has dissolved. While waiting for the sugar to melt, occasionally tilt and turn the pan, but do not stir. Not even if you are tempted. Once the sugar has all melted and turned a deep amber colour, remove the pan from the heat to slightly cool until it begins to thicken.

Use a cocktail stick to push into each pecan part. Prep the floor by the pan with a sheet of baking paper or a silicone mat to catch any drips of caramel. Get some tape at the ready. Dip each pecan into the caramel, making sure it is generously coated before removing from the pan and taping the end of the cocktail stick to your worktop. This allows the pecan and caramel to hang off the edge to create a drip. Repeat for all the pecans and leave to set and harden.

Arrange the pecan shards on top of the cake to complete.

Banana, Choc and Butterscotch Traybake with Whipped Coconut Cream and Ginger Crumb

This naughty little number started out originally as a plant-based bake – it's a banana-butterscotch bonanza. A lot of the time, a stacked cake isn't always the best option. With a traybake, you can slice, scoop, pop in a bowl, and it feels like a warming, albeit lightly spiced, hug.

I know it's fifty shades of beige, but it has flavours of cinnamon, coconut, ginger and chocolate, all drowning in butterscotch sauce. This cake is almost verging on a pud with the number of layers and how it eats, but, most importantly, the skill set required to nail the bake is super minimal.

On the off chance that you aren't after something that will make 20 portions, halve the quantities overleaf for a smaller bake, use a 23-cm/9-in. square cake tin and reduce the baking time by 10 minutes, keeping an eye on it until it is done. It keeps well in the fridge once made, freezes well once baked and eats well when done. Let's get to it.

Banana, Choc and Butterscotch Traybake with Whipped Coconut Cream and Ginger Crumb

Serves: 20

For the Sponge
4 large ripe bananas
100 ml full-fat milk, room temp
110 ml vegetable oil
2 large eggs
2 tsp vanilla bean paste
150 g light soft brown sugar
385 g self-raising flour, sifted
1¼ tbsp sweetened ground cinnamon
pinch of sea salt
200 g dark chocolate, chunks or callets

For the Butterscotch Sauce
300 ml single cream
80 g unsalted butter, room temp
150 g light soft brown sugar
1 tsp vanilla bean paste

For the Coconut Whipped Cream
170 g cream cheese
300 ml double cream
75 g sweetened desiccated coconut
50 g caster sugar, or to taste
1½ tsp vanilla bean paste

For the Ginger Biscuit Crumb
6 ginger snap biscuits, blitzed or bashed
   to crumbs

deep 20 x 30-cm/8 x 12-in. cake tin, greased
   and lined (allow the paper to come up over
   the sides)

Pop that oven on to 155°C fan/175°C/gas mark 4.

In a medium bowl, mash the bananas to a purée. Add the milk, vegetable oil, eggs and vanilla bean paste to the bowl before mixing well with a balloon whisk to help emulsify all the liquids. Next in is the sugar; mix well until fully combined.

In a separate large bowl, add the sifted flour and cinnamon. Add the salt before combining the dry ingredients with the wet. I like to begin mixing by using a balloon whisk to help incorporate all the ingredients, before scraping down the bowl sides and bottom with a rubber spatula.

Complete the sponge batter by folding in the chocolate chunks before transferring to the prepared tin. Use the back of a spoon or an offset palette knife to help even out the mix before placing in the oven and baking for 24–26 minutes. I always like to go for less time, for a gooey, slightly under-done middle.

Meanwhile, make the butterscotch sauce. It's super simple – all you gotta do is chuck all the ingredients into a saucepan and cook over a gentle heat until the butter has melted, sugar has dissolved, and the liquid begins to bubble and thicken. This should take about 15 minutes. Remove from the heat and leave to cool.

Once the sponge is baked and still warm, poke a few holes in the top using a toothpick and then use a pastry brush to coat generously with some of the butterscotch sauce. The holes will soak up all that goodness, leaving a super-moist and flavorsome sponge. Leave in the tin to cool completely.

When the sponge has cooled, make the coconut whipped cream by adding the cream cheese to the bowl of a stand mixer and whisking until smooth. Add the remaining ingredients and whisk until it's at medium peaks; we want this to be a silky, spreadable, but firm consistency. You can either pipe on the cream, swirl it, or level it out, but once added, pop the tin in the fridge for about 30 minutes to set.

To finish, pour on the remaining cooled butterscotch sauce, sprinkle the ginger biscuit crumbs on top and leave to set for another 30 minutes before carefully removing the stacked sponge from the tin and serving yourself a slice.

Plant-Based Banana, Choc and Butterscotch Traybake with Whipped Coconut Cream and Ginger Crumb

Serves: 20

For the Sponge
4 large ripe bananas
100 ml soy milk, room temp
110 ml vegetable oil
2 tsp vanilla bean paste
150 g light soft brown sugar
2 tsp apple cider vinegar
385 g self-raising flour, sifted
1¼ tsp sweetened ground cinnamon
pinch of sea salt
200 g dark chocolate, chunks or callets

For the Butterscotch Sauce
300 ml plant-based single cream
80 g plant-based unsalted butter, room temp
150 g light soft brown sugar
1 tsp vanilla bean paste

For the Coconut Whipped Cream
300 g plant-based cream cheese
300 ml plant-based whipping cream
75 g sweetened desiccated coconut
50 g caster sugar, or to taste
1½ tsp vanilla bean paste

For the Ginger Biscuit Crumb
6 ginger snap biscuits, blitzed or bashed
   to crumbs

deep 20 x 30-cm/8 x 12-in. cake tin, greased
   and lined (allow the paper to come up over
   the sides)

Pop that oven on to 155°C fan/175°C/gas mark 4.

In a medium bowl, mash the bananas to a purée. Add the milk, vegetable oil and vanilla bean paste to the bowl before mixing well with a balloon whisk to help emulsify all the liquids. Next in is the sugar; mix well until fully combined. Pour in the apple cider vinegar and give it all a good mix before leaving to one side.

In a separate large bowl, add the sifted flour and cinnamon together. Add a good pinch of salt before combining the dry ingredients with the wet. I like to begin mixing by using a balloon whisk to help incorporate all the ingredients, before scraping down the bowl sides and bottom with a rubber spatula.

Complete the sponge batter by folding in the chocolate chunks before transferring to the prepared tin. Use the back of a spoon or an offset palette knife to help even out the mix before placing in the oven and baking for 26–28 minutes. I always like to go for less time, for a gooey, slightly under-done middle.

Meanwhile, make the butterscotch sauce. It's super simple – all you gotta do is chuck all the ingredients into a saucepan and cook over a gentle heat until the butter has melted, sugar has dissolved, and the liquid begins to bubble and thicken. This should take about 15 minutes. Remove from the heat and leave to cool.

Once the sponge is baked and still warm, poke a few holes in the top using a toothpick and then use a pastry brush to coat generously with some of the butterscotch sauce. The holes will soak up all that goodness, leaving a super-moist and flavorsome sponge. Leave the sponge in the tin to cool completely.

When the sponge has cooled, make the coconut whipped cream by adding the cream cheese to the bowl of a stand mixer bowl and whisking until smooth. Add the remaining ingredients f and whisk until it's at medium peaks; we want this to be a silky, spreadable, but firm consistency. You can either pipe on the cream, swirl it, or level it out, but once added, pop the tin in the fridge for about 30 minutes to set.

To finish, pour on the remaining cooled butterscotch sauce, sprinkle the ginger biscuit crumbs on top and leave to set for another 30 minutes. To serve, carefully remove the stacked sponge from the tin and slice.

Cardamom and Raspberry Cake with White Chocolate and Pistachio

This is the cake I would always make back in the day when I first started baking because a) the flavour combo is bomb dot com and b) I really thought I was doing something new and inventive out here with the ingredients. Turns out I was just reinventing the cake wheel, but sometimes a classic combo is all you truly need.

This is such a crowd-pleasing cake – there is nothing rogue with the flavours at all, despite my many attempts to tweak it. It's a trusty, tried-and-tested combination: the lightly spiced sponge works incredibly well with the tartness from the fresh raspberries, sweetness from the whipped white chocolate cream, and nuttiness from the pistachio crumb. I have never had a complaint from anyone who's gobbled this cake and long will it stay that way.

Cardamom and Raspberry Cake with White Chocolate and Pistachio

Serves: 8

For the Sponge
260 g unsalted butter or baking margarine,
    room temp
260 g golden caster sugar
4 large eggs
2 tsp vanilla bean paste
50 g soured cream, room temp
1½ tsp ground cardamom
275 g self-raising flour, sifted

For the Filling
400 g raspberries
1 tsp caster sugar
squeeze of lemon juice
50 g pistachios, blitzed to a crumb

For the White Chocolate Whipped Cream
430 ml double cream
10 g icing sugar, sifted
1½ tsp vanilla bean paste
70 g white chocolate, melted and cooled

For the Sugar Syrup
1 quantity simple vanilla syrup (see page 303)

2 x 18-cm/7-in. cake tins, greased with
    coconut oil and lined (base and sides)

Preheat the oven to 155°C fan/175°C/gas mark 4.

In a stand mixer fitted with the paddle attachment, beat the butter and sugar until light and fluffy. Make sure you give this a few minutes to do its thing, this is a key stage to building those airy, fluffy, life-changing sponges. Add the eggs to the stand mixer, one at a time, mixing well between each addition, allowing the eggs to emulsify with the butter. Add the vanilla bean paste and soured cream and mix again for a few rotations to distribute.

Add the cardamom to your flour and mix. I like to do this before it goes into the stand mixer to make sure all that heavenly, fragrant spice is distributed evenly. Add one-third of the cardamom flour to the stand mixer and mix well. Remove the bowl from the stand and fold in the remaining two-thirds of flour by hand using a rubber spatula. You'll find this easier and less of a workout if you do this in two stages – this will also minimise flour clumps once your sponge has baked.

Divide the batter evenly between the prepared tins and bake in the oven for 35–38 minutes, until the sponge has started to come away from the sides of the tin. Prick the middle with a toothpick to ensure you only bring back crumbs, if you want to be super-duper sure.

Remove from the oven and leave to sit for a few minutes before turning the sponges out onto a cooling rack. Let them sit there at room temp for about 30 minutes before wrapping in clingfilm and leaving to cool completely. Wrapping them locks in all that moistness and ensures no dry, sad sponges.

For the filling, add three-quarters of the raspberries and all the sugar to a bowl. Squeeze over a bit of lemon juice and break down with the back of a fork.

The last thing to make is the white chocolate cream. You can sub this out for a Swiss meringue buttercream (see page XXX, the only one I ever use), but let's make something even better and simpler. Add all the ingredients to a bowl and whisk until it's at a medium peak. Because this isn't going to be a three-sponge bonanza, a looser cream is fine (and also preferred for a silkier finish). Work the rest of the cream by hand until you get it to a consistency you feel comfortable with.

Let's construct the cake. Remove the cakes from the wrap and level out any domed tops with a serrated knife. Using a pastry brush, liberally coat the tops and sides of the sponges with the vanilla sugar syrup. Dollop a good helping of the white chocolate cream on top, saving some for later. Swirl around for an even layer before topping with half of the raspberry filling and a handful of the blitzed pistachios.

Sandwich the cake with the remaining sponge, bottom-side up (for a super-flat top) and add the remaining cream. I like to go rustic and just use the back of the spoon to swirl loosely. To finish this beauty off, top with the remaining raspberry mix and scatter over the rest of the pistachios. This fragrant beauty is now complete to eat.

Plant-Based Cardamom and Raspberry Cake with White Chocolate and Pistachio

We are using a whipped plant-based white chocolate cream to sandwich, but if you are after something sturdier for a stacked bonanza, make sure you switch this up to an American-style buttercream filling. Despite me vowing to never use it, sometimes you also just don't want your cake to collapse. Ya, know? So, use your better judgment.

Serves: 8

For the Sponge
300 ml almond milk
1 tsp apple cider vinegar
350 g self-raising flour, sifted
1½ tsp ground cardamom
1 tsp bicarbonate of soda, sifted
½ tsp baking powder, sifted
235 g caster sugar
115 ml sunflower oil
35 g plant-based unsalted butter, melted
2 tsp vanilla bean paste

For the Filling
400 g raspberries
1 tsp caster sugar
squeeze of lemon juice
50 g pistachios, blitzed to a crumb

For the White Chocolate Whipped Cream
100 g plant-based cream cheese
430 ml plant-based double cream
10 g icing sugar, sifted
1½ tsp vanilla bean paste
70 g plant-based white chocolate, melted
    and cooled

For the Sugar Syrup
1 quantity simple vanilla syrup (see page 000)

2 x 18-cm/7-in. cake tins, greased with
    coconut oil and lined (base and sides)

Preheat the oven to 150°C fan/175°C/gas mark 4.

This sponge is so low key – you'll have it whipped up and made in no time. Firstly, add the almond milk and apple cider vinegar to a large bowl. Give it a little mix and let it sit for 10 minutes to curdle. This will make a vegan buttermilk equivalent to ensure a super-soft, moist sponge.

In the meantime, add all the dry ingredients to a separate large bowl and mix to combine.

Once the milk has done its thing, add the oil, melted butter and vanilla bean paste. Give this a good stir before pouring into the dry ingredients. Use a balloon whisk to mix until everything has just incorporated.

Divide the batter evenly between the two prepared tins and pop in the oven to bake for 28–30 minutes until the sponge has started to come away from the sides of the tin. Prick the middle with a toothpick and ensure you only bring back crumbs.

Remove the tins from the oven and leave to sit for a few minutes before turning the sponges onto a cooling rack. Let them sit at room temp for 30 minutes before wrapping in clingfilm and leaving to cool completely.

For the filling, add three-quarters of the raspberries and all the sugar to a bowl. Squeeze over a bit of lemon juice and break down with the back of a fork. Leave to one side.

The last thing to make is the white chocolate whipped cream. Add the cream cheese to a bowl and mix until smooth. Add all the remaining cream ingredients to the bowl and whisk to stiff peaks (because we are using a plant-based cream, you really want this to be stable, so take it past the point of medium peaks to give yourself a solid stacking foundation). I like to pop this into the fridge for at least 30 minutes before using, to allow it to solidify.

Now, let's construct the cake. Remove the cakes from the wrap and level out any domed tops with a serrated knife. Using a pastry brush, liberally coat the tops and sides of the sponges with the vanilla sugar syrup. Dollop a good helping of the white chocolate cream on top, saving some of the cream for later. Swirl around for an even layer before topping with half of the raspberry filling. Sprinkle over a generous handful of the blitzed pistachios.

Sandwich the cake with the remaining sponge, bottom-side up (for a super-flat top) and add the remaining cream. I like to go rustic and just use the back of the spoon to swirl loosely.

To finish this beauty off, top with the remaining raspberry mix and scatter over the rest of the pistachios.

Self-saucing Sticky Toffee Pud Tray-Cake with Stem Ginger and Chocolate

When I think of this tray-cake, I imagine eating it stonkingly hot, drowning in a vanilla-overdosed crème Anglaise on a cold winter's day. Equally, I also imagine eating this cold, topped with a scoop or two of vanilla ice cream on a warm summer's day. If you can't do the maths here, this is a bake that is great all-year-round. Just my cup of tea. And talking of tea, if you are wanting to make this into individual portions to serve up to guests at a dinner party, just divide the recipe by two and then divvy up the sauce and batter into individual ramekins and bake for one-third of the time.

Serves: 8 generous portions

For the Date Purée
225 g Medjool dates, destoned
350 ml boiling water
275 ml water
1 tsp bicarbonate of soda

For the Sauce
150 ml water
245 ml double cream
225 g dark soft brown sugar
100 g unsalted butter, diced
20 g dark chocolate, chopped
30 g cocoa powder, sifted

For the Sponge
115 g unsalted butter or baking margarine, room temp
75 g dark soft brown sugar
75 g light soft brown sugar
1 tsp vanilla bean paste
2 large eggs
260 g self-raising flour, sifted
1½ tsp ground ginger
1 bulb preserved stem ginger, finely chopped
35 g dark chocolate, chopped
40 g milk chocolate, chopped

deep 35 x 25-cm/14 x 10-in. baking tray

To begin with, we want to get rid of the skins on the dates for a silky smooth purée. Add the dates to a bowl, along with the boiling water. Sprinkle in the bicarbonate of soda, give it all a stir, and allow them to sit and soften for 20–25 minutes. Once softened, drain the water and remove the skins from the dates. Fill the bowl back up with the 275 ml of water before blitzing using a hand blender or popping into a food processor. We want to make sure there are no lumps, so keep going until it is lovely and smooth. Set aside.

Preheat the oven to 160°C fan/180°C/gas mark 4.

Add all the ingredients for the sauce to a saucepan and mix well using a balloon whisk. Let the butter and chocolate melt, bringing the sauce up to the boil before turning the heat down and reducing to a simmer for a few minutes. Once slightly thickened, take off the heat and allow to cool while you get cracking with the sponge.

Cream together the room temp butter, sugar and vanilla bean paste in a stand mixer fitted with the whisk attachment until light and fluffy. Add the eggs, one by one, making sure you mix well between each addition – we want the mixture to be fully emulsified before moving on. Sift in the flour and ground ginger, mixing well before folding in the chopped stem ginger, date purée and chocolate.

Transfer the cake batter to the prepared baking tray. Pour the cooled chocolate sauce on top. It may look weird, it may feel weird, but trust me – it is all part of the process! Pop the tray in the oven for 35–38 minutes until the sponge is jusssst cooked through. I personally like to remove this on the slightly under-done side for extra gooeyness, but you do you.

Once removed, leave to sit for 5–10 minutes before tucking in with a serving of vanilla ice cream.

TIP For a super-naughty dessert, serve this up alongside my cinnamon and rum ice cream (see pages 178–9) for ultimate and I mean ULTIMATE indulgence.

Plant-Based Self-saucing Sticky Toffee Pud Tray-Cake with Stem Ginger and Chocolate

Shall I tell you a secret? I actually think the plant-based version of this recipe is my favourite out the two – the sponge is delicately soft. When you are short on eggs, dairy fans I URGE you to make this one to see whether you can taste the difference. The exact same flavour, all the same yums, just simpler, easier and less faff.

Serves: 8 generous portions

For the Date Purée
225 g Medjool dates, destoned
350 ml boiling water
275 ml water
1 tsp bicarbonate of soda

For the Sauce
150 ml water
245 ml plant-based double cream
225 g dark soft brown sugar
100 g plant-based unsalted butter, diced
20 g plant-based dark chocolate, chopped
30 g cocoa powder, sifted

For the Sponge
115 g plant-based unsalted butter
75 g dark soft brown sugar
75 g light soft brown sugar
1 tsp vanilla bean paste
4 tbsp water
4 tsp baking powder
2 tsp vegetable oil
260 g self-raising flour, sifted
½ tsp bicarbonate of soda
1½ tsp ground ginger
1 bulb preserved stem ginger, finely chopped
75 g plant-based dark chocolate, chopped

deep 35 x 25-cm/14 x 10-in. baking tray

To begin with, we want to get rid of the skins on the dates for a silky smooth purée. Add the dates to a bowl, along with the boiling water. Sprinkle in the bicarbonate of soda, give it all a stir, and allow them to sit and soften for 20–25 minutes. Once softened, drain the water and remove the skins from the dates. Fill the bowl back up with the 275 ml of water before blitzing using a hand blender or popping into a food processor. We want to make sure there are no lumps, so keep going until it is lovely and smooth. Set aside.

Preheat the oven to 160°C fan/180°C/gas mark 4.

Add all the ingredients for the sauce to a saucepan and mix well using a balloon whisk. Let the butter and chocolate melt, bringing the sauce up to the boil before turning the heat down and reducing to a simmer for a few minutes. Once slightly thickened, take off the heat and allow to cool while you get cracking with the sponge.

The sponge for this is super easy – another two-bowl mixy-mix. Add the butter, sugars and vanilla bean paste to a pan and gently heat until the butter has melted and sugar has dissolved. Take off the heat and give this a real good mix.

Add the date purée and stir well. In a small bowl, mix together the water, baking powder and vegetable oil – this is your egg replacement. Add this to the pan.

Into another bowl, add the flour, bicarb and ground ginger before mixing to combine. Pour in the butter mix and give it all a really good stir until smooth. Add the stem ginger and chocolate, and fold in.

Transfer the cake batter to the prepared baking tray. Pour the cooled chocolate sauce on top.

Pop the tray in the oven and cook for 40 minutes until the sponge is just cooked through. I personally like to remove this on the slightly under-done side for extra gooeyness, but you do you. Once removed, leave to sit for 5–10 minutes before tucking in with a serving of plant-based vanilla ice cream.

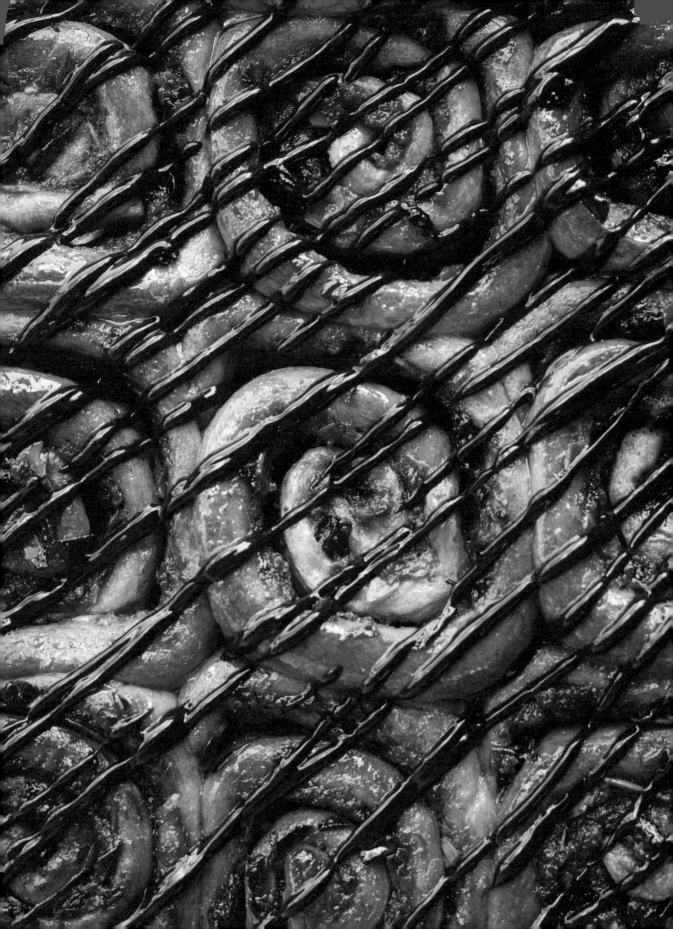

Breaking Bread

Carbs, glorious carbs!

Cinnamon Rolls with Cream Cheese Frosting

Holy crummage. This recipe is foolproof – it doesn't matter what they come out of the oven looking like, because as soon as you slather on the vanilla-laden frosting, it hides a myriad of problems, and before you know it, you're three rolls deep and wondering whether eating a fourth would be a good idea.

The key to these being the best you've ever had is the tangzhong – an additional step I throw into lots of my bread recipes. This Japanese method of bread baking sees you cooking out a percentage of the flour alongside the milk to form a gelatinous paste. You add this to the dough ingredients at the start and the results are always worth the extra effort, as the bread stays softer and tender for longer. But the good news is, you can prep this a day or two in advance and store it in your fridge until you need it.

Yes, bread can be time-consuming. But it's also thought-consuming, soul-consuming – your focus is all on the making, the baking, and the eating. The voices in your head quieten, your breathing becomes deeper, slower, more intentional. Following instructions and instinctively doing becomes almost like a guided meditation. Whatever the outcome, whatever presents itself is yours. For the soul and for those you choose to share it with. It is, quite simply, therapy. Try it and you'll see what I mean.

Cinnamon Rolls with Cream Cheese Frosting

Makes: 12

For the Tangzhong
50 g strong white bread flour, sifted
170 ml full-fat milk

For the Dough
170 ml lukewarm full-fat milk (38–40°C/
    100–104°F)
12 g active dried yeast
55 g golden caster sugar
420 g strong white bread flour, sifted, plus
    extra for dusting
9 g salt
1 large egg
1 egg yolk
¼ tsp ground cardamom
1½ tsp vanilla bean paste
80 g unsalted butter, room temp

For the Filling
125 g light soft brown sugar
110 g unsalted butter, room temp
1½ tbsp ground cinnamon, sifted
1¼ tbsp cocoa powder, sifted
1½ tsp vanilla bean paste

For the Icing
180 g icing sugar, sifted
60 g unsalted butter, room temp
65 g cream cheese
1 tsp vanilla bean paste
1 tbsp full-fat milk

For the tangzhong, add the flour to a pan. Slowly add the milk, using a balloon whisk to ensure no lumps. Place the pan over a medium heat and whisk until thickened – think gloopy wallpaper-paste consistency. Leave to cool at room temperature, covering the surface of the tangzhong with some clingfilm or baking paper to avoid it crusting over.

Once cooled, move onto the dough. Add the lukewarm milk to a bowl with the yeast and a pinch of the sugar. Leave for 10–15 minutes until the milk is bubbly and frothy.

Scoop the cooled tangzhong to the bowl of a stand mixer and add the flour, remaining sugar, salt, egg, egg yolk, cardamom, vanilla bean paste and the yeasty milk. Mix on low speed with the dough hook attachment for 6–8 minutes until soft and stretchy. Add the butter and mix on medium–high speed for 5 minutes until it is fully incorporated, the dough has started to come away from the sides and is smooth. Mix on low speed for another 5 minutes.

Transfer the dough to a lightly oiled large bowl before placing it in a proving bag or covering with clingfilm. Leave to prove for 2 hours in an unheated oven with a tray of freshly boiled water at the bottom to create a steamy environment.

While proving, make the filling. Add all the ingredients to the bowl of a stand mixer fitted with the paddle attachment, and mix until well combined (or mix using an electric hand whisk). Set aside at room temperature.

Turn the proved dough out onto a lightly floured surface. Gently knock back the dough before rolling out into a large rectangle about 7.5 mm/⅓ in. thick.

Spread the spiced butter filling (reserving 1 tbsp) evenly onto the dough using a palette knife or the back of a spoon – go all the way to the edges. Warning: The dough will be super soft and needs a bit of a gentle touch when handling, so have a bit of chill when spreading the butter. If you're in struggle city, transfer the butter to a piping bag

and warm the bag up with your hands, before piping out the butter and then spreading.

You have two options here for rolling. Option 1: From the long end, tightly roll the dough, leaving the seam at the bottom. Divide the dough into twelve before using sharp knife/floss to cut. Option 2: Trim the edges of your rolled-out dough to a nice, neat rectangle. Divide this dough evenly into twelve on the long edge. Use a knife or a pizza cutter to cut each strip, before rolling each one individually for a neater finish.

Use the reserved 1 tbsp of spiced butter to grease the bottom of a deep, large baking tray. Place the rolls in the tray, leaving a bit of space between them, if possible. Cover with a proving bag or clingfilm to prove for 1 hour. I'd recommend the hot tray of water and oven combo again.

Once proved, remove tray from bag/clingfilm. Don't worry about any butter pooling on the top; that'll soak back into the dough during baking.

Now's the time to preheat the oven to 160°C fan/180°C/gas mark 4.

Bake for 28–30 minutes, placing a sheet of foil on top after 25 minutes to prevent further browning – we are after a deep golden-brown colour, not burnt and charred. Use a thermometer probe to check if the dough has reached at least 92°C/198°F once baked. Leave to cool.

To finish, make the icing by adding the icing sugar and butter to a mixing bowl and beating until combined. Add the cream cheese and vanilla and whisk until smooth, before adding a splash of milk to loosen it slightly to a spreadable consistency. Slather over the cooled rolls, really spreading the icing into the nooks and crannies. Frost the buns while still slightly warm for a super smushy texture and then proceed to devour them.

Plant-Based Cinnamon Rolls with Cream Cheese Frosting

Makes: 12

For the Tangzhong
50 g strong white bread flour, sifted
170 ml soy milk

For the Dough
195 ml lukewarm soy milk (38–40°C/
  100–104°F)
12 g active dried yeast
55 g golden caster sugar
420 g strong white bread flour, sifted,
  plus extra for dusting
¼ tsp ground cardamom
1½ tsp vanilla bean paste
9 g salt
80 g unsalted plant-based butter, room temp

For the Filling
125 g light soft brown sugar
115 g plant-based unsalted butter, room temp
1½ tbsp ground cinnamon
1¼ tbsp cocoa powder
1½ tsp vanilla bean paste

For the Icing
170 g icing sugar, sifted
60 g plant-based unsalted butter, room temp
65 g plant-based cream cheese
1 tsp vanilla bean paste
1 tbsp plant-based milk

Let's begin with making the tangzhong. Add the flour to a pan. Slowly add the milk, using a balloon whisk to ensure no lumps. Place the pan over a medium heat and whisk until thickened – think gloopy wallpaper-paste consistency. Leave to cool at room temperature, covering the surface of the tangzhong with clingfilm or baking paper to avoid it crusting over.

Once cooled, move onto the dough. Add the milk to a bowl with the yeast and a pinch of the sugar. Leave for 10–15 minutes until frothy.

Scoop the cooled tangzhong into the bowl of a stand mixer and add the flour, cardamom, vanilla bean paste, salt and remaining sugar before pouring in the yeasty milk. Mix on low speed with the dough hook attachment for 6–8 minutes until soft and stretchy. Add the butter and mix on medium–high speed for 5 minutes until fully incorporated, the dough has started to come away from the sides and smooth. Turn the speed down to low and mix for another 5 minutes. Don't add more flour, even if the dough feels wet to touch.

Transfer the dough to a lightly oiled large bowl before placing it in a proving bag or covering with clingfilm. Leave to prove for 2 hours in an unheated oven with a tray of freshly boiled water at the bottom to create a steamy environment.

While proving, make the filling. Add all the ingredients to the bowl of a stand mixer fitted with the paddle attachment, and mix until well combined (or mix using an electric hand whisk). Set aside at room temperature.

Turn the proved dough out onto a lightly floured surface. Gently knock back the dough before rolling out into a large rectangle about 7.5 mm/ ⅓ in. thick.

Spread the spiced butter filling (reserving 1 tbsp) evenly onto the dough using a palette knife or the back of a spoon – go all the way to the edges. Warning: The dough will be super soft and needs

a bit of a gentle touch when handling, so have a bit of chill when spreading the butter. If you're in struggle city, transfer the butter to a piping bag and warm the bag up with your hands, before piping out the butter and then spreading.

You have two options here for rolling. Option 1: From the long end, tightly roll the dough, leaving the seam at the bottom. Divide the dough into twelve before using sharp knife or floss to cut. Option 2: Trim the edges of your rolled-out dough to a nice, neat rectangle. Divide this dough evenly into twelve on the long edge. Use a knife or a pizza cutter to cut each strip, before rolling each one individually for a neater finish.

Use the reserved 1 tbsp of spiced butter to grease the bottom of a deep, large baking tray. Place the rolls in the tray, leaving a bit of space between them, if possible. Cover with a proving bag or clingfilm again to prove for 1 hour.

Once proved, remove tray from bag/clingfilm. Don't worry about any butter pooling on the top; that'll soak back into the dough during baking.

Now's the time to preheat the oven to 160°C fan/180°C/gas mark 4.

Bake for 28–30 minutes, placing a sheet of foil on top after 25 minutes to prevent further browning – we are after a deep golden-brown colour. Use a thermometer probe to check if the dough has reached at least 92°C/198°F once baked. Leave to cool.

To finish, make the icing by adding the icing sugar and butter to a mixing bowl and beating until combined. Add the cream cheese and vanilla bean paste and whisk until smooth, before adding a splash of plant-based milk to loosen to a spreadable consistency. Slather over the cooled rolls, really spreading the icing into the nooks and crannies. Frost the buns while still slightly warm for a super smushy texture and then proceed to devour them.

Malt Choco-Nut Babka
with Streusel Top

There is something so special about Babka — the slice falling flat on its face to show you its intertwined, chocolatey guts, just gets me every single time. We are ramping up the flavour of the dough with a punch of malty, vanilla bean goodness, a filling of homemade Nutella and then we finish off the bake with a nutty almond and macadamia streusel top for added texture and indulgence. A really homely, comforting treat. Best eaten on the day and with good company.

There are bits of the recipe where you can get ahead, making the actual bake day far less daunting. Prep the homemade Nutella and streusel the day before, allowing you to breeze through the recipe and get that Babka in the belly quicker than a blink of an eye (if the blink was actually you going to sleep and waking up again).

Malt Choco-Nut Babka with Streusel Top

Serves: 6

For the Dough
70 ml lukewarm full-fat milk (38–40°C/
    100–104°F)
6 g fast-action dried yeast
45 g golden caster sugar
330 g strong white bread flour, sifted,
    plus extra for dusting
45 g malt powder
5 g salt
2 large eggs
1 large egg yolk
2 tsp vanilla bean paste
90 g unsalted butter, room temp
1 egg, beaten, for brushing

For the Filling
1 quantity homemade Nutella (see page 288)

For the Streusel Topping
25 g unsalted butter, fridge temp and diced
25 g golden caster sugar
20 g plain flour
10 g ground almonds
15 g flaked almonds
15 g macadamia nuts, roughly chopped
1 tsp vanilla bean paste
½ tsp almond extract

For the Sugar Syrup
½ quantity simple vanilla syrup (see page 303)

2-kg/900-g loaf tin, greased and lined
    (allow the paper to come up over the sides)

Start by activating the yeast. Pour the milk into a bowl and sprinkle the yeast and 1 tsp of the sugar on top. Give it a mix and set aside to do its thing for 10 minutes until bubbly and frothy.

Add the remaining dough ingredients, except the butter and the beaten egg for brushing, to the bowl of a stand mixer. Pour in the yeasty milk and mix on low–medium speed for 5 minutes to combine all the ingredients and roughly form a dough. Add the butter and mix on medium speed for 3 minutes to incorporate, then turn the speed down to low and mix for 10 minutes. We are after a soft, stretchy dough – be careful not to overmix as it will break the gluten strands. This is an enriched dough, so it may feel slightly wet to touch, don't overload it with more flour.

Transfer the dough to a large, lightly oiled bowl and cover. Leave to prove for 1½–2 hours in an unheated oven with a tray of freshly boiled water at the bottom to create a steamy environment.

Turn out the dough onto a lightly floured worktop. Roll out the dough into a 40 x 30-cm/16 x 12-in. rectangle, about 7.5 mm/⅓ in. thick.

Evenly spread the homemade Nutella on top of the dough, all the way to the edges, using a palette knife or the back of a spoon. Be generous and slather evenly. Starting with the long edge closest to you, begin to roll up the dough into a tight spiral, finishing with the dough seam at the base.

Rotate the dough so the short edge is now closest to you. Trim off the edges of the roll to neaten up, before using a pizza cutter or sharp knife to slice lengthways down the middle, cutting the dough into two pieces, exposing the chocolate layers. Working cut-face up, carefully braid the two pieces around each other to create a two-strand plait. I find it easier to start by overlapping them both in the middle as an anchor point and then continuing to braid either side. If that proves a nightmare, gently tack the two ends on one side together and braid top to bottom instead.

Seal the bottom of each strand together and fold underneath to hide the seam. Carefully lift the loaf into the prepared tin, cover and leave to prove for 45 minutes, or until the dough has doubled in size.

Preheat the oven to 170°C fan/190°C/gas mark 5.

While you are waiting for the oven to preheat and the dough to prove, make the streusel topping by adding all the ingredients to a bowl and working with your fingertips until it resembles clumpy breadcrumbs. Alternatively, you can pop this into a food processor and pulse. Set aside.

Once the dough has doubled in size, use a pastry brush to gently brush over the beaten egg. This will act as a glue for the streusel.

Generously load up the streusel on top of the loaf before popping into the oven. Bake for 20 minutes, then lower the oven temperature to 150°C fan/170°C/gas mark 3 and bake for a further 20 minutes. Check to see whether the top is browning a little too much. If so, place a foil tent over the top to avoid incinerating the streusel. Bake for another 15–20 minutes. Check the dough has cooked by using a thermometer probe, or by poking it with a wooden skewer to ensure no raw dough returns. You want to see a temperature of at least 92°C/198°F in the thickest part to know the dough is baked.

Once baked, remove from the oven and leave to sit in the tin for 10 minutes before carefully removing by lifting the loaf up by the overlined paper. Liberally brush the sides and any exposed dough with the sugar syrup. This dough is damn delicious either warm or cold – my only advice is to keep any leftovers well wrapped or in a sealed container.

Plant-Based Malt Choco-Nut Babka with Streusel Top

Because this is an enriched dough, we need to do a little extra work with getting it lovely, fluffy and moist without using eggs. Here we are using a tangzhong to help with that, alongside the addition of unsweetened apple sauce. To get a head start, you can make the tangzhong a day or two in advance, just store, covered, in the fridge until it is needed.

Serves: 6

For the Tangzhong
30 g strong white bread flour, sifted
50 ml soy or almond milk

For the Dough
100 ml lukewarm soy or almond milk
   (38–40°C/100–104°F)
6 g fast-action dried yeast
45 g golden caster sugar
345 g strong white bread flour, sifted,
   plus extra for dusting
45 g malt powder
5 g salt
115 g unsweetened apple sauce
   (see page 302)
2 tsp vanilla bean paste
75 g plant-based unsalted butter, room temp
5 ml maple syrup, for brushing

For the Filling
1 quantity homemade Nutella (see page 288)

For the Streusel Topping
25 g plant-based unsalted butter, diced
25 g golden caster sugar
20 g plain flour
10 g ground almonds
15 g flaked almonds
15 g macadamia nuts, roughly chopped
1 tsp vanilla bean paste
½ tsp almond extract

For the Sugar Syrup
½ quantity simple vanilla syrup (see page 303)

2-kg/900-g loaf tin, greased with coconut oil
   and lined (let the paper to come over sides)

For the tangzhong, add the flour to a pan. Slowly add the milk, using a balloon whisk to mix to ensure no lumps. Place the pan over a medium heat and whisk until thickened to a gloopy, wallpaper-paste consistency. Leave to sit at room temperature, covering the tangzhong with some clingfilm or baking paper to avoid it crusting over.

Pour the milk into a bowl and sprinkle the yeast and 1 tsp of the sugar on top. Give it a mix and leave for 15 minutes until bubbly and frothy.

Add the remaining dough ingredients, except the butter and maple syrup, to the bowl of a stand mixer and add the yeasty milk. Mix on low–medium speed for 5 minutes to combine and roughly form a dough. Add the butter and mix on medium speed for 3 minutes to incorporate, then turn the speed down to low and mix for 10 minutes. We are after a soft, stretchy dough – be careful not to overmix as we don't want to break the gluten strands. This is an enriched dough, so it may feel slightly wet to touch, don't overload it with more flour.

Transfer the dough to a large, lightly oiled bowl and cover. Leave to prove for 1½–2 hours in an unheated oven with a tray of freshly boiled water at the bottom to create a steamy environment.

Turn out the dough onto a lightly floured worktop. Roll out the dough into a 40 x 30-cm/16 x 12-in. rectangle, about 7.5 mm/⅓ in. thick.

Evenly spread the homemade Nutella on top of the dough, all the way to the edges, using a palette knife or the back of a spoon. Be generous and slather evenly. Starting with the long edge closest to you, begin to roll up the dough into a tight spiral, finishing with the dough seam at the base.

Rotate the dough so the short edge is now closest to you. Trim the edges of the roll to neaten up before using a pizza cutter or sharp knife to slice lengthways down the middle, cutting the dough into two pieces, exposing the chocolate layers. Working cut-face up, carefully braid the two pieces around each other to create a two-strand plait. I find it easier to start by overlapping them both in the middle as an anchor point and then continuing to braid either side. If that proves a nightmare, gently tack the two ends on one side together and braid top to bottom instead.

Seal the bottom of each strand together and fold underneath to hide the seam. Carefully lift the loaf into the lined tin, cover and leave to prove for 45 minutes, or until the dough has doubled in size. Preheat the oven to 170°C fan/190°C/gas mark 5.

While you are waiting for the oven to preheat and the dough to prove, make the streusel topping by adding all the ingredients to a bowl and working with your fingertips until it resembles clumpy breadcrumbs. Alternatively, you can pop this into a food processor and pulse. Set aside.

Once the dough has doubled in size, use a pastry brush to gently brush over the maple syrup. This will act as a glue for the streusel.

Generously load up the streusel on top of the loaf before popping into the oven. Bake for 20 minutes, then lower the oven temperature to 150°C fan/170°C/gas mark 3 and bake for a further 20 minutes. Check to see whether the top is browning a little too much: If so, place a foil tent over the top to avoid incinerating the streusel. Bake for another 15–20 minutes. Check the dough has cooked by using a thermometer probe, or by poking it with a wooden skewer to ensure no raw dough returns. You want to see a temperature of at least 92°C/198°F in the thickest part to know the dough is baked.

Once baked, remove the loaf from the oven and leave to sit in the tin for 10 minutes before lifting out with the overlined paper. Liberally brush the sides and any exposed dough with the sugar syrup. Serve warm or cold – keep any leftovers well wrapped or in a sealed container.

Salted Caramel Doughnuts with Orange and Cinnamon

I used to love nothing more than tucking into one of those pre-packaged doughnuts you'd get from the supermarket. You know the type where it's laden with sugar and when you'd bite into it, the jam would inevitably spill out the other side and the sides of your mouth, and somehow even your cheek would be covered in that sweet, sticky, sugary glitter.

These doughnuts do just that, except better. They have the fluffiest doughnut dough that is spiced with a hint of cinnamon and lifted with orange zest, packed with a salted caramel pastry cream and then classically finished with a dip in caster sugar. That first bite of pillowy soft dough is so satisfying.

This recipe was originally double all the quantities, but upon testing, I thought that making twenty doughnuts in one go was *slightly* excessive? Just double the quantities below and keep the method the same, if you too, want to be drowning in doughnuts.

Salted Caramel Doughnuts with Orange and Cinnamon

Makes: 10

For the Dough
170 ml lukewarm full-fat milk (38–40°C/
   100–104°F)
7 g fast-action dried yeast
60 g golden caster sugar
350 g strong white bread flour, sifted
5 g salt
1 large egg
1 large egg yolk
1 tbsp ground cinnamon
grated zest of 1 large orange
1 tsp vanilla bean paste
60 g unsalted butter, room temp

For the Filling
375 ml full-fat milk
1½ tsp vanilla bean paste
5 medium egg yolks
75 g caster sugar
22 g cornflour, sifted
15 g plain flour, sifted
110 g salted caramel sauce (see page 290 or
   use store-bought, shhh don't tell anyone)

For Frying
1 litre vegetable oil

To Finish
caster sugar, for dusting

Add the milk to a bowl and sprinkle the yeast and a pinch of the sugar on top. Give it a stir and leave to sit for 15 minutes until bubbly and frothy.

Add the flour, remaining sugar, the salt, egg, egg yolk, cinnamon, orange zest and vanilla bean paste to the bowl of a stand mixer before pouring in the yeasty milk. Mix on low speed with the dough hook attachment for 6–8 minutes until soft and stretchy. Add the butter and mix on medium–high speed for 5 minutes until it is fully incorporated, the dough has started to come away from the sides, and is soft and smooth. This is quite a wet dough, so don't be tempted to add more flour if it feels wet to the touch.

Transfer the dough to a lightly oiled large bowl, then into a proving bag or cover with clingfilm.

Leave to prove for 2 hours in an unheated oven with a tray of freshly boiled water at the bottom to create a steamy environment. Alternatively, if you are making these on a warm day, leaving the bowl covered in the sunshine will also work a treat.

The base of the filling is a thickened pastry cream (or crème pâtissière if you want to be fancy about it). Pour the milk and vanilla bean paste into a saucepan over a medium heat and bring to a near boil.

While the milk is heating up, whisk the egg yolks, sugar and both flours in a separate bowl. Work past that gritty, lumpy stage until the yolks are smooth.

Once the milk is simmering, pour one-third onto the mixed egg yolks and whisk immediately until smooth. Work quickly to avoid scrambling the eggs; make sure the mixture is free from lumps before pouring back into the saucepan of milk. Cook, stirring often, while the cream begins to thicken, for about 5 minutes. I begin mixing with a balloon whisk and then switch to a rubber spatula towards the end to ensure the cream doesn't catch on the bottom.

When the cream begins to bubble in the middle, remove from the heat. Cover the surface with some clingfilm or baking paper to avoid it forming a skin and leave to cool completely.

Once the crème pât is cool, combine with the salted caramel and mix until smooth. Set aside.

Cut out ten squares of greaseproof paper for each doughnut to prove on individually – this will also help when you add to the pan for frying.

Turn out the dough onto a lightly floured surface and roll out the dough to 1.5 cm/½ in. thick. Use a 9-cm/3½-in. cookie cutter to cut out the doughnut rounds and place each one on top of a greaseproof square. Alternatively, you can divide the dough evenly into ten and roll into balls with your hands. Place onto a tray and cover for 50 minutes for the last prove.

Heat the vegetable oil in a large deep saucepan over a medium–high heat, or in a deep-fryer, until it reaches a temperature of 180°C/356°F.

Working in batches, add each square of greaseproof paper with the doughnut to the fryer using a fish slice. This will save your hands from getting burnt. Don't overload the pan with doughnuts as this will lower the temperature of the oil. Fry for 2 minutes on each side until they have puffed up and are golden all over. Remove using a slotted spoon and place onto some kitchen paper to drain and cool.

Transfer the caramel custard to a piping bag with a small nozzle attached. To fill the doughnuts, make a hole in the side of each one on the crease line (the light line of dough). Use a metal straw, a knife, or skewer to help. Pipe a generous amount of cream into each doughnut – when the cream begins to pour out of the top, you know it's time to stop.

Pour some caster sugar into a shallow tray and toss the filled doughnuts in the sugar to coat. Now, tuck in and enjoy.

Plant-Based Salted Caramel Doughnuts with Orange and Cinnamon

Okay, so I am going rogue and giving another filling alternative here because I tried it not long ago and I think it would be verging on sacrilege if I kept this information to myself. Instead of filling the doughnuts with a salted caramel custard, give it a go with the dulce de leche filling we use for the plant-based chocolate alfajores (see pages 216–17).

Makes: 10

For the Tangzhong
25 g strong white bread flour, sifted
85 ml soy milk

For the Dough
150 ml lukewarm soy milk (38–40°C/
    100–104°F)
8 g fast-action dried yeast
60 g golden caster sugar
350 g strong white bread flour, sifted
5 g salt
55 g unsweetened apple sauce (see page 302)
1 tbsp ground cinnamon
grated zest of 1 large orange
1 tsp vanilla bean paste
65 g plant-based unsalted butter, room temp

For the Filling
375 ml coconut or almond milk
1½ tsp vanilla bean paste
75 g caster sugar
30 g cornflour, sifted
15 g plain flour, sifted
110 g plant-based salted caramel sauce
    or dulce de leche, (see page 290 or use
    store-bought, shhh don't tell anyone)

For Frying
1 litre vegetable oil

To Finish
caster sugar, for dusting

Let's start with the dough base. Make the tangzhong by adding the flour to a pan. Slowly add the milk, using a balloon whisk to mix.

Place the pan over a medium heat and whisk until thickened. Leave to sit at room temperature, covering the tangzhong with some clingfilm or baking paper to avoid it crusting over.

For the dough, add the lukewarm milk to a bowl and sprinkle the yeast and a pinch of the sugar on top. Give it a good stir and leave to sit for 15 minutes until bubbly and frothy.

Add flour, remaining sugar, the salt, apple sauce, cinnamon, orange zest and vanilla bean paste, before pouring in the yeasty milk. Mix on low speed with the dough hook attachment for 6–8 minutes until soft and stretchy. Add the butter and mix on low–medium speed for 8–10 minutes until it is fully incorporated, the dough has started to come away from the sides and is soft and smooth. This is quite a wet dough, so don't be tempted to add more flour if it feels wet to the touch.

Transfer the dough to a lightly oiled large bowl before placing in a proving bag or covering with clingfilm. Leave to prove for 1½–2 hours (but no more) in an unheated oven with a tray of freshly boiled water at the bottom to create a steamy environment. Alternatively, if you are making these on a warm day, leaving the bowl covered in the sunshine will also work a treat.

While the dough is proving, start making the salted caramel cream filling. The base of the filling is a thick pastry cream (crème pâtissière). Pour the milk and vanilla bean paste into a saucepan, place over a medium heat and bring to a near boil.

While the milk is heating up, whisk the caster sugar and both flours in a separate bowl. Once the milk is simmering, pour one-third onto the flours and whisk immediately until smooth. Pour back into the saucepan. Cook, stirring often, for about 5 minutes until the cream begins to thicken.

Ensure it doesn't catch and burn on the bottom.

When the cream begins to bubble in the middle and drops from a spoon, as opposed to pouring off, remove from the heat. Cover the surface with some clingfilm or baking paper to avoid the crème pât from forming a skin and leave to cool completely. Once the crème pât is cool, combine with the salted caramel until smooth.

Cut out ten squares of greaseproof paper so each doughnut can prove individually – this will also help when you add to the pan for frying.

Turn out the dough onto a lightly floured surface and roll out the dough to 1.5 cm/½ in. thick. Use a 9-cm/3½-in. cookie cutter to cut out the doughnut rounds and place each one on top of a greaseproof square. Alternatively, you can divide the dough evenly into ten and roll into balls with your hand. Place onto a tray and cover for 55 minutes for the second prove.

Heat the vegetable oil in a large deep saucepan over a medium–high heat, or in a deep-fryer, until it reaches a temperature of 180°C/356°F.

Working in batches, add each square of greaseproof paper with the doughnut to the fryer using a fish slice, to save your hands from getting burnt. Don't overload the pan with doughnuts as this will lower the temperature of the oil. Fry for 2 minutes on each side until they have puffed up and are golden all over. Remove using a slotted spoon and place onto some kitchen paper to drain and cool.

Transfer the caramel custard to a piping bag with a small nozzle attached. To fill the doughnuts, make a hole in the side of each one on the crease line (the light line of dough). Use a metal straw, a knife, or skewer to help.

Pipe a generous amount of cream into each doughnut – stopping when the cream begins to spill out of the top. Pour some caster sugar into a shallow tray and toss the filled doughnuts in the sugar to coat. Now, tuck in!

Lemon Skoleboller with Almond Pastry Cream and Raspberry Jam

These sweet, custardy buns are a Norwegian childhood staple – the name skoleboller translates into 'school buns' – and these delicious treats are often packed into lunchboxes or sold at bake sales. All I'm gonna say is, I wish I went to school in Norway, cause my packed lunch looked nothing like this.

The dough we are using here is heavily spiked with lots of lemon zest and the buns are filled with an almond pastry cream, which sits on top of a tart raspberry jam to cut through all that sweetness. It's finished with a generous sprinkling of desiccated coconut.

These are best eaten the day they are made so, for me, are the perfect slow weekend sort of bake. That being said, there are steps in the recipe you can definitely make ahead to save yourself some time. Get the tangzhong made a day or two in advance, as well as the almond pastry cream and jam.

Lemon Skoleboller with Almond Pastry Cream and Raspberry Jam

If you haven't quite guessed, the secret to majority of my bread recipes is an additional step for making either a yudane or tangzhong. Both require you to cook out some of the flour with the milk before adding it to the rest of the ingredients and while it may seem like a massive faff, it is so worth it.

Makes: 9 large or 12 small

For the Tangzhong
50 g strong white bread flour, sifted
170 ml full-fat milk

For the Dough
170 ml lukewarm full-fat milk (38–40°C/
    100–104°F)
10 g fast-active dried yeast
70 g caster sugar
420 g strong white bread flour, sifted,
    plus extra for dusting
9 g salt
1 large egg
grated zest of 3 lemons
1½ tsp vanilla bean paste
90 g unsalted butter, room temp
1 egg, beaten, for brushing (optional)

For the Almond Pastry Cream
200 ml full-fat milk
50 ml double cream
1 tsp vanilla bean paste
1½ tsp almond extract
3 large egg yolks
50 g caster sugar
10 g cornflour, sifted
10 g plain flour, sifted

For the Raspberry Jam
½ quantity raspberry jam (see page 297 or use
    store-bought, shhh don't tell anyone)

To Finish
105 g icing sugar, sifted
25 ml water
handful of desiccated coconut

2 baking trays, lined

For the tangzhong, add the flour to a pan. Slowly add the milk, using a balloon whisk to mix to ensure no lumps. Place the pan over a medium heat and whisk until thickened to a gloopy, wallpaper-paste consistency. Leave to sit at room temperature, covering the tangzhong with some clingfilm or baking paper to avoid it crusting over.

Pour the milk into a bowl and sprinkle the yeast and 1 tsp of the sugar on top. Mix and leave for 15 minutes until bubbly and frothy.

In the bowl of a stand mixer, add the flour, remaining sugar, the salt, egg, lemon zest and vanilla bean paste, before going in with the cooled tangzhong and the yeasty milk. Mix using a dough hook on low speed for 7 minutes to bring all the ingredients together into a rough but smooth dough. Begin to add the butter, a bit at a time, with the mixer still going on low–medium speed. Once all the butter has been added, reduce the speed to low and mix for 10 minutes until the dough is smooth and not sticky.

Transfer the dough to a well-oiled large bowl and cover with either clingfilm or a tea towel. Leave to prove in a warm environment – I always go for the oven with a tray of hot water sat at the base for the perfect temperature. Let it rest for 2–2½ hours until doubled in size.

While the dough is proving, make the almond pastry cream by adding the milk, cream, vanilla bean paste and almond extract to a saucepan. Mix well and place over a medium heat.

In a small bowl, add the egg yolks, sugar and both flours, and whisk until smooth.

Once the milk is near boiling, pour half on top of the egg yolks and start whisking immediately to prevent scrambling. Pour the eggy milk back into the saucepan and continue to stir. This will begin to thicken after a few minutes, so keep an eye on it and stir often. Once it has thickened past the point of a pourable custard, remove from the heat and strain through a sieve to remove any lumps. Cover and leave to cool. Once cooled, add the strained pastry cream to a piping bag and set aside.

Once the dough has doubled in size, turn it out onto a lightly floured surface. Gently knock back the dough before dividing it equally into nine large or twelve small buns. Roll these into seamless balls and place onto the prepared baking trays, leaving ample space between them all. Cover and leave to prove once again for 45 minutes–1 hour until they have doubled in size.

Preheat the oven to 200°C fan/220°C/gas mark 7.

Lightly dust the base of a small flat-bottomed glass and press it into the middle of each proved bun, pressing it all the way down to the bottom, leaving a border of dough. Alternatively, you can use your fingers to press into the dough. Use a pastry brush to gently brush over some beaten egg. This step isn't essential but it will give the buns a nice glossy finish when done.

Add 1 tsp of jam to the bottom of each indent, then pipe some almond pastry cream on top to cover. Repeat for all the dough balls and use up all of that almond pastry cream.

Bake for 7 minutes before reducing the temperature to 180°C fan/200°C/gas mark 6 and baking for another 8–10 minutes until the buns are beautifully golden brown. Carefully transfer the buns to cooling racks.

Once they are cool to touch, finish them off with the icing glaze. Add the icing sugar and water to a bowl and mix until smooth. Use a pastry brush to brush the glaze liberally over the exposed sides of the buns before scattering a generous sprinkling of the desiccated coconut on top. Let the icing set before tucking in. I am so jealous you are about to eat these.

Plant-Based Lemon Skoleboller with Almond Pastry Cream and Raspberry Jam

Makes: 9 large or 12 small

For the Tangzhong
50 g strong white bread flour, sifted
170 ml soy milk

For the Dough
170 ml lukewarm soy milk (38–40°C/
   100–104°F)
10 g fast-active dried yeast
70 g caster sugar
455 g strong white bread flour, sifted,
   plus extra for dusting
9 g salt
80 g unsweetened apple sauce (see page 302)
grated zest of 3 lemons
1½ tsp vanilla bean paste
90 g plant-based unsalted butter, room temp
10 ml maple syrup (optional)

For the Almond Pastry Cream
250 ml almond milk
1 tsp vanilla bean paste
1½ tsp almond extract
60 g caster sugar
12 g cornflour, sifted
10 g plain flour, sifted
yellow food colouring

For the Raspberry Jam
½ quantity raspberry jam (see page 297 or use
   store-bought, shhh don't tell anyone)

To Finish
105 g icing sugar, sifted
25 ml water
handful of desiccated coconut

For the tangzhong, add the flour to a pan. Slowly add the milk, using a balloon whisk to mix to ensure no lumps. Place the pan over a medium heat and whisk until thickened to a gloopy, wallpaper-paste consistency. Leave to sit at room temperature, covering the tangzhong with some clingfilm or baking paper to avoid it crusting over.

Pour the lukewarm milk into a bowl and sprinkle the yeast and 1 tsp of the sugar on top. Give it a little mix and leave to do its thing for 15 minutes until bubbly and frothy.

Put the flour, remaining sugar, the salt, apple sauce, lemon zest and vanilla bean paste in the bowl of a stand mixer and then add the cooled tangzhong and yeasty milk. Mix using a dough hook on low speed for 7 minutes to bring all the ingredients together into a rough but smooth dough. Begin to add the butter, a bit at a time, with the mixer on low–medium speed. Once all the butter has been added, reduce the speed to low and mix for 10 minutes until the dough is smooth and not sticky.

Transfer the dough to a well-oiled large bowl and cover with either clingfilm or a tea towel. Leave to prove in a warm environment – I always go for the oven with a tray of hot water sat at the base for the perfect temperature. Let it do its thing for 2–2½ hours until doubled in size.

While the dough is proving, make the almond pastry cream by adding the milk, vanilla bean paste, almond extract and a touch of yellow food colouring to a saucepan. Mix well and place over a medium heat.

In a small bowl, add the sugar and both flours, and mix well with a balloon whisk until smooth.

Once the milk is near boiling, pour half into the flour bowl and whisk well immediately. We don't want no lumps in our cream! Pour the mixture back into the saucepan and continue to stir. This will begin to thicken after a few minutes so keep an eye on it and make sure you stir this often. Once it has thickened past the point of a pourable custard, remove from the heat and strain through a sieve to remove any lumps. Cover and leave to cool. Once cooled, add the strained pastry cream to a piping bag and set aside.

Once the dough has doubled in size, turn it out onto a lightly floured surface. Gently knock back the dough before dividing it equally into nine large or twelve small buns. Roll these into seamless balls and place onto the prepared baking trays, leaving ample space between them all. Cover and leave to prove again for 45 minutes–1 hour until they have doubled in size.

Preheat the oven to 200°C fan/220°C/gas mark 7.

Lightly dust the base of a small flat-bottomed glass and press it into the middle of each proved bun, pressing it all the way down to the bottom, leaving a border of dough. Alternatively, you can use your fingers to press into the dough. Use a pastry brush to gently brush over some maple syrup. This step isn't essential but it will just give the buns a nice glossy finish when done.

Add 1 tsp of jam to the bottom of each indent, then pipe some almond pastry cream on top to cover. Repeat for all the dough balls and use up all of that almond pastry cream – do not let this taste of heaven go to waste.

Bake for 7 minutes, then reduce the temperature to 180°C fan/200°C/gas mark 6 and bake for another 8–10 minutes until the buns are beautifully golden brown. Carefully transfer the buns to cooling racks.

Once they are cool to touch, finish them off with the icing glaze. Add the icing sugar and water to a bowl and mix until smooth. Use a pastry brush to brush the glaze liberally over the exposed sides of the buns before scattering over a generous sprinkling of the desiccated coconut on top. Let the icing set before tucking in.

Fruited Focaccia with Plums, Cherries and Lemon Thyme

This one is for my mum. I spent years of my childhood standing by her side in the kitchen when I was growing up. She leans more towards the savoury side of life, and when she does eat something sweet, chocolate does not float her boat. I know, right, like how are we even related? The mystery remains unsolved.

So, I've taken something inherently savoury and teamed the flavour of olive oil with a heady mix of stone fruit and lemon thyme. The combination may seem unusual, but drown a piece in icing sugar and it's like a more sophisticated version of a tea cake.

If the fruit listed overleaf doesn't tickle your pickle, swap them out for whatever does. My fruited focaccia is a real all-year-round belly-pleaser, so mix up the fruit as the seasons change and continue to reap the delicious rewards as the months go by.

Fruited Focaccia with Plums, Cherries and Lemon Thyme

Serves: 6-8

For the Dough
500 g strong white bread flour, sifted
12 g sea salt
30 g Demerara sugar
12 g fast-action dried yeast
4 lemon thyme sprigs, leaves only
45 ml olive oil, plus extra for greasing
350 ml cool water

For the Fruit Topping
3 plums, stoned and sliced
250 g cherries, stoned and halved
4–5 lemon thyme sprigs, leaves only
50 ml olive oil
40 g Demerara sugar

To Finish
icing sugar, for dusting

deep 18 x 24-cm/7 x 9½-in. dish,
    generously oiled

In a large mixing bowl, add the flour, salt and sugar to one side, and the yeast and lemon thyme leaves to the other. Add the olive oil and three-quarters of the water to the bowl, using your hand to stir and turn the mixture. Slowly add the remaining water, a bit at a time, until the sides of the bowl are clean of flour. You may need less or more water, but we are looking for a very soft, wetter than normal bread dough, so don't be shy!

Keep mixing with your hand until it forms a rough dough. Leave to sit for 5 minutes for the flour to hydrate.

You can use a stand mixer for the next step, however, I have always hand-kneaded this dough with great results. Yes, it is messy, but it is also weirdly therapeutic and satisfying. If you choose to do that, use some oil to coat the worktop lightly and then tip the dough onto it and begin to knead.

Knead for 7–10 minutes until you have worked through the wet stage and the dough begins to soften and become elasticated. Do not add more flour, even if you think it is very wet – trust the process!

If you do want to save yourself the mess, pop the dough into the bowl of a stand mixer, attach the dough hook and mix for 8 minutes on low–medium speed.

Transfer the dough into the prepared dish, cover with clingfilm or a tea towel and leave to prove in a warm environment or proving drawer for 2–3 hours (the longer the better). You could, alternatively, go for a slow prove overnight in the fridge.

Once the initial prove is complete, gently fold the top half of the dough over the bottom half. Turn the dough 90 degrees, before repeating. Gently stretch out the dough to cover the base of the dish, cover and prove again for 1 hour, or until the dough has doubled in size.

Preheat the oven to 200°C fan/220°C/gas mark 7.

Add the plums and cherries to a bowl and use either a potato masher or the base of a flat-bottomed glass to lightly squash them, releasing lots of juice and gently breaking down the fruit. Add the lemon thyme leaves to the bowl. Pour in the olive oil and mix well, coating all the fruit and incorporating the citrussy notes from the lemon thyme.

Once the second prove has completed, use the tips of your fingers to make dimples in the focaccia, pressing them all the way through the dough to the bottom. Try not to disturb any large air bubbles formed in the dough; these bubbles are exactly what we are after.

Gently drizzle the fruit topping over the dough, then sprinkle over the Demerara sugar to finish.

Place the tray into the oven and bake for 25 minutes until golden brown on top and cooked through (you are after an internal temperature of 92°C/198°F or higher). Leave it to sit in the dish for 30 minutes, before transferring to a wire rack to cool completely.

Once cooled, dust over a generous sprinkling of icing sugar, if you prefer it on the sweeter side of life. Trust me, there's no such thing as too much icing sugar on this one, so go to town.

All that's left to do is dunk it into tea, slather it with some butter or eat it as it is. Enjoy.

Cranberry, Apricot and Almond Couronne with Apricot Glaze

I baked something very similar to this on Bread Week for *Bake Off*. We had to make an enriched bread that was worthy of a celebration – I chose the sob story for my bake to be my parents' wedding cake, because some centuries ago, when they did get married, they never had one. How mental is that?! I think if there was no cake at my wedding, I'd just flat-out refuse to participate. No cake, no wedding.

This is a buttery, almond-laden dough packed full of dried apricots and cranberries, and then glazed in an apricot jam and scattered with toasted almond flakes. Full of romance.

Cranberry, Apricot and Almond Couronne with Apricot Glaze

Serves: 12

For the Dough
135 ml full-fat milk
1½ tsp vanilla bean paste
1½ tsp almond extract
9 g fast-action dried yeast
260 g strong white bread flour, sifted,
   plus extra for dusting
7 g salt
1 medium egg
80 g unsalted butter, room temp
vegetable oil, for greasing

For the Filling
100 g unsalted butter, room temp
80 g light muscovado sugar
175 g dried apricots, roughly chopped
125 g dried cranberries
75 g flaked almonds
75 g marzipan, diced

For the Glaze
3 tbsp apricot jam
100 g icing sugar
handful of flaked almonds

In a small heavy-bottomed saucepan set over a low heat, combine the milk, vanilla bean paste and almond extract. Mix well until *just* lukewarm and remove from the heat. We are looking for a temperature of around 38–40°C/100–104°F. It's important the milk isn't hot, as this will create an overactive yeast. Add the yeast to the milk and leave to sit for 15 minutes to activate.

Place the flour into the bowl of a stand mixer, add the salt to one side of the bowl and the milky yeast to the other – sounds pedantic, but we want the yeast to thrive. Next in is the egg. Place the bowl into the stand fitted with the dough hook and mix on low–medium speed for 5 minutes.

Once the dough has formed a smooth skin, begin to add the butter with the mixer still running. Once the butter has incorporated, turn the speed down to low and mix for another 8 minutes.

To test the dough's gluten development, stretch a bit of dough between your thumbs. You'll know you're good if the dough stretches without tearing or breaking, and results in a thin, translucent membrane. If you can't, continue to either knead by hand for a further 5 minutes or pop back into the stand mixer.

Once the dough is all good, lightly oil a large bowl and place the mixed dough inside. Cover with clingfilm or a cloth and leave in a warm place to rise for 2 hours (I leave mine in the oven with a tray of hot water sitting on the base.)

In the meantime, make the filling by using an electric hand whisk to cream together the butter and sugar until light and fluffy. Add the apricots, cranberries, almonds and marizpan and mix until thoroughly combined. You want the fruit to be coated in that naughty sugary butter mix. Set aside until the dough has finished its first prove.

Lightly flour your worktop and turn out the dough. Roll the dough out into a rectangle about 5 mm/ ¼ in. thick, making sure the long edge is facing towards you. Tack the edge closest to you down to the worktop using your thumb – this will 'glue' the edge to help when it comes to rolling.

Use a spatula to distribute the filling across the dough and use a palette knife to spread it evenly. Starting at the end furthest away from you, begin to roll the dough like a Swiss roll towards you, tightly and as neatly as you can.

Use a sharp knife to cut the dough lengthways down the middle, making sure to leave one end still adjoined. Gently twist each strand around each other – like a two-strand plait – and join the two ends together by pressing the dough down tightly to form a 'crown'.

I like to use a pizza oven tray to bake this but if you don't have one you can also use a large baking tray, lined with baking paper. Carefully transfer to the tray and pop into a proving bag (or large, clean bin bag – there's no shame in it) for 45 minutes–1 hour in a warm place.

In the meantime, ensure your oven is preheated to 180°C fan/200°C/gas mark 6.

Once the bread has finished its final prove, pop it into the oven for 40 minutes. If the bread looks like it is browning too quickly (this may happen due to the high sugar content), remove from the oven, cover the top in foil and place back in the oven. One way to check your bread is baked is to prod into the middle with a thermometer – the temperature we are looking for here is a steady minimum of 92°C/198°F. If you don't have a probe, gently lift up the bread and tap the bottom for a hollow sound. Remove from the oven and carefully transfer to a cooling rack.

While still hot, use a pastry brush to coat the crown with 2 tbsp of the apricot jam. Mix the icing sugar with enough water for a loose glaze, mix in the remaining 1 tbsp of apricot jam and then pour or drizzle over the couronne. Sprinkle on the flaked almonds and then you are free to enjoy lightly warm or cold.

Plant-Based Cranberry, Apricot and Almond Couronne with Apricot Glaze

For the plant-based version of this bread, we are going to use the yudane method, which is similar to tangzhong, except the flour is hydrated with boiling water to gelatinise and then is left for a few hours – or preferably overnight – for mega-fluffy, super-tasty dough.

Serves: 12

For the Yudane
50 g strong white bread flour, sifted
10 ml hot water
40 ml boiling water

For the Dough
135 ml soy or almond milk
1½ tsp vanilla bean paste
2 tsp almond extract
9 g fast-action dried yeast
235 g strong white bread flour, sifted,
    plus extra for dusting
7 g salt
40 g unsweetened apple sauce (see page 302)
100 g plant-based unsalted butter, room temp
vegetable oil, for greasing

For the Filling
100 g plant-based unsalted butter, room temp
80 g light muscovado sugar
175 g dried apricots, roughly chopped
125 g dried cranberries
75 g flaked almonds
75 g marzipan, diced

For the Glaze
2½ tbsp apricot jam
90 g icing sugar, sifted
handful of flaked almonds

The day before, make the yudane. Put the flour in a medium bowl and mix in the hot water. Once mixed, add the boiling water and mix until smooth. The temperature of dough we are after here is about 50°C/122°F. Cover the bowl and leave to cool at room temperature for an hour before transferring to the fridge overnight. On the day of baking, remove the yudane from the fridge and allow it to come to room temperature.

In a small heavy-bottomed saucepan set over a low heat, combine the milk, vanilla bean paste and almond extract. Mix well until *just* lukewarm (38–40°C/100–104°F) and then remove from the heat – it is super-important the milk isn't hot, as this will create an overactive yeast. Add the yeast to the milk and leave to sit for 10–15 minutes to activate.

Place the flour into the bowl of a stand mixer, add the salt and apple sauce to one side of the bowl and the milky yeast to the other – sounds pedantic but we want the yeast to thrive. Next in is the room-temp yudane. Place the mixer bowl into the stand fitted with the dough hook and mix on low–medium speed for 5 minutes.

Once the dough has formed a smooth skin, begin to add the butter with the mixer still running. Once the butter has incorporated, turn the speed down to low and mix for another 8 minutes.

To test the dough's gluten development, stretch a bit of dough between your thumbs. It should be a thin, translucent membrane. If it breaks, continue to either knead by hand for a further 5 minutes or pop back into the stand mixer.

Lightly oil a large bowl and place the mixed dough inside. Cover with clingfilm or a cloth and leave in a warm place to rise for 2 hours.

In the meantime, make the filling by using an electric hand whisk to cream together the butter and sugar until light and fluffy. Add the apricots, cranberries, almonds and diced marzipan, and mix well until thoroughly combined. Leave to one side until the dough has finished its first prove.

Lightly flour your worktop and turn out the dough. Roll the dough out into a rectangle about 5 mm/¼ in. thick, making sure the long edge is facing towards you. Tack the edge closest to you down to the worktop using your thumb – this will 'glue' the edge to help when it comes to rolling. Use a spatula to distribute the filling across the dough and use a palette knife to spread it evenly. Starting at the end furthest away from you, begin to roll the dough like a Swiss roll towards you, tightly and as neatly as you can.

Use a sharp knife to cut the dough lengthways down the middle, making sure to leave one end still adjoined. Gently twist each strand around each other – like a two-strand plait – and join the two ends together by pressing the dough down tightly to form a 'crown'.

I like to use a pizza oven tray to bake this but you can also use a large baking tray, lined with baking paper. Carefully transfer to the tray and pop into a proving bag (or large, clean bin bag – no shame) for 45 minutes–1 hour in a warm place

In the meantime, ensure your oven is preheated to 180°C fan/200°C/gas mark 6.

Once the bread has finished its final prove, bake in the oven for 40 minutes. If it looks like it is browning too quickly, remove, cover the top in foil and return to oven. Check your bread is baked by prodding the centre with a thermometer probe – it should be at least 92°C/198°F. Alternatively, lift up the bread and tap the bottom for a hollow sound. Remove from the oven and carefully transfer to a cooling rack.

While still hot, use a pastry brush to coat the crown with 2 tbsp of the apricot jam. Mix the icing sugar with enough water for a loose glaze, mix in the remaining 1 tbsp of apricot jam and then pour or drizzle over the couronne. Sprinkle on the flaked almonds and enjoy.

Carrot Halwa and Chai Chelsea Buns with Medjool Dates, Raisins and Dark Chocolate

The major difference between a roll and a bun, despite looking exactly the same is that a Chelsea bun has a fruit filling, with a sticky glazed top, whereas a roll contains a sugared filling with a thicker, cream-based top.

My Chelsea buns are filled with a classic Indian dessert which I have grown up with. No wedding or celebration is complete without a serving of *gujarela*, also known as carrot halwa – a sweet carrot filling, which is laden with almonds and raisins that have been soaked and simmered in cardamom milk. You'll often find it served with a scoop of vanilla ice cream to really clog up those arteries, but this time we are using it as the filling for our buns, which are then glazed in a sticky orange syrup and heavily drizzled with a chocolate ganache.

Carrot Halwa and Chai Chelsea Buns with Medjool Dates, Raisins and Dark Chocolate

Makes: 12

For the Carrot Filling
500 g carrots, peeled and grated
750 ml full-fat milk
6 green cardamom pods
¾ tbsp ghee
1 tbsp caster sugar
75 g Medjool dates, roughly chopped
40 g blanched almonds, roughly chopped
150 g raisins

For the Dough
285 ml lukewarm full-fat milk (38–40°C/
    100–104°F)
10 g fast-active dried yeast
65 g golden caster sugar
475 g strong white bread flour, sifted,
    plus extra for dusting
9 g salt
1 large egg
1 egg yolk

2 tsp chai spice mix (see pages 196–7)
1½ tsp vanilla bean paste
90 g unsalted butter, room temp

For the Orange Glaze
100 ml water
100 ml freshly squeezed orange Juice
150 g caster sugar
grated zest of 1 large orange

For the Butter Filling
40 g unsalted butter, room temp
45 g golden caster sugar

For the Chocolate Drizzle
80 ml double cream
95 g dark chocolate
1 tbsp golden syrup

deep baking tray, lightly buttered

Let's start with the carrot filling. Place the grated carrot into a large saucepan and pour in the milk. Use a knife to pierce a hole into each of the cardamom pods and add them to the pan. Use a wooden spoon to give everything a good mix before placing over a low–medium heat. We want to cook the carrots until the milk reduces and evaporates, so let this do its thing for about 45 minutes–1 hour, but make sure you stir occasionally to avoid the bottom catching.

Once the milk has evaporated, add the ghee to the pan and continue cooking for 15 minutes. Stir in the sugar, chopped dates, almonds and raisins. Cook for a further 5 minutes, stirring occasionally, before removing from the heat and transferring to a shallow baking tray to cool.

Next up is the dough. Add the milk to a bowl and sprinkle in the yeast. Add a pinch of the sugar, mix, and leave to sit for about 15 minutes until bubbly and frothy.

Transfer the dough to a lightly oiled large bowl, cover with either clingfilm or a cloth and leave to prove until doubled in volume; 2–3 hours should be perfect. I like to pop the bowl into an oven with a tray of hot water sitting at the base. This creates the perfect steamy environment for the dough to thrive.

While the dough is proving, get the orange glaze made. Pop all the ingredients into a saucepan and place over a medium heat for 15 minutes. We want this to reduce to a sticky, syrupy consistency. Remove from the heat and set aside to cool.

Once the dough has doubled in volume, on a lightly floured surface, roll it out into a large rectangle, 1 cm/½ in. thick.

Mix the butter filling together before mixing it into the cooled carrot filling. We want that sugary goodness to coat all of the fruit. Spread the sugared carrot filling evenly over the dough.

You have two options for rolling. Option 1: From the long end, tightly roll the dough, leaving a seam at the bottom. Divide the dough into twelve before using sharp knife or floss to cut. Option 2: Trim the edges of your rolled-out dough to a nice, neat rectangle. Divide this dough up evenly into twelve on the long edge. Use a knife or a pizza cutter to cut each strip, before rolling each one individually for a neater finish.

Transfer the rolls to the prepared baking tray, spacing them out slightly if possible. Cover the tray with clingfilm or a cloth and leave to prove until doubled in size; approximately 1 hour.

Meanwhile, make the chocolate drizzle by warming the cream in a pan over a medium heat. Once the cream is near boiling, remove from the heat and add the chocolate. Set aside for 1 minute with a plate on top to trap the heat, then remove and use a balloon whisk or rubber spatula to mix until smooth. Add the golden syrup and mix again. Set aside to cool.

Preheat the oven to 160°C fan/180°C/gas mark 4.

Bake the rolls for 30–32 minutes. Use a thermometer to check the dough temperature, we are after anything over 92°C/198°F.

Leave the buns to cool in the tray for 15 minutes before liberally brushing the tops with the orange glaze. Let the buns sit for 15 minutes to soak up that sugary goodness, then generously drizzle over the chocolate ganache to finish.

Plant-Based Carrot Halwa and Chai Chelsea Buns with Medjool Dates, Raisins and Dark Chocolate

Makes: 12

For the Carrot Filling
500 g carrots, peeled and grated
750 ml full-fat coconut milk
6 green cardamom pods
¾ tbsp plant-based unsalted butter
1 tbsp caster sugar
75 g Medjool dates, roughly chopped
40 g almonds, blanched and roughly chopped
150 g raisins

For the Tangzhong
50 g strong white bread flour, sifted
165 ml full-fat soy or coconut milk

For the Dough
160 ml lukewarm full-fat soy or coconut milk
    (38–40°C/100–104°F)
12 g fast-active dried yeast
470 g strong white bread flour, sifted
55 g golden caster sugar
9 g salt

60 g unsweetened apple sauce (see page 302)
2 tsp chai spice mix (see pages 196–7)
1½ tsp vanilla bean paste
80 g plant-based unsalted butter, room temp

For the Orange Glaze
100 ml water
100 ml freshly squeezed orange Juice
150 g caster sugar
grated zest of 1 large orange

For the Butter Filling
40 g plant-based unsalted butter, room temp
45 g golden caster sugar

For the Chocolate Drizzle
80 ml coconut cream
95 g plant-based dark chocolate
1 tbsp golden syrup

deep baking tray, lightly buttered

Let's start with the carrot filling. Place the grated carrot into a large saucepan and pour in the coconut milk. Use a knife to pierce a hole into each of the cardamom pods and add to the pan. Use a wooden spoon to give everything a mix before placing over a low–medium heat. Cook the carrots for about 45 minutes–1 hour until the milk evaporates, stirring occasionally to avoid the bottom catching.

Once the milk has evaporated, add the butter to the pan and continue cooking for 15 minutes. Stir in the sugar, chopped dates, almonds and raisins. Cook for a further 5 minutes, stirring occasionally, before removing from the heat and transferring to a shallow baking tray to cool.

For the tangzhong, add the flour to a saucepan and slowly pour in the milk. Whisk together and place over a medium heat. Continue to mix until it thickens to a wallpaper-paste consistency. Leave to cool completely.

Once the tangzhong is cool, move onto making the dough. Add the milk to a bowl and sprinkle in the yeast. Add a pinch of the sugar, mix and leave to sit for about 15 minutes until bubbly and frothy.

Put the cooled tangzhong into the bowl of a stand mixer with all the remaining dough ingredients, except the butter. Add the milky yeast and mix using the dough hook on low speed for 5 minutes to bring all the ingredients together. Add the plant-based butter before turning up the speed a notch to low–medium and mixing for a further 10 minutes.

Transfer the dough to a lightly oiled large bowl, cover with clingfilm and leave to prove until doubled in volume; 2–3 hours should be perfect.

While the dough is proving, get the orange glaze made. Pop all the ingredients into a saucepan and place over a medium heat for 15 minutes to reduce to a sticky, syrupy consistency. Remove from the heat and set aside to cool.

Once the dough has doubled in volume, on a lightly floured surface, roll it out into a large rectangle, 1 cm/½ in. thick.

Mix the butter filling together before mixing it into the cooled carrot filling. Spread the sugared carrot filling evenly over the dough.

You have two options for rolling. Option 1: From the long end, tightly roll the dough, leaving the seam at the bottom. Divide the dough into twelve before using sharp knife or floss to cut. Option 2: Trim the edges of your rolled-out dough to a nice, neat rectangle. Divide this dough up evenly into twelve on the long edge. Use a knife or a pizza cutter to cut each strip, before rolling each one individually for a neater finish.

Transfer the rolls to the prepared baking tray, spacing them out slightly if possible. Cover the tray with clingfilm or a cloth and leave to prove until doubled in size; approximately 1 hour.

While you are waiting, make the chocolate drizzle by warming the coconut cream in a pan over a medium heat. Once the cream is near boiling, take it off the heat and add the chocolate. Set aside for 1 minute with a plate on top to trap the heat, then remove the plate and use a balloon whisk or rubber spatula to mix until smooth. Add the golden syrup and mix again. Set aside to cool.

Preheat the oven to 160°C fan/180°C/gas mark 4.

Bake the rolls for 30–32 minutes. Use a thermometer probe to check dough temperature is over 92°C/198°F.

Leave the buns to sit in the tray for 15 minutes before liberally brushing the tops with the orange glaze. Let the buns sit for another 15 minutes to soak up that sugary goodness before generously drizzling over the chocolate drizzle to finish.

Banoffee Monkey Bread with Salted Peanuts and Toffee Sauce

Monkey Bread is a real soft, sweet, sticky treat, which is often served up for breakfast over in America (what a way to start the day, am I right?), but I love nothing more than picking off the buttery, syrup-drenched dough with my fingers and eating it with a cup of tea in the afternoon.

This version has all those soul-pleasing flavours of banoffee – and in abundance, too. The ripe bananas lightly caramelise on top and turn to mush in the middle, while the toffee sauce smothers every piece of dough, creating something so moreish and sticky, you'll be licking your fingers clean at the end.

This is a lovely afternoon treat or an alternative celebration masterpiece. If you don't have a bundt tin, or are after a smaller treat, use a loaf tin or a 20-cm/8-in. cake tin to stack the dough.

Banoffee Monkey Bread with Salted Peanuts and Toffee Sauce

Serves: 9

For the Dough
250 ml lukewarm full-fat milk (38–40°C/
   100–104°F)
10 g fast-action dried yeast
540 g strong white bread flour, sifted,
   plus extra for dusting
50 g golden caster sugar
10 g salt
1 tbsp vanilla bean paste
2 medium eggs
125 g milk chocolate, roughly chopped
   or callets
85 g unsalted butter, room temp

For the Salted Toffee Sauce
150 ml double cream
45 g unsalted butter
50 g light soft brown sugar
pinch of sea salt

To Assemble
150 g light soft brown sugar
2½ tbsp cocoa powder
250 g ripe bananas (approx. 3 large), blitzed
   to a chunky purée
80 g salted peanuts, roughly chopped
100 g milk chocolate, roughly chopped
   or callets

For the Glaze
30 g unsalted butter
½ tsp vanilla bean paste
2 tbsp full-fat milk
pinch of ground cinnamon
25 g milk chocolate, roughly chopped or callets
70 g icing sugar, sifted

25-cm/10-in. bundt tin, lightly greased

We gotta start with the dough, as this will take up most of the time. Add the lukewarm milk to a bowl and sprinkle the dried yeast on top. Cover the bowl and leave to sit for 10–15 minutes until the milk has turned frothy and slightly bubbly.

Into the bowl of a stand mixer bowl fitted with the dough hook, add the flour, sugar, salt and vanilla bean paste. Pour in the yeasty milk, followed by the eggs, and mix on low speed for a few minutes to form a rough dough. Leave to sit for 5 minutes to allow the flour to hydrate.

Mix on low speed for 5 minutes until all the ingredients have come together, then add the chocolate and butter. Continue to mix on low speed until the butter has incorporated, then mix on low–medium speed for 10 minutes. When the dough is smooth and not sticky, stop mixing.

Place the dough in a lightly oiled large bowl, cover with clingfilm and leave to prove for 1 hour in a warm place – you can place the bowl in an oven with a tray of hot water at the base for the perfect proving environment.

Time to make the salted toffee sauce by adding all the ingredients, except the salt, to a saucepan. Place over a medium heat and gently cook until the butter has melted. Stir the sauce often to avoid it catching on the bottom and continue to cook until it has turned a golden brown colour. Remove from the heat, sprinkle in the sea salt and give it a stir. Set aside to cool.

Into a separate bowl, add the sugar and cocoa powder for assembling. Mix well to combine.

Into the bottom of the prepared bundt tin, spoon 1 tbsp of the cocoa sugar, a few spoonfuls of the chunky banana purée, and a good handful of the chopped peanuts and chocolate.

Once the dough has proved, divide the dough into little balls (slightly smaller than a golf ball). Take each ball, roll it in the cooled toffee sauce to coat, then dunk it in the cocoa sugar and place into the tin. Continue to form one layer around the tin. Add a generous handful of the chocolate chunks, peanuts and banana purée across the dough. Really work the purée into the nooks and crannies for full flavour impact once baked.

Use the rest of the dough balls to continue to fill the bundt tin. Top with any remaining peanuts, sugar mix, and banana purée to finish. Cover the tin with clingfilm and leave to prove for 50 minutes, or until doubled in volume. Make sure you keep any remaining toffee sauce to one side as this will be a great addition to the glaze.

Preheat the oven to 160°C fan/180°C/gas mark 4.

Bake the bread for 40 minutes until gorgeously golden on top. Double-check the internal dough temperature has hit at least 92°C/198°F before removing from the oven. Allow the tin to cool until just warm and then turn out onto a serving plate – be proud of yourself right now CAUSE LOOK AT IT!!

For the glaze, add the butter to a saucepan alongside any remaining toffee sauce and gently melt. Once melted, add all the remaining ingredients, mix well with a whisk and generously pour over the monkey bread. Tear and share (or not), and most importantly, enjoy.

Plant-Based Banoffee Monkey Bread with Salted Peanuts and Toffee Sauce

Serves: 9

For the Dough
250 ml lukewarm soy or coconut milk
   (38–40°C/100–104°F)
10 g fast-action dried yeast
550 g strong white bread flour, sifted,
   plus extra for dusting
50 g golden caster sugar
10 g salt
1 tbsp vanilla bean paste
100 g unsweetened apple sauce
   (see page 302)
125 g plant-based milk or dark chocolate,
   roughly chopped or callets
90 g plant-based unsalted butter, room temp

For the Salted Toffee Sauce
150 ml plant-based double cream
45 g plant-based unsalted butter
50 g light soft brown sugar
½ tsp cornflour, sifted
pinch of sea salt

To Assemble
150 g light soft brown sugar
2 tbsp cocoa powder
250 g ripe bananas (approx. 3 large), blitzed
   to a chunky purée
75 g salted peanuts, roughly chopped
100 g plant-based milk or dark chocolate,
   roughly chopped or callets
1 tbsp ground cinnamon

For the Glaze
30 g plant-based unsalted butter
½ tsp vanilla bean paste
2 tbsp soy or coconut milk
pinch of ground cinnamon
25 g plant-based milk or dark chocolate,
   roughly chopped or callets
90 g icing sugar, sifted

25-cm/10-in. bundt tin, lightly greased

Start with the dough. Add the lukewarm milk to a bowl and sprinkle the dried yeast on top. Cover the bowl and leave to sit for 10–15 minutes until the milk has turned frothy and slightly bubbly.

Into the bowl of a stand mixer bowl fitted with the dough hook, add the flour, sugar, salt, and vanilla bean paste. Pour in the yeasty milk, followed by the apple sauce, and begin to mix on low speed for a few minutes to form a rough dough. Leave to sit for 5 minutes to allow the flour to hydrate.

Mix on low speed for 5 minutes until all the ingredients have come together, then add the chocolate and butter. Continue to mix on low speed until the butter has incorporated, then mix on low–medium speed for 10 minutes. When the dough is smooth and not sticky, stop mixing.

Place the dough in a lightly oiled large bowl, cover with clingfilm and leave to prove for 1 hour in a warm place – you can place the bowl in an oven with a tray of hot water at the base for the perfect proving environment.

Time to make the salted toffee sauce by adding all the ingredients, except the salt, to a saucepan. Place over a medium heat and gently cook until the butter has melted. Stir the sauce often to avoid it catching on the bottom and continue to cook until it has turned a golden brown colour. Remove from the heat, sprinkle in the sea salt and give it a stir. Set aside to cool.

Into a separate bowl, add the sugar and cocoa powder for assembling. Mix well to combine.

Into the bottom of the prepared bundt tin, spoon 1 tbsp of the cocoa sugar, a few spoonfuls of the chunky banana purée, and a good handful of the chopped peanuts and chocolate.

Once the dough has proved, divide the dough into little balls (slightly smaller than a golf ball). Take each ball, roll it in the cooled toffee sauce to coat, then dunk it in the cocoa sugar and place into the tin. Continue to form one layer around the tin. Add a generous handful of the chocolate chunks, peanuts and banana purée across the dough. Really work the purée into the nooks and crannies for full flavour impact once baked.

Use the rest of the dough balls to continue to fill the bundt tin. Top with any remaining peanuts, sugar mix, and banana purée to finish. Cover the tin with clingfilm and leave to prove for 50 minutes, or until doubled in volume. Make sure you keep any remaining toffee sauce to one side as this will be a great addition to the glaze.

Preheat the oven to 160°C fan/180°C/gas mark 4.

Bake the bread for 40 minutes until gorgeously golden on top. Double-check the internal dough temperature has hit at least 92°C/198°F before removing from the oven. Allow the tin to cool until just warm and then turn out onto a serving plate and feel proud!

For the glaze, add the butter to a saucepan alongside any remaining toffee sauce and gently melt. Once melted, add all the remaining ingredients, mix well with a whisk and generously pour over the monkey bread. Tear away!

Cherry and Chocolate Maritozzi

Maritozzi are incredibly light, gorgeously sweet, brioche-style filled buns. They look incredible and, fortunately, taste just as good. These have a heavenly chocolate dough encasing an almondy cherry compote and a super-light whipped mascarpone cream, which is drowning in vanilla bean. It gives off a real Black Forest (sans booze) sort of vibe. It's a tried and tested combo of yum.

That being said, this bake is just a bake that keeps on giving. You can really have a bit of fun with these and change up the fillings, the dough flavourings, and the cream you are using. Add zest to the dough, some chai spice, maybe even some herbs against a vanilla dough, and then go wild on the fillings. Change up the compote to a jam (I have a section dedicated to all things saucy to help you out on page 297), add in fresh fruit, maybe a ganache but always, always, ALWAYS finish it with lashings of sweetened whipped cream.

Granted, these beauties are best gobbled fresh and on the day. If you are making these in advance, bake the dough, but don't fill until serving to keep them fresh.

Cherry and Chocolate Maritozzi

Makes: 12 small or 9 large

For the Tangzhong
40 g strong white bread flour, sifted
100 ml full-fat milk

For the Dough
110 ml lukewarm full-fat milk (38–40°C/
   100–104°F)
7 g fast-active dried yeast
70 g caster sugar
390 g strong white bread flour, sifted,
   plus extra for dusting
60 g cocoa powder, sifted
6 g salt
3 large eggs
120 g unsalted butter, room temp
1 egg, beaten, for brushing

For the Cherry Compote
500 g maraschino or amarena cherries,
   plus 3 tbsp syrup from the jar
squeeze of lemon juice

For the Whipped Mascarpone Cream
150 g mascarpone cheese, room temp
50 g icing sugar, sifted
400 ml double cream
2 tsp vanilla bean paste

To Finish
icing sugar, for dusting

2 baking trays, lined

130

First up, make the tangzhong. Add the flour to a saucepan and pour in the milk. Use a balloon whisk to mix until smooth, then place over a medium heat. You want to cook out the flour until it forms a thick paste – think wallpaper paste consistency. Remove from the heat and transfer to a bowl to cool to room temperature.

Add the lukewarm milk to a bowl and sprinkle in the yeast. Add a pinch of the sugar before covering with a tea towel for 10–15 minutes until the milk is bubbly and frothy.

Add the flour, cocoa powder, remaining sugar, the salt and eggs to the bowl of a stand mixer with the cooled tangzhong. Pour in the yeasty milk and use the dough hook to mix the ingredients together on low speed for a few minutes. Once the ingredients have roughly come together, allow the dough to sit for 5 minutes to hydrate, then mix the dough on low speed for 6–8 minutes until the dough has started to come away from the sides. Begin to add the butter to the bowl, continuing to mix on low–medium speed. Once all the butter has been added, keep the mixer going for a further 10 minutes on low speed.

By now the gluten should have developed and the dough should be smooth and not sticky. To test the dough's gluten development, stretch a bit of dough between your thumbs. You'll know you're good if the dough stretches without tearing or breaking, and results in a thin, translucent membrane. Place the dough into an oiled large bowl and cover with either clingfilm or a tea towel. Pop in a warm place to prove for 2–2½ hours until the dough has at least doubled in size.

Once the dough has proved, lightly flour your worktop before turning it out. Gently knock back (i.e., flatten it with your hands) and divide the dough into either twelve small buns or nine large. Roll the dough into seamless balls. If you know how to make a cob loaf, use this method to shape the balls, or use your hand as a cage to roll.

Place the dough balls on the prepared baking trays, leaving plenty of space between them, and cover once again for the second prove. Pop into a proving drawer or leave to prove again for 45 minutes–1 hour until doubled in size.

Meanwhile, preheat the oven to 160°C fan/180°C/gas mark 4.

While you are waiting for the bread to prove, make the cherry compote. We aren't looking for this to be super-smushy, we want the cherries to break down slightly and release some of their juices. Pop the cherries, reserved syrup from the jar and lemon juice into a saucepan and place over a medium heat. Cook the cherries for 5–10 minutes, stirring occasionally, then leave to cool.

For the whipped mascarpone cream, place the mascarpone and icing sugar in a bowl and mix until smooth. Pour in the double cream and vanilla bean paste and mix on low until everything comes together to a medium peak. Don't overwork because we want this silky-smooth and it will continue to thicken when you scoop it out. Transfer the cream to a piping bag.

One the dough has proved, use a pastry brush to gently glaze with the beaten egg. Pop the trays into the oven and bake for 12 minutes. Once baked, let the maritozzi sit on the trays for a minute before carefully transferring to a rack to cool completely.

Once they are completely cool, use a serrated knife to cut the bread in half horizontally, leaving the bread 'hinged' at one side. Carefully open and spoon in a good helping of the cherry compote at the hinge of the bread. This should naturally keep the bread top open at an angle. Repeat for all the maritozzi.

Next, pipe the cream into the buns to fill them completely. Use a palette knife to scrape any cream from the outsides for that seamless bun finish. Lightly dust over a sprinkling of icing sugar to finish.

Plant-Based Cherry and Chocolate Maritozzi

Makes: 12 small or 9 large

For the Tangzhong
40 g strong white bread flour, sifted
100 ml soy milk

For the Dough
110 ml lukewarm soy milk (38–40°C/
   100–104°F)
7 g fast-active dried yeast
80 g caster sugar
400 g strong white bread flour, sifted
50 g cocoa powder, sifted
6 g salt
220 g unsweetened apple sauce
   (see page 302)
120 g plant-based unsalted butter, room temp
maple syrup, to glaze

For the Cherry Compote
500 g maraschino or amarena cherries,
   plus 3 tbsp syrup from the jar
squeeze of lemon juice

For the Whipped Cream
500 ml plant-based double cream
50 g icing sugar, sifted
2 tsp vanilla bean paste

To Finish
icing sugar, for dusting

2 baking trays, lined

First up, make the tangzhong. Add the flour to a saucepan and pour in the soy milk. Use a balloon whisk to mix until smooth, then place over a medium heat. You want to cook out the flour until it forms a thick paste – think wallpaper paste consistency. Remove from the heat and transfer to a bowl to cool to room temperature.

Add the lukewarm soy milk to a bowl and sprinkle the yeast on top. Add a pinch of the sugar before covering with a tea towel for 10–15 minutes until the milk is bubbly and frothy.

Add the flour, cocoa powder, remaining sugar, the salt and apple sauce to the bowl of a stand mixer with the cooled tangzhong. Pour in the yeasty milk and use the dough hook to mix the ingredients together on low speed for a few minutes. Once the ingredients have roughly come together, allow the dough to sit for 5 minutes to hydrate, then mix the dough on low speed for 6 minutes until the dough has started to come away from the sides and is smooth. Begin to add the butter to the bowl, continuing to mix on low–medium speed. Once all the butter has been added, keep the mixer going for a further 10 minutes on low speed.

By now the gluten should have developed and the dough should be gloriously smooth and not sticky. To test the dough's gluten development, stretch a bit of dough between your thumbs. You'll know you're good if the dough stretches without tearing or breaking, and results in a thin, translucent membrane. Place the dough into an oiled large bowl and cover with clingfilm. Pop in a warm place to prove for 2–2½ hours until the dough has at least doubled in size.

Once the dough has proved, lightly flour your worktop before turning it out. Gently knock back (i.e., flatten it with your hands) and divide the dough into either twelve small buns or nine large. Roll the dough into seamless balls. If you know how to make a cob loaf, use this method to shape the balls, or use your hand as a cage to roll.

Place the dough balls on the prepared baking trays, leaving plenty of space between them, and cover once again for the second prove. Pop into a proving drawer or leave to prove again for 45 minutes–1 hour until doubled in size.

Meanwhile, preheat the oven to 160°C fan/180°C/gas mark 4.

While you are waiting for the bread to prove, make the cherry compote. We aren't looking for this to be super-smushy, we just want the cherries to break down slightly and release some of their juices. Pop the cherries, reserved syrup from the jar and lemon juice into a saucepan and place over a medium heat. Cook the cherries for 5–10 minutes, stirring occasionally, then leave to cool.

The bit I love most about maritozzi is the sweetened cream. Put the double cream, icing sugar and vanilla bean paste into the bowl of a stand mixer and mix on low until everything comes together to a medium peak. Don't overwork it because we want this silky-smooth and it will continue to thicken when you scoop it out. Transfer the cream to a piping bag.

One the dough has proved, use a pastry brush to gently glaze with the maple syrup. Pop the trays into the oven and bake for 15 minutes. Remove and let the maritozzi sit on the trays for a minute before carefully removing and transferring to a rack to cool completely.

Once they are completely cool, use a serrated knife to cut the bread in half horizontally, leaving the bread 'hinged' at one side. Carefully open and spoon in a good helping of the cherry compote at the hinge of the bread. This should naturally keep the bread top open at an angle. Repeat for all the maritozzi.

Pipe the cream into the buns to fill them completely. Use a palette knife to scrape any cream from the outsides for that seamless bun finish. Lightly dust over a sprinkling of icing sugar to finish.

Easy as Pie

Slice, slice baby

Peach and Lime Crostata with Whipped Basil Yoghurt

For me, peaches in the summer is what it is all about. I'm talking about that gorgeously juicy, ripe flesh and the inevitable drip of sweet, peachy nectar running down your chin once you've taken a bite. Whether you call these crostatas or galettes, they are very versatile and easy to make. I love how easy it is to whack the pastry together – it's a real low-key vibe so something great to whip up when you're short on time or are after something satisfyingly simple.

The deep, fragrant flavour of ripe peaches works so well with the zesty sharpness of the lime, and provides a suitably delicious base for a sweetened, coconutty, basil-spiked whipped yoghurt.

I know this is a dessert, but there's also something a little brunchy about it – serve these up alongside some Bellinis for a real bougie, boozy brunch affair (just make sure you send me an invite, too).

Peach and Lime Crostata with Whipped Basil Yoghurt

Makes: 6

For the Crostata Dough
300 g plain flour, sifted, plus extra if needed
  and for dusting
½ tsp baking powder, sifted
145 g caster sugar
1 large egg
1 large egg yolk
pinch of salt
2 tsp vanilla bean paste
160 g unsalted butter, fridge temp and diced,
  plus extra if needed
grated zest and freshly squeezed juice of
  2 limes, plus extra if needed

For the Filling
6 peaches, stoned and halved
1 quantity simple vanilla syrup (see page 303),
  plus extra if needed

grated zest of 2 limes
pinch of salt
1 tsp cornflour, sifted, if needed

To Glaze
15 ml double cream
6 pinches of Demerara sugar

For the Whipped Yoghurt
400 g Greek yoghurt
25 g icing sugar, sifted
155 g double cream
25 g coconut cream
75 g desiccated coconut
1 basil leaf, finely chopped
1 tsp vanilla bean paste

The easiest way to bring this pastry dough together is by using a food processor. You can do this by hand (and by hand, I mean your fingers) but let's save the faff and a few minutes of your life, if possible. Add the flour, baking powder, sugar, egg, egg yolk, salt and vanilla bean paste to a food processor. Pulse a few times to blitz the ingredients together. Next, add the cold, diced butter. Pulse until the mixture resembles clumpy breadcrumbs. Go in with the lime zest and juice, and pulse again to bring the dough together. We don't want sticky dough, so if the dough feels a little wet, add another 5 g of flour before pulsing again. Likewise, if the dough feels too dry, add another 5 g of butter or lime juice to soften.

Turn out the dough onto a lightly floured surface and bring it together to form a disc. Lightly dust the dough with flour before wrapping in clingfilm and popping in the fridge to chill for 30 minutes.

Set aside six peach halves. Roughly chop the remaining six peach halves and add to a bowl. Mix the sugar syrup with the lime zest and add one-quarter of the zesty syrup to the chopped peaches. Either use a potato masher or hand blender to lightly mash the peaches to a chunky purée. Give this a good stir to distribute the syrup and zest. Add salt to taste and sprinkle in the cornflour if the mixture is too loose. If you think it needs a touch more sweetness, add more sugar syrup, 1 tsp at a time, until you're a happy bunny.

Once the dough has chilled, divide it into six pieces and roll out each one into a 10-cm/4-in. round (I like to draw around a bowl on a sheet of greaseproof paper, turn the paper over and roll out the dough on top, using the lines as a guide). Or alternatively, you can use mini tart tins and gently press in the dough.

Add 1 tbsp of the mashed peaches to the middle of each round, leaving a 2.5-cm/1-in. border all the way round. Fold the edges of the dough up, over the peaches, encasing all the juicy goodness. This will look super rustic and a little rough, but don't worry, it all adds to the overall vibe we are after.

Repeat for each dough round before nestling the remaining peach halves, cut-side down, into the middle of each crostata.

Transfer to baking sheets and leave to chill in the fridge for up to an hour, but no less than 30 minutes. We want the butter to firm up in the pastry before we bake to prevent it leaking, which would leave us with sad pastry.

Preheat the oven to 180°C fan/200°C/gas mark 6.

Before baking, brush the edges of the dough with the double cream and sprinkle a pinch of Demerara sugar all over the top. Pop into the oven and bake for 25 minutes.

While you are waiting for those beauties to bake, make the whipped yoghurt by adding the yoghurt to a bowl with the icing sugar. Mix until smooth with either a balloon whisk or electric hand whisk. Add the remaining ingredients, then mix until thickened and the cream has hit a medium peak. Leave in the fridge until serving.

Remove the crostatas from the oven and carefully peel off the peach skin.

Brush the remaining zesty sugar syrup over each peach half and place back in the oven for a further 10 minutes until the peaches are bubbling and pastry has turned a lovely golden brown.

Leave to cool for 20 minutes if serving warm. Serve with a scoop of whipped yoghurt sitting on top or on the side.

Plant-Based Peach and Lime Crostata with Whipped Basil Yoghurt

Makes: 6

For the Crostata Dough
400 g plain flour, sifted
60 g caster sugar
pinch of salt
2 tsp vanilla bean paste
180 g plant-based unsalted butter, fridge temp and diced
grated zest and freshly squeezed juice of 2 limes, plus extra if needed
100 ml cold water

For the Filling
6 peaches, stoned and halved
1 quantity simple vanilla syrup (see page 303), plus extra if needed
grated zest of 2 limes

pinch of salt
1 tsp cornflour, sifted, if needed

To Glaze
15 ml maple syrup
6 pinches of Demerara sugar

For the Whipped Yoghurt
400 g plant-based Greek-style yoghurt
25 g icing sugar, sifted
155 g plant-based double cream
25 g coconut cream
75 g desiccated coconut
1 basil leaf, finely chopped
1 tsp vanilla bean paste

The easiest way to bring this pastry dough together is by using a food processor. You can do this by hand (and by hand, I mean your fingers) but let's save the faff and a few minutes of your life, if possible. Add the flour, sugar, salt and vanilla bean paste to a food processor. Pulse a few times to blitz the ingredients together. Next, add the cold, diced butter. Pulse until the mixture resembles clumpy breadcrumbs. Go in with the lime zest, juice and cold water, and pulse again to bring the dough together. We don't want sticky dough, so if the dough feels a little wet, add another 5 g of flour before pulsing again. Likewise, if the dough feels too dry, add another 5 g of butter or lime juice to soften.

Turn out the dough onto a lightly floured surface and bring it together to form a disc. Lightly dust the dough with flour before wrapping in clingfilm and popping in the fridge to chill for 30 minutes.

Set aside six peach halves. Roughly chop the remaining six peach halves and add to a bowl. Mix the sugar syrup with the lime zest and add one-quarter of the zesty syrup to the chopped peaches. Either use a potato masher or hand blender to lightly mash the peaches to a chunky purée. Give this a good stir to distribute the syrup and zest. Add salt to taste and sprinkle in the cornflour if the mixture is too loose. If you think it needs a touch more sweetness, add more sugar syrup, 1 tsp at a time, until you're a happy bunny.

Once the dough has chilled, divide it into six pieces and roll out each one into a 10-cm/4-in. round (I like to draw around a bowl on a sheet of greaseproof paper, turn the paper over and roll out the dough on top, using the lines as a guide). Or alternatively, you can use mini tart tins and gently press in the dough.

Add 1 tbsp of the mashed peaches to the middle of each round, leaving a 2.5-cm/1-in. border all the way round. Fold the edges of the dough up, over the peaches, encasing all the juicy goodness. This will look super rustic and a little rough, but don't worry, it all adds to the overall vibe we are after.

Repeat for each dough round before nestling the remaining peach halves, cut-side down, into the middle of each crostata.

Transfer to baking sheets and leave to chill in the fridge for up to an hour, but no less than 30 minutes. We want the butter to firm up in the pastry before we bake to prevent it leaking, which would leave us with sad pastry.

Preheat the oven to 180°C fan/200°C/gas mark 6.

Before baking, brush the edges of the dough with the maple syrup and sprinkle a pinch of Demerara sugar all over the top. Pop into the oven and bake for 25 minutes.

While you are waiting for those beauties to bake, make the whipped yoghurt by adding the yoghurt to a bowl with the icing sugar. Mix until smooth with either a balloon whisk or electric hand whisk. Add the remaining ingredients, then mix until thickened and the cream has hit a medium peak. Leave in the fridge until serving.

Remove the crostatas from the oven and carefully peel off the peach skin.

Brush the remaining zesty sugar syrup over each peach half and place back in the oven for a further 10 minutes until the peaches are bubbling and the pastry has turned a lovely golden brown.

Leave to cool for 20 minutes if serving warm. Serve with a scoop of whipped yoghurt sitting on top or on the side. Remember to keep a napkin by your side to mop up that peach chin juice.

Spiced Apple and Stem Ginger Tart with Macadamia Streusel

Streusel or crumble, whatever you wanna call it, are essentially the same thing. One is generally more clumpy, which, for a first in baking, is a good thing. The other tends to be more of a crumb. When it comes to a pie or tart topping, the clumpier the better for me.

Spiced, stewed apples and stem ginger nuggets encased in a stem ginger sweet pastry and topped with lots of clumpy, vanilla streusel – this is best eaten when piping hot and drowning in custard, and with a silly, goofy grin slapped across your face.

Spiced Apple and Stem Ginger Tart with Macadamia Streusel

Serves: 8

For the Pâté Sucrée
125 g unsalted butter, room temp
50 g caster sugar
1 tsp vanilla bean paste
1 medium egg
225 g plain flour, sifted, plus extra for dusting
2 tbsp stem ginger syrup
1 egg, beaten, for brushing

For the Filling
6 Granny Smith apples, peeled and diced
4 preserved stem ginger pieces, finely chopped
2 tsp ground cinnamon
1 tsp chai spice mix (see pages 196–7 or use store-bought)
1½ tsp vanilla bean paste

50 g unsalted butter, diced
1 star anise
100 g light soft brown sugar
15 g cornflour

For the Macadamia Streusel
75 g unsalted butter, fridge temp and diced
75 g golden caster sugar
50 g plain flour, sifted
25 g ground almonds
1 tsp vanilla bean paste
½ tsp almond extract
110 g macadamia nuts, roughly chopped

23-cm/9-in tart tin, buttered

Start with the pastry as this must chill in the freezer for an hour before we do anything else.

Into the bowl of a stand mixer (or large mixing bowl), add the butter, sugar and vanilla bean paste. Cream together using the paddle attachment on medium speed or 5 minutes until light and fluffy. Next in is the egg, mix again, making sure this has emulsified before moving onto the next step. Add the sifted flour and stem ginger syrup, and mix until just combined.

Turn out the dough onto a lightly floured surface and bring together to form a disc, about 1.5 cm/½ in. thick. Lightly dust the dough with flour before wrapping in clingfilm and chilling in the fridge for 30 minutes.

Make a start on the fruit filling by adding the apples, stem ginger, cinnamon, chai spice mix and vanilla bean paste to a bowl. Mix well and let the apples marinate for 30 minutes to soak up the spice.

Time to go back to our pastry, while the fruit is doing its thing. Lay out greaseproof paper onto your worktop and lightly sprinkle with flour. Place the chilled dough on top and use a rolling pin to roll out to about 3 mm/⅛ in. thick. Try and keep this as circular as you can. Doing this on top of greaseproof paper will mean you don't have any pastry stuck to your worktop.

Carefully peel off the rolled dough and gently line the base of the prepared tart tin, coaxing the dough into the sides, overlining the edges. I find using a scrap bit of dough covered in clingfilm and dipped in flour is the best way to work the pastry into the base edge without it sticking.

Cut off the excess dough with either a knife or by rolling a rolling pin across the top, and use a fork to prick the base gently. Place into the freezer for at least 45 minutes until frozen through – this prevents shrinkage and butter leakage later on.

Meanwhile, back to the filling. Add the butter and star anise to a large pan and warm over a low heat. When the butter has melted, remove the star anise. Pop the marinated apples into the pan, followed by the sugar, and mix.

Once the sugar has been cooked out, mix the cornflour with 2 tbsp of water to create a slurry, then add to the apples. Stir to combine and leave over a medium heat for 5–10 minutes until the liquid released from the apples has thickened slightly. Set aside to cool.

Preheat the oven to 170°C fan/190°C/gas mark 5.

When your pastry has frozen through, scrumple up some greaseproof paper and use it to line the base and sides. Add some baking beans or dried rice to blind bake. Place the tin onto a baking tray and bake in the oven for 15 minutes, then gently remove the baking beans and greaseproof paper. Using a pastry brush, gently brush over the beaten egg to seal the pastry, then place back in the oven for a further 7 minutes.

Add the cooled spiced apples to the pastry case and set aside while you prepare the streusel. Place all the ingredients, except the macadamia nuts, into a food processor and pulse to a chunky crumb. Add the macadamia nuts, and pulse once or twice to distribute. Layer on top of the apples. Build it up, baby!

Turn down the oven to 150°C fan/170°C/gas mark 3 before popping the tart back into the oven for a further 30 minutes until the streusel top is crisp and golden brown.

Remove the baked tart from the oven and leave to sit for a few minutes before gently releasing it from the tin. If you find you have any cracks in your pastry or the tart is too soft to release, leave it in the tin to cool completely before removing – this should give you some stability.

Drown immediately in custard (see page 285 for the perfect accompaniment).

Plant-Based Spiced Apple and Stem Ginger Tart with Macadamia Streusel

Serves: 6

For the Pâté Sucrée
125 g plant-based unsalted butter, room temp
50 g caster sugar
1 tsp vanilla bean paste
150 g plain flour, sifted, plus extra for dusting
75 g ground almonds
2 tbsp maple syrup, plus extra for brushing

For the Filling
6 Granny Smith apples, peeled and diced
4 preserved stem ginger pieces, finely chopped
2 tsp ground cinnamon
2 tsp chai spice mix (see pages 196–7 or use store-bought)
1½ tsp vanilla bean paste
50 g plant-based unsalted butter

1 star anise
100 g light soft brown sugar
15 g cornflour

For the Macadamia Streusel
75 g plant-based unsalted butter, fridge temp and diced
75 g golden caster sugar
50 g plain flour, sifted
25 g ground almonds
1 tsp vanilla bean paste
½ tsp almond extract
110 g macadamia nuts, roughly chopped

23-cm/7-in tart tin, greased with plant-based butter

Start with the pastry as this must chill in the freezer for an hour before we do anything else.

Into the bowl of a stand mixer (or large mixing bowl), add the butter, sugar and vanilla bean paste. Cream together using the paddle attachment on medium speed for about 5 minutes until light and fluffy. Add the flour, ground almonds and maple syrup, and mix until just combined.

Turn out the dough onto a lightly floured surface and bring it together to form a disc, about 1 cm/½ in. thick. Lightly dust the dough with flour before wrapping in clingfilm and chilling in the fridge for 30 minutes.

Make a start on the fruit filling by adding the apples, stem ginger, cinnamon, chai spice mix and vanilla bean paste to a bowl. Mix well and let the apples marinate for 30 minutes to soak up the spice.

Time to go back to our pastry, while the fruit is doing its thing. Lay out greaseproof paper onto your worktop and lightly sprinkle with flour. Place the chilled dough on top and use a rolling pin to roll out to about 3 mm/⅛ in. thick. Try and keep this as circular as you can. Doing this on top of greaseproof paper will mean you don't have any pastry stuck to your worktop.

Carefully peel off the rolled dough and gently line the base of the prepared tart tin, coaxing the dough into the sides, overlining the edges. I find using a scrap bit of dough covered in clingfilm and dipped in flour is the best way to work the pastry into the base edge without it sticking.

Cut off the excess dough with either a knife or by rolling a rolling pin across the top, and use a fork to prick the base gently. Place into the freezer for at least 45 minutes until frozen through – this prevents shrinkage and butter leakage later on.

Meanwhile, back to the filling. Add the butter and star anise to a large pan and warm over a low heat. When the butter has dissolved, remove the star anise. Pop the marinated apples into the pan, followed by the sugar, and mix.

Once the sugar has been cooked out, mix the cornflour with 2 tbsp of water to create a slurry, then add to the apples. Stir to combine everything and leave over a medium heat for 5–10 minutes until the liquid released from the apples has thickened slightly. Set aside to cool.

Preheat the oven to 170°C fan/190°C/gas mark 5.

When your pastry has frozen through, scrumple up some greaseproof paper and use it to line the base and sides. Add some baking beans or dried rice to blind bake. Place the tin onto a baking tray and bake in the oven for 15 minutes, then gently remove the baking beans and greaseproof paper. Using a pastry brush, gently brush over the beaten egg to seal the pastry, then place back in the oven for a further 7 minutes.

Add the cooled spiced apples to the pastry case and set aside while you prepare the streusel. Place all the ingredients, except the macadamia nuts, into a food processor and pulse to a chunky crumb. Add the macadamia nuts, and pulse once or twice to distribute. Layer on top of the apples. Build it up, baby!

Turn down the oven to 150°C fan/170°C/gas mark 3 before popping the tart back into the oven for a further 30 minutes until the streusel top is crisp and golden brown.

Remove the baked tart from the oven and leave to sit for a few minutes before gently releasing it from the tin. If you find you have any cracks in your pastry or the tart is too soft to release, leave it in the tin to cool completely before removing – this should give you some stability.

Drown immediately in custard (see page 285 for the perfect accompaniment). Enjoy every last sweet pastry crumb.

Cherry and Almond Pie

This is one of my favourite pies to make. Not just because it's stupidly delicious hot or cold, but because it is also pretty simple. There's plenty of steps in this recipe where you can make bits ahead and keep chilled until the big bake day. I have doubled the quantities for the dough because, a) it's so simple, and b) it freezes well.

I have some real firm favourites when it comes to flavour pairings, if you haven't already noticed. Basically anything almond and custard based. However, the filling is a versatile little number – if cherries aren't your thing (weird, but okay), then swap them out for another firm stone fruit. Plums would be delicious, or even unripe nectarines. In fact, peaches would work a dream in this, turning a slightly autumnal bake into a lovely summery number. Change the recipe seasonally. Work with what is best right now. The more you bake, the more confident you will get at changing things up.

Cherry and Almond Pie

Serves: 6

For the Almond Sweet Shortcrust Pastry
250 g unsalted butter, room temp
1 tsp vanilla bean paste
1 tsp almond extract
100 g caster sugar
2 medium eggs
200 g '00' or plain flour, sifted, plus extra
    for dusting
200 g ground almonds
1 egg, beaten, for brushing

For the Cherry Filling
1 kg fresh cherries, stoned (you can also use
    tinned or frozen)
150 g caster sugar
30 ml freshly squeezed lemon juice
½ tsp almond extract
120 ml water
35 g cornflour, sifted

23-cm/9-in. tart tin, buttered

Let's start with the pastry so this baby can get in the fridge to chill before we do anything else. In a stand mixer or large bowl, add the butter, vanilla bean paste, almond extract and sugar. Mix well until light and fluffy. Add the eggs and mix until fully incorporated. This may take a minute or two to emulsify completely. Next, in goes the flour and ground almonds. Mix until just combined.

Flatten out the dough with your hands on a piece of clingfilm to about 1 cm/½ in. thickness. Lightly sprinkle with flour and then wrap it tightly and place the covered dough onto a baking tray. Pop the tray into the fridge to chill for about 1 hour – this will make it miles easier for you to roll out and handle once the butter has firmed up a notch.

Sprinkle a little flour onto the worktop and use a rolling pin to roll the chilled dough to 3 mm/⅛ in. thick. You may find it easier to roll your pastry directly onto some baking paper to prevent any sticking.

Carefully line the base of the prepared tin, gently pressing in the pastry at the base edges before cutting off the excess dough. Keep the surplus dough to one side to use for your top decoration. Use a fork to gently prick the base of the lined tart tin and place it into the freezer for at least 45 minutes to freeze through completely.

While the tart is in the freezer, make your decorations to top your tart. Whether you choose to lattice, use a stencil, or use cutters, set the decorations aside and place in the freezer to set firm.

Preheat the oven to 170°C fan/190°C/gas mark 5.

Now that everything is chilling, let's move on to make the cherry filling. In a saucepan, add the cherries, sugar, lemon juice and almond extract. In a bowl, add the water and cornflour and mix to make a slurry. Pour into the saucepan. Place the saucepan over a medium heat and bring to the boil. Reduce the heat and cook the cherries low and slow, stirring often, for about 20 minutes until thickened. Once the liquid has reduced and coats the back of a spoon, remove from the heat and leave to cool. I pour this into a large, shallow baking tray for a speedier cool down.

When the pastry shell is frozen through, scrumple up some greaseproof paper, unfold it and place on top of the base. Pour in some baking beans or dried rice to blind bake for 15 minutes.

Remove from the oven and take out the baking beans (be careful, these will be super-hot!) and greaseproof paper. Use a pastry brush to brush beaten egg liberally over the bottom and sides to seal the pastry and ensure zero soggy bottom. Place back in the oven for a further 5 minutes toocook the egg wash.

Now spoon the cooled cherry filling into the pie case. Once filled, place your frozen pastry decoration on top and brush with egg wash. Place back into the oven for a further 20 minutes to bake.

Once the pie is out of the oven, allow to cool for 15 minutes in the tin, then carefully remove from the tin before slicing and serving warm. This is also killer when cold and sets nicely for a clean, sharp slice.

Either way, fill your plates, fill your bellies. Happy chappy.

Plant-Based Cherry and Almond Pie

Serves: 6

For the Almond Sweet Shortcrust Pastry
250 g plant-based unsalted butter, room temp
1 tsp vanilla bean paste
1 tsp almond extract
100 g caster sugar
200 g '00' or plain flour, sifted, plus extra
    for dusting
200 g ground almonds
2 tbsp water
1 tsp maple syrup, for brushing

For the Cherry Filling
1 kg fresh cherries, stoned (you can also use
    tinned or frozen)
30 ml freshly squeezed lemon juice
150 g caster sugar
½ tsp almond extract
35 g cornflour, sifted
120 ml water

23-cm/9-in. tart tin, greased with plant-based
    butter

Let's start with the pastry so this baby can get in the fridge to chill before we do anything else. In a stand mixer or large bowl, add the butter, vanilla bean paste, almond extract and sugar. Mix well until light and fluffy. Next, in goes the flour, ground almonds and water. Mix until just combined. If the dough feels a little dry, increase the amount of water 1 tbsp at a time – we want no visible streaks of flour but likewise, we don't want a sticky mess.

Flatten out the dough with your hands on a piece of clingfilm to about 1 cm/½ in. thickness. Lightly sprinkle with flour and then wrap it tightly and place the covered dough onto a baking tray. Pop the tray into the fridge to chill for about 1 hour – this will make it miles easier for you to roll out and handle once the butter has firmed up a notch.

Sprinkle a little flour onto the worktop and use a rolling pin to roll the chilled dough to 3 mm/⅛ in. thick. You may find it easier to roll your pastry directly onto some baking paper to prevent any sticking.

Carefully line the base of the prepared tin, gently pressing in the pastry at the base edges before cutting off the excess dough. Keep the surplus dough to one side to use for your top decoration. Use a fork to gently prick the base of the lined tart tin and place it into the freezer for at least 45 minutes to freeze through completely.

While the tart is in the freezer, make your decorations to top your tart. Whether you choose to lattice, use a stencil, or use cutters, set the decorations aside and place in the freezer to set firm.

Preheat the oven to 170°C fan/190°C/gas mark 5.

Now that everything is chilling, let's move on to make the cherry filling. In a saucepan, add the cherries, sugar, lemon juice and almond extract. In a bowl, add the water and cornflour and mix to make a slurry. Pour this into the saucepan. Place the saucepan over a medium heat and bring to the boil. Reduce the heat and cook the cherries low and slow, stirring often, for about 20 minutes until thickened and glossy. Once the liquid has reduced and coats the back of a spoon, remove from the heat and leave to cool. I pour this into a large, shallow baking tray for a speedier cool down.

When the pastry shell is frozen through, scrumple up some greaseproof paper, unfold it and place on top of the base. Pour in some baking beans or dried rice to blind bake for 15 minutes.

Remove from the oven and take out the baking beans (be careful, these will be super-hot!) and greaseproof paper. Pop back in the oven for 5 minutes.

Remove once again and this time use a pastry brush to brush the bottom and sides liberally with the maple syrup. This will seal the pastry and ensure zero soggy bottom. Place back in the oven for a further 5 minutes.

Now spoon the cooled cherry filling into the pie case. Once filled, place your frozen pastry decoration on top, brush with maple syrup and place back into the oven for a further 20 minutes to bake.

Once the pie is out of the oven, allow to cool for 15 minutes before removing from the tin, slicing and serving warm. This is also great cold – it sets nicely for a clean, sharp slice.

Dark Chocolate Velvet Tart with Dulce de Leche, Strawberries and Macadamia Nuts

This was initially named 'silk tart' because of its gloriously smooth, silky consistency, but apparently that's already a thing, so here is my dark chocolate velvet tart!

My key bit of advice for pastry is to read the recipe once, read it twice, then highlight the key bits of info that you KNOW you GOTTA do. Grab a pen, scribble on the page, use this book as your scrapbook. Underline, add sticky note tabs, add arrows, the whole lot. This is how I tackle new recipes (and technical challenges on *Bake Off*) – the only thing we need going in blind here, is an unbaked pastry crust, NOT YOU.

This tart looks more complicated than it is. A lovely one to share, and an indulgent bake to treat yourself to. Go on, *you* deserve it.

Dark Chocolate Velvet Tart with Dulce de Leche, Strawberries and Macadamia Nuts

Serves: 6

For the Dulce De Leche
397-g tin condensed milk

For the Chocolate Pastry
125 g unsalted butter, room temp
1 tsp vanilla bean paste
50 g caster sugar
1 medium egg
200 g plain flour, sifted, plus extra for dusting
25 g cocoa powder, sifted
1 egg, beaten, for brushing

For the Chocolate Ganache
275 ml double cream
20 g golden caster sugar
pinch of sea salt
375 g dark chocolate, callets or chopped
75 g unsalted butter, room temp
85 ml full-fat milk
1 tsp vanilla bean paste

To Finish
fresh strawberries, sliced
macadamia nuts, roughly chopped

23-cm/9-in. tart tin, buttered

First up, let's start with the thing that needs some time and care, which is the dulce de leche, the star of the show in my eyes. Preheat the oven to 220°C/gas mark 7 (don't use fan assist).

Pour the condensed milk into a deep cake tin and cover with foil – I am talking top, sides and bottom. Place the cake tin into a baking tray before pouring in enough water to come halfway up the sides of the tin. Bake in the oven for 1¾–2 hours; check halfway through to ensure enough water is still in the tray. Once done, remove the foil to see if the condensed milk has turned a deep golden colour and leave to cool. If it hasn't, pop it back in the oven for a further 30 minutes to thicken.

Next, let's get cracking with the pastry. In the bowl of a stand mixer (or large mixing bowl), add the butter, vanilla bean paste and sugar. Mix well with the paddle attachment until light and fluffy. Add the egg, making sure you mix well to allow all the ingredients to emulsify fully.

Stir the flour and cocoa powder together in a separate bowl to combine, then add to the butter mixture. Mix all the ingredients on low speed until they have just combined.

Turn out the dough onto a floured worktop and bring it all together with your hands, then flatten out the dough to about 1 cm/½ in. thickness. Transfer the dough to a sheet of clingfilm, lightly sprinkle with flour, then wrap it and pop into the fridge to chill for 30 minutes to allow the butter to solidify. Don't skip this bit – it will make the pastry far easier to work with if you give it a little time to chill.

Lightly flour the worktop and use a rolling pin to roll out the chilled dough to about 3 mm/⅛ in. thickness. Line the base of the prepared tin, cut off the excess dough and use a fork to prick the base gently. Pop into the freezer for at least 45 minutes to freeze completely. This will help minimise any pastry shrinkage in the oven.

Preheat the oven to 180°C fan/200°C/gas mark 4.

Once chilled, line the tart base with greaseproof paper and add in some baking beans or dried rice to blind bake. Place the tart tin onto a flat baking sheet and pop it into the oven for 12 minutes. Remove from the oven and gently remove the baking beans and greaseproof paper, before placing back in the oven for a further 5 minutes to continue drying out the pastry.

Use a pastry brush to brush over the beaten egg, then pop back into the oven for a final 5 minutes to seal. We don't want no soggy bottoms here, not on my watch! Remove the tin from the oven and leave to cool completely.

Once cooled, add a generous layer of dulce de leche to the base of the pastry tart and place in the fridge to set. Any remaining dulce de leche can be stored in the fridge for up to a week – add this to buttercreams or biscuit fillings (check out pages 212–17 for my chocolate alfajores), or drizzle on top of ice cream.

In the meantime, let's make the chocolate ganache. Add the cream, sugar and salt to a saucepan and bring to a simmer. Once the cream is simmering, add the chocolate and butter, and stir continuously until melted. Once melted, take off the heat and allow to cool slightly for about 10–15 minutes.

Stir in the cold milk with a balloon whisk until velvety (see, it makes sense now, right?) smooth. Pour the chocolate on top of the set dulce de leche, gently tap to even out, and allow to cool completely at room temperature for 2 hours. Finally, top with the strawberries and a scattering of macadamia nuts, then use a hot knife to serve up a slice of indulgence.

Plant-Based Dark Chocolate Velvet Tart with Dulce de Leche, Strawberries and Macadamia Nuts

The dairy-free version of this recipe is super easy. But a nifty little tip for anyone after yet another cheat code, swap out the homemade pastry for blitzed-up Oreo cookies (hi, accidentally plant-based goodness) and some melted butter like you would with a cheesecake base and use that buttery crumb to serve as the base for your tart. Just as delicious, just delicious made easier.

Serves: 6

For the Dulce De Leche
397-g tin coconut condensed milk

For the Chocolate Pastry
125 g plant-based unsalted butter, room temp
50 g caster sugar
1 tsp vanilla bean paste
200 g plain flour, sifted, plus extra for dusting
25 g cocoa powder, sifted
2 tbsp maple syrup, plus extra for brushing

For the Chocolate Ganache
350 ml tinned coconut milk (solids only), fridge temp

50 g golden caster sugar
pinch of sea salt
1 tbsp cornflour, sifted
1 tsp vanilla bean paste
300 g plant-based dark chocolate, callets or chopped
10 g plant-based unsalted butter, room temp

To Finish
fresh strawberries, sliced
macadamia nuts, roughly chopped

23-cm/9-in. tart tin, greased with plant-based butter

First up, let's start with the thing that needs some time and care, which is the dulce de leche, the star of the show in my eyes. Preheat the oven to 220°C/gas mark 7 (don't use fan assist).

Pour the coconut condensed milk into a deep cake tin and cover with foil – I am talking top, sides, and bottom. Place the cake tin into a baking tray before pouring in enough water to come halfway up the sides of the tin. Place into the oven and bake for 1¾–2 hours; check halfway through to ensure enough water is still in the tray. Once done, remove the foil to see if the condensed milk has turned a deep golden colour and leave to cool. If it hasn't, pop it back in the oven for a further 30 minutes to thicken.

Next, let's get cracking with the pastry, as this baby must get into the freezer to chill for about 1 hour before we do anything else. In the bowl of a stand mixer (or large mixing bowl), add the butter, sugar and vanilla bean paste. Cream together using the paddle attachment for about 5 minutes on medium speed until light and fluffy.

Add the sifted flour, cocoa powder and maple syrup to the mixer and mix until just combined.

Turn the dough out onto a floured surface and flatten it out to about 1 cm/½ in. thickness. Place it onto a piece of lightly floured clingfilm and wrap it tightly. Place it onto a baking tray and pop it into the fridge to chill for 30 minutes.

Lay a sheet of greaseproof paper on your worktop and lightly sprinkle with some flour. Place the chilled dough on top and use a rolling pin to roll out to 3 mm/⅛ in. thickness. Doing this on top of greaseproof paper will mean you don't have any pastry stuck to your worktop and will make it easier to transfer to your tin.

Carefully peel off the rolled dough and gently line the base of the prepared tart tin, coaxing the dough into the sides and overlining the edges. Cut off the excess dough with either a knife or by rolling a rolling pin across the top. Use a fork to prick the base gently. Pop this onto a baking tray and place into the freezer for at least 45 minutes until frozen through.

Preheat the oven to 170°C fan/190°C/gas mark 5.

When your pastry has frozen through, scrumple up some greaseproof paper, open it out, and use it to line the base and sides of the pastry. Add in some baking beans or dried rice to blind bake.

Place the tin onto a baking tray and pop into the oven to bake for 20 minutes, then remove the baking beans and greaseproof paper, and use a pastry brush to gently brush over some maple syrup to seal the pastry. Pop it back in the oven for a further 5 minutes. Once baked, allow the tart to cool completely in the tart tin.

Once cooled, add a generous layer of dulce de leche to the base of the tart and place in the fridge to set. Any remaining dulce de leche can be stored in the fridge for up to a week – add this to buttercreams or biscuit fillings (check out pages 212–17 for my chocolate alfajores), or drizzle on top of ice cream.

In the meantime, let's make the chocolate ganache. Add the coconut milk, sugar and salt to a saucepan and bring to a simmer. Once the cream is simmering, mix 1 tbsp of the hot milk with the cornflour to make a slurry, then add it back to the pan, along with the vanilla bean paste, chocolate and butter. Mix until smooth and glossy. Leave to cool for 15 minutes.

Pour the velvety smooth chocolate on top of the set dulce de leche and gently tap to even out. Allow to cool completely at room temperature for 2–3 hours. Top with the sliced strawberries and a scattering of macadamia nuts to serve. Use a hot knife to slice it.

Sweet Samosas with Medjool Date and Orange

I got so much sh*t on *Bake Off* for uttering the most blasphemous thing I could ever say as an Indian person. I nonchalantly declared that 'I don't even like samosas'. From that point on, half the South Asian population in the UK disowned me, and I am pretty sure all my ancestors turned in their graves. And so, to all those haters I say... SORRY. Yes, that's right. Turns out I was *gulp* wrong. Samosas are truly glorious.

Sweet or savoury, whatever triangular shape they may come in, whether they have been baked or fried, whether they are served hot or cold. These little golden parcels of deliciousness are truly something special and making them from scratch puts these flavour bombs on a whole new level. We're cheating a lil here by using filo pastry as opposed to samosa pastry, but the filo gives the necessary crunch. Super-delicious, super-versatile... and handshake worthy.

Sweet Samosas with Medjool Date and Orange

Makes: 12

For the Filling
300 g Medjool dates, stoned
1 tsp cumin seeds
100 g unsalted butter
120 ml freshly squeezed orange juice
1 tsp almond extract
½ tbsp almond butter
grated zest of 1 large orange

For the Pastry
6 filo pastry sheets, plus extra *just* in case
15 g unsalted butter, melted

For the Dipping Custard
175 ml full-fat milk
125 ml double cream
4 whole cardamom pods
1½ tsp vanilla bean paste
grated zest of 1 large orange
3 large egg yolks
50 g caster sugar
10 g plain flour
5 g cornflour

baking tray, lined

Place the Medjool dates into a food processor and blitz to a paste. If it gets too clumpy, add 1 tsp of water to loosen, before blitzing again.

Put the cumin seeds in a small pan and dry-toast over a low–medium heat for a few minutes until the cumin begins to 'pop' and your kitchen is smelling gloriously spiced. Transfer to a mortar and use a pestle to grind the cumin down. Place back into the pan, add the butter and orange juice, and heat until butter has fully melted.

Next, add the date purée to the pan and stir well using a wooden spoon. You want to make sure the butter emulsifies properly with the purée. And by this, I mean, stir the crap out of it until it is smooth AF and not two separate liquids. Keep on the heat for 10 minutes, stirring often to ensure the bottom doesn't catch. Once the liquid has all cooked out, remove the pan from the heat and add the almond extract, almond butter and orange zest. Stir well and then transfer to a baking tray to cool.

When the mixture has cooled, begin to construct the samosas. Fold each sheet of filo in half on the short end and use the line as a guide to slice each sheet in two (so you now have twelve sheets).

Brush a sheet of filo liberally with the melted butter (a pastry brush is best here, but if you don't have one, use your fingers – washed obvs – to distribute). Add 2 tbsp (or more if needed) of the date mixture on one side of the pastry sheet, shaping it into a rough triangle shape. Fold the triangle diagonally over, back and forth, sealing the pastry shut. By repeating the folds, we are eliminating the possibility of any spillages, keeping that delicious mixture all inside. Repeat with the remaining filo and filling. Brush the tops and bottoms with the melted butter and set aside.

Preheat the oven to 160°C fan/180°C/gas mark 4.

Place the samosas onto the prepared baking tray and bake for 20–25 minutes, flipping them over halfway through, until beautifully crisp and golden brown. Alternatively, these also work well shallow-fried in a generous glug of vegetable oil.

While they are baking, make the dipping custard. I call it dipping, I would rather drown in it. Put the milk, double cream, cardamom pods, vanilla bean paste and orange zest into a saucepan and place it over a medium heat.

Meanwhile, add the egg yolks, caster sugar and both flours to a bowl. Mix thoroughly using a balloon whisk.

When the milk is hot but not boiling, pour a little into the egg mix and whisk immediately with a balloon whisk. You want to work quickly here to avoid any lumps. Pour this egg mixture back into the pan and continue stirring until the custard coats the back of a spoon, then pour into a serving bowl.

Remove the baked samosas and serve with the custard. The custard and the samosas both taste great hot or cold – so a little treat for now and a little snack for later.

Plant-Based Sweet Samosas with Medjool Date and Orange

(EF)

Makes: 12

For the Filling
300 g Medjool dates, stoned
1 tsp cumin seeds
100 g plant-based unsalted butter
120 ml freshly squeezed orange juice
½ tbsp almond butter
1 tsp almond extract
grated zest of 1 large orange

For the Pastry
6 filo pastry sheets, plus extra *just* in case
15 g plant-based unsalted butter, melted

For the Dipping Custard
250 ml almond milk
4 whole cardamom pods
1½ tsp vanilla bean paste
grated zest of 1 large orange
50 g caster sugar
10 g plain flour
5 g cornflour

baking tray, lined

Place the Medjool dates into a food processor and blitz to a paste. If it gets too clumpy, add 1 tsp of water to loosen, before blitzing again.

Put the cumin seeds in a small pan and dry-toast over a low–medium heat for a few minutes until the cumin begins to 'pop' and your kitchen is smelling gloriously spiced. Transfer to a mortar and use a pestle to grind the cumin down. Place back into the pan, add the butter and orange juice, and heat until the butter has fully melted.

Next, add the date purée to the pan and stir well using a wooden spoon. You want to make sure the butter emulsifies properly with the purée. And by this, I mean, stir the crap out of it until it is smooth AF and not two separate liquids. Keep on the heat for 10 minutes, stirring often to ensure the bottom doesn't catch. Once the liquid has all cooked out, remove the pan from the heat and add the almond extract, almond butter and orange zest. Stir well and then transfer to a baking tray to cool.

When the mixture has cooled, begin to construct the samosas. Fold each sheet of filo in half on the short end and use the line as a guide to slice each sheet in two (so you now have twelve sheets).

Brush a sheet of filo liberally with the melted butter (a pastry brush is best here, but if you don't have one, use your fingers – washed obvs – to distribute). Add 2 tbsp (or more if needed) of the date mixture on one side of the pastry sheet, shaping it into a rough triangle shape. Fold the triangle diagonally over, back and forth, sealing the pastry shut. By repeating the folds, we are eliminating the possibility of any spillages, keeping that delicious mixture all inside. Repeat with the remaining filo and filling, Brush the tops and bottoms with the melted butter and set aside.

Preheat the oven to 160°C fan/180°C/gas mark 4.

Place the samosas onto the lined baking tray and bake for 20–25 minutes, flipping them over halfway through, until beautifully crisp and golden brown. Alternatively, these also work well shallow-fried in a generous glug of vegetable oil.

While they are baking, make the glorious dipping custard. Put the almond milk, cardamom pods, vanilla bean paste and orange zest into a saucepan and place over a medium heat.

Meanwhile, add the caster sugar and both flours to a bowl. Mix thoroughly using a balloon whisk.

When the milk is hot but not boiling, pour a little into the flour mix and whisk immediately with a balloon whisk. You want to work quickly here to avoid any lumps. Pour this flour mixture back into the pan and continue stirring until the custard coats the back of a spoon, then pour into a serving bowl.

Remove the baked samosas and serve with the custard. The custard and the samosas both taste great hot or cold.

PB and J Millefeuille Cake with Peanut Butter Crème Pâtissière and White Chocolate Whipped Cream

Here's a cake for anyone who doesn't want the faff of making a cake. Something that looks super impressive but is a breeze to make. Something quicker to make, a little lighter, a little more unique, and a little more wow.

Go big or go small with this one, adapt the size to suit your preference, make as one big whole cake or miniature-sized for individual servings. This bake has plenty of steps that can be done in advance, meaning on the day of serving, you are barely breaking a sweat.

My KEY bit of advice to you is to construct this *just* before serving, so you keep that pastry gloriously crisp. If you are making this as one large cake, one serving would be a single layer. Don't try cutting it into actual cake slices because it does NOT WORK. Yes, experience taught me well.

PB and J Millefeuille Cake with Peanut Butter Crème Pâtissière and White Chocolate Whipped Cream

Serves: 6–8

For the Filo Layers
8 filo pastry sheets
20 g coconut oil, melted
10 g caster sugar
handful of desiccated coconut

For the Peanut Butter Crème Pâtissière
250 ml full-fat milk
4 medium egg yolks
50 g caster sugar
15 g cornflour, sifted
10 g plain flour, sifted
120 g crunchy peanut butter
good pinch of salt

For the White Chocolate Cream
175 g mascarpone cheese, room temp
100 g white chocolate, melted and cooled
175 ml double cream
1 tsp vanilla bean paste

To assemble
300 g fresh raspberries
icing sugar, for dusting (optional)

baking tray, lined with a silicone mat
    or greaseproof paper

Preheat the oven to 180°C fan/200°C/gas mark 6.

Let's get our filo layers made. Lay out a sheet of filo and use a pastry brush to liberally brush over the coconut oil. Sprinkle over a generous pinch of sugar and scatter the desiccated coconut to evenly cover. Place another sheet of filo directly on top of the coconut sugar mix and repeat the process three times, so you are left with one sheet made up of four layers of filo. Repeat the above process with the remaining four sheets of filo.

Grab a bowl the size of the cake you want to make. Turn the bowl upside down and use this as your guide to carefully cut around with a sharp knife or a scalpel. Repeat this as many times as the bowl fits on the sheets. Then repeat with the remaining four sheets. Remove the excess pastry and save to make kataifi for my Peach and Amaretto Cheesecake (see pages 260–3).

Place the layered discs on to the lined baking tray. Add another sheet of greaseproof paper on top of the filo discs and place a baking tray on top, to flatten. We want super-thin layers, not puffy circles, so it's important we keep them weighted down to avoid this from happening.

Place in the oven and bake for 10 minutes. Carefully remove the top tray and greaseproof paper before popping back into the oven and baking for another 2–3 minutes until the tops are dark golden brown. Once baked, allow them to sit on the tray for a few minutes before transferring to a cooling rack.

For the peanut butter pastry cream, start with a normal pastry cream base by adding the milk to a saucepan and placing it over a medium heat.

In the meantime, add the egg yolks, sugar and both flours to a bowl. Whisk this super-well with a balloon whisk, taking it from the gritty bitty stage to the smooth stage. Once the milk is near boiling, pour half the milk into the bowl with the egg yolks and mix well. Pour the mixture back into the saucepan and continue to stir until thickened. We are after a consistency where it has gone past pourable and is more scoopable.

Once at the scoopy stage, remove the pan from the heat. Add the peanut butter and salt and give it a good mix to combine. Taste it, because OMG, heaven, but also to check the salt levels. Adjust if necessary. Leave this to cool before transferring into a piping bag with a nozzle attached if you wanna get fancy.

Next, let's make the white chocolate cream. I like the cream with a bit of texture. If this sounds like it floats your boat, use the chocolate when it is still slightly warm. If you want a cream that is smooth, allow the chocolate to cool completely first.

Add the mascarpone to the bowl of a stand mixer and mix using the whisk attachment until smooth. Add the white chocolate and mix again until combined, then add the cream and vanilla bean paste. Mix this to medium peaks and work the rest of the mixture by hand whisk a balloon whisk to get a good piping consistency. Transfer to a piping bag with nozzle attached.

Let's finally construct this beauty. Place one of the crisp golden filo discs onto your serving plate. Pipe the peanut butter and cream in whatever pattern you fancy – I go for alternating, adding a fresh raspberry in between to help cut through the sweetness. Once you have piped over the first filo disc, place the second layer onto the worktop. Yes, worktop. It is far easier to pipe onto a flat surface, as opposed to piping when the filo is layered. Once piped, carefully place the second layer on top of the first layer and repeat for the remaining discs.

Finish off the top layer however you want. Go for a full top of raspberries, or maybe you want to add more of the peanut butter cream, or keep it simple with just a dusting of icing sugar. Whichever way you choose to finish it, serve it within the hour and enjoy demolishing.

Plant-Based PB and J Millefeuille Cake with Peanut Butter Crème Pâtissière and White Chocolate Whipped Cream

Serves: 6–8

For the Filo Layers
8 filo pastry sheets
20 g coconut oil, melted
10 g caster sugar
handful of desiccated coconut

For the Peanut Butter Crème Pâtissière
250 ml coconut milk
50 g caster sugar
25 g cornflour, sifted
10 g plain flour, sifted
110 g crunchy peanut butter
good pinch of salt

For the White Chocolate Cream
100 g plant-based cream cheese
100 g plant-based white chocolate, melted
  and cooled
175 ml plant-based double cream
1 tsp vanilla bean paste

To assemble
300 g fresh raspberries
icing sugar, for dusting (optional)

baking tray, lined with a silicone mat
  or greaseproof paper

Preheat the oven to 180°C fan/200°C/gas mark 6.

Lay out a sheet of filo and use a pastry brush to liberally brush over the coconut oil. Sprinkle over a generous pinch of sugar and scatter the desiccated coconut to evenly cover. Place another sheet of filo directly on top of the coconut sugar mix and repeat the process three times, so you are left with one sheet made up of four layers of filo. Repeat the above process with the remaining four sheets of filo.

Grab a bowl the size of the cake you want to make. Turn the bowl upside down and use this as your guide to carefully cut around with a sharp knife or a scalpel. Repeat this as many times as the bowl fits on the sheets. Then repeat with the remaining four sheets. Remove the excess pastry and save to make kataifi for my Peach and Amaretto Cheesecake (see pages 260–3).

Place the layered discs on to the prepared baking tray. Add another sheet of greaseproof paper on top of the filo discs and place a baking tray on top, to flatten. We want super-thin layers, not puffy circles, so it's important we keep them weighted down to avoid this from happening.

Place in the oven and bake for 10 minutes. Carefully remove the top tray and greaseproof paper before popping back into the oven and baking for another 2–3 minutes until the tops are all dark golden brown. Once baked, allow them to sit on the tray for a few minutes before transferring to a cooling rack.

To make the peanut butter pastry cream, start by adding the coconut milk to a saucepan and placing it over a medium heat. Meanwhile, add the sugar and both flours to a bowl. Whisk to combine. Once the milk is near boiling, pour half the milk into the bowl and mix well. Pour the mixture back into the saucepan and continue to stir until thickened. We are after a consistency where it has gone pass pourable and more... scoopable. Once at that scoopy stage, remove

the pan from the heat. Add the peanut butter and salt, and give it a good mix to combine. Give it a taste (hi, heaven) to check the salt and adjust if necessary. Leave to cool before transferring to a piping bag with a nozzle attached if you wanna get fancy.

Next, let's make the white chocolate cream. I like the cream with a bit of texture. If this sounds like it floats your boat, use the chocolate when it is still slightly warm. If you want a cream that is smooth, allow the chocolate to cool completely first.

Add the cream cheese and white chocolate to the bowl of a stand mixer and mix using a whisk attachment until smooth before going in with the cream and vanilla bean paste. Mix this to medium peaks and work the rest of the mixture by hand whisk a balloon whisk to get a good piping consistency. Transfer to a piping bag with nozzle attached.

Let's finally construct this beauty. Place one of the crisp golden filo discs onto your serving plate. Pipe the peanut butter and cream in whatever pattern you fancy – I go for alternating, adding a fresh raspberry in between to help cut through the sweetness. Once you have piped over the first filo disc, place the second layer onto the worktop. Yes, worktop. It is far easier to pipe onto a flat surface, as opposed to piping when the filo is layered. Once piped, carefully place the second layer on top of the first layer and repeat for the remaining discs.

Finish off the top layer however you want. Go for a full top of raspberries, or maybe you want to add more of the peanut butter cream, or keep it simple with just a dusting of icing sugar. Whichever way you choose to finish it, serve it within the hour and enjoy demolishing.

Banana and Pecan Tarte Tatin with Cinnamon and Rum Ice Cream

I've binned the apples and we're using bananas instead. Once you have made it my way, you'll soon realise what a game-changing move this is. The bananas caramelise on top, they hold their shape while being cooked until tender and soft, the caramel hugs each piece in a velvety smooth sauce and the pecans add a crunchy nuttiness that brings it all together.

This is my go-to recipe when short on time, and when times are SUPER TIGHT, I scrap making the base from scratch and buy a block of ready-made puff pastry from the shops – after all, if it's good enough for Mary Berry, it's good enough for us.

I love adding a spoonful of my no-churn cinnamon and rum ice cream on top for a ridiculously filthy, adults-only dessert. Don't you fret, I have included the recipe for that here, too. If you want to get your chops on the entire shebang, make sure you make the no-churn ice cream the day before – this will need to set overnight (or for 6 hours at least) to ensure you aren't serving up boozy (but delicious) slop.

Banana and Pecan Tarte Tatin with Cinnamon and Rum Ice Cream

Serves: 6

For the Cinnamon and Rum Ice Cream
397-g tin condensed milk
550 ml double cream
25 g light soft brown sugar, or to taste
2 tsp vanilla bean paste
1 tbsp ground cinnamon
2½ tbsp coconut rum, or to taste (optional)

For the Rough Puff Pastry
250 g strong white bread flour, sifted,
    plus extra for dusting
pinch of salt
1½ tsp vanilla bean paste

225 g unsalted butter, frozen and grated
110 ml ice-cold water

For the Caramel
225 g caster sugar
1 cinnamon stick
1 vanilla pod, sliced in half
50 g unsalted butter

For the Tart Filling
75 g pecans, roughly chopped
4–5 large bananas, on the riper side of life
2 tbsp Demerara sugar

If you are going for the boozy ice cream, make this first by adding all the ingredients to a bowl and whisking to medium peaks. We don't want this whisked to a firm consistency as we want the ice cream to be gloriously smooth when set, so whisk the rest by hand to bring this to just before stiff peaks. Have a little taste of the cream and adjust the sweetness or booziness accordingly before transferring to a freezer-proof container. Cover and pop into the freezer overnight or for at least 6 hours.

Let's move on to the pastry. We aren't going for a full puff, so it's super important before you begin that the butter is frozen through and the water is ice-cold. Place the flour into a large mixing bowl with the salt, vanilla bean paste and frozen grated butter. Lightly mix until the butter has just mixed through, then add the water and mix until a dough forms. We really want to keep the butter as intact as possible – you want to be able to see streaks of unmixed butter throughout the dough. Form the dough into a rough rectangle and flatten before wrapping in clingfilm and popping in the fridge for 30 minutes to allow the butter to harden.

Lightly dust the worktop with flour and roll out the dough into a rectangle, 40 x 20 cm/16 x 8 in. in size. Fold the dough into three by folding the bottom third up and then top third on top. This is one fold. Rotate the pastry a quarter turn and roll the pastry out again to 40 x 20 cm/16 x 8 in. in size. Fold it into three again, making it two folds. Wrap the dough tightly in clingfilm before placing it back in the fridge for 30 minutes.

Remove the pastry and follow the folding and turning process twice more, meaning you have folded the dough four times in total. Wrap again and chill until needed.

Preheat the oven to 160°C fan/180°C/gas mark 4.

Put the sugar, cinnamon stick, and vanilla pod into an ovenproof pan and set over a medium heat. Cook until the sugar has dissolved and turned a caramel colour. Add the butter and mix until melted. Remove the pan from the heat and discard the cinnamon stick.

Scatter half the chopped pecans into the caramel, distributing evenly. Slice the bananas in half lengthways and carefully place them flat-side down into the caramel to cover the entire base of the pan. Once the bananas are nestled into the caramel, sprinkle the demerara sugar on top of the bananas to gently caramelise when baking. Scatter over the remaining pecans.

Remove the pastry dough from the fridge and lightly flour your worktop. Roll the dough out into a rough circle, 4 mm/1/8 in in. thick. Gently lift the rolled dough and carefully place on top of the bananas. Press the dough into the nooks and crannies around the outside to minimise any caramel seepage once we turn it out.

Pop the pan into the oven and bake for 45 minutes, or until crisp and golden brown.

Allow the pan to cool slightly once removed from the oven, then turn it out onto your serving plate. Serve up generous slices topped with a scoop of cinnamon and rum ice cream, or drown in custard and enjoy.

Plant-Based Banana and Pecan Tarte Tatin with Cinnamon and Rum Ice Cream

Serves: 6

For the Cinnamon and Rum Ice Cream
397-g tin plant-based condensed milk
550 ml plant-based double cream
25 g light soft brown sugar, or to taste
2 tsp vanilla bean paste
1 tbsp ground cinnamon
1½ tbsp dark rum, or to taste (optional)

For the Rough Puff Pastry
250 g strong white bread flour, sifted,
    plus extra for dusting
pinch of salt
1½ tsp vanilla bean paste

225 g plant-based unsalted butter, frozen
    and grated
110 ml ice-cold water

For the Caramel
225 g caster sugar
1 cinnamon stick
1 vanilla pod, sliced in half
50 g plant-based unsalted butter

For the Tart Filling
4–5 large bananas, on the unripe side of life
75 g pecans, roughly chopped

If you are going for the boozy ice cream, make this first by adding all the ingredients to a bowl and whisking to medium peaks. We don't want this whisked to a firm consistency as we want the ice cream to be gloriously smooth when set, so whisk the rest by hand to bring this to just before stiff peaks. Have a little taste of the cream and adjust the sweetness or booziness accordingly before transferring to a freezer-proof container. Cover and pop into the freezer overnight or for at least 6 hours.

Let's move on to the pastry. We aren't going for a full puff, so it's super important before you begin that the butter is frozen through and the water is ice-cold. Place flour into a large mixing bowl with the salt, vanilla bean paste and frozen grated butter. Lightly mix until the butter has just mixed through, then add the water and mix until a dough forms. We really want to keep the butter as intact as possible – you want to be able to see streaks of unmixed butter throughout the dough. Form the dough into a rough rectangle and flatten before wrapping in clingfilm and popping in the fridge for 30 minutes to allow the butter to harden.

Lightly dust the worktop with flour and roll out the dough into a rectangle, 40 x 20 cm/16 x 8 in. in size. Fold the dough into three by folding the bottom third up and then top third on top. This is one fold. Rotate the pastry a quarter turn and roll the pastry out again to 40 x 20 cm/16 x 8 in. in size. Fold it into three again, making it two folds. Wrap the dough tightly in clingfilm before placing it back in the fridge for 30 minutes.

Remove the pastry and follow the folding and turning process twice more, meaning you have folded the dough four times in total. Wrap again and chill until needed.

Preheat the oven to 160°C fan/180°C/gas mark 4.

Put the sugar, cinnamon stick and vanilla pod into an ovenproof pan and set over a medium heat. Cook until the sugar has dissolved and turned a caramel colour. Add the butter and mix until melted. Remove the pan from the heat and take out the cinnamon stick.

Scatter half the chopped pecans into the caramel, distributing evenly. Slice the bananas in half lengthways and carefully place them flat-side down into the caramel to cover the entire base of the pan. Scatter over the remaining chopped pecans.

Remove the pastry dough from the fridge and lightly flour your worktop. Roll the dough out into a rough circle, 4 mm/⅛ in. thick. Gently lift the rolled dough and carefully place on top of the bananas. Press the dough into the nooks and crannies around the outside to minimise any caramel seepage once we turn it out.

Pop the pan into the oven and bake for 45 minutes, or until crisp and golden brown.

Allow the pan to cool slightly once removed from the oven, then turn it out onto your serving plate. Serve up generous slices topped with a scoop of cinnamon and rum ice cream or plenty of custard.

Taking the Biscuit

To dunk or not to dunk? That is the question...

Stem Ginger, Cardamom and Orange Gingerbread

(EF)

Nothing gets me quite as stressed as making a gingerbread house during Christmas. I honestly think my architecture background doesn't help. It's like I challenge myself every year to go bigger and better, just so I can prove to myself that all those years studying for my masters was worth it.

This is the perfect quantity if you're going big, but works just as well halving it for a smaller batch of biscuits. These warming treats will stay fresh for up to a week in a sealed container once baked, or can stay in the freezer for up to 3 months pre-baked. Try them dunked in some homemade chocolate spread (see page 288). The depth of spice works so well with the zesty orange. Incredibly moreish and stupidly easy to make.

Makes: 1 large gingerbread house or 2 small

For the Biscuit
390 g unsalted butter or plant-based unsalted butter, diced
315 g dark soft brown sugar
170 g golden syrup
60 g preserved stem ginger, finely chopped
1 tbsp stem ginger syrup from the jar

1 kg plain flour, sifted
1 tbsp bicarbonate of soda, sifted
1 tsp ground cardamom
2½ tbsp ground ginger
grated zest of 1 large orange

gingerbread house cutters or stencils

Add the butter, sugar and golden syrup to a pan over a medium heat and gently cook until the butter has melted and the sugar has dissolved. Keep on cooking and stirring for a further 5 minutes before removing.

Next, add the stem ginger and ginger syrup to the pan, and use a balloon whisk to mix, making sure the butter is thoroughly incorporated.

In a large bowl, add the flour, bicarbonate of soda, cardamom, ground ginger and orange zest. Use a balloon whisk or fork to mix well to ensure they have all blended together. Get all those flavours intertwined with each other.

Pour the warm, melted butter mixture into the flour and use a wooden spoon to bring the dough together. This will require a teeny bit of elbow grease, but this is about as technical and tricky as it gets.

When the dough is still warm, but cool enough to touch, lightly knead and bring together with your hands. Making sure you work at it while it is still warm means a pliable dough, making it easier for you to roll out, shape, cut, and make whatever floats your boat.

My top tip for rolling out the dough: Roll it out directly onto a silicone mat or piece of greaseproof paper – the dough is quite soft, so trying to transfer these individually onto a baking tray will be a nightmare. Save yourself the heartache and hassle. Lightly flour the silicone mat or greaseproof paper, before placing some of the dough on top. Keep the remaining dough in the bowl and cover it with a tea towel or clingfilm to keep warm.

Gently press the dough down to flatten before placing another sheet of greaseproof paper on top. Use a rolling pin on top of this sheet to roll out to about 2.5 mm/⅛ in. thick. This will prevent the dough sticking to the rolling pin and create a smooth and even surface. Remove the top sheet of greaseproof paper and leave to one side to use again.

Use your gingerbread house cutters to cut out shapes (or stencils to cut around shapes) before carefully removing any excess dough. I find it useful to use a thin palette knife for this. Keep the excess dough to one side to re-use.

Place your tray of cut-out biscuits into the freezer for at least 30 minutes. We want them to be frozen through before they go into the oven to prevent any shrinkage, or, even worse, the shapes turning into splodges. I like to pre-cut all my biscuits and have them all frozen before I preheat my oven.

If you find the dough has begun to harden and dry, simply pop the bowl of dough, covered, into a microwave and heat in short, sharp bursts to warm up the butter again.

When you are ready to bake, preheat the oven to 180°C fan/200°C/gas mark 6.

Place the biscuits (nicely spaced out) into the oven and bake for 12–13 minutes until gorgeously golden and lightly browned on the edges. They may feel soft when removed but they will go hard once cooled. Leave to sit on the tray for a few minutes before transferring to a cooling rack to cool completely.

Decorate, if you wish, once cool, or sprinkle over a light dusting of icing sugar to enjoy as a warming, gently spiced treat.

Note: If you are using this gingerbread to make a house at Christmas, see page 305 for my go-to Royal icing recipe, which I use as the glue for my masterpieces. Sturdy, easy to make, and quick-drying – everything you need while you are busy drowning in stress.

Chocolate Wagon Wheels with Raspberry Jam and Hazelnut Biscuit

These old-school biscuits deserve to be bought back, updated and jazzed up. We made these on the first week of the show as our technical bake and, quite frankly, it was these biscuits that saved my ass from being kicked off. Nailed it, didn't I? (By some prayer and miracle.) They are quite the undertaking and I would suggest only tackling these on a mentally strong day, as they will break even the strongest of wills in the blink of an eye.

Despite being a bit of a faff, they are incredibly worth it. The homemade versions are far superior to anything wrapped and multi-packed. The buttery shortbread biscuit, the tart raspberries and the vanilla mallow, all encased in glossy, dark chocolate. Don't even get me started on that *snap* when you first break into it. Break down the stages to make it manageable for yourself; preparation is key.

Chocolate Wagon Wheels with Raspberry Jam and Hazelnut Biscuit

Makes: 12–14

For the Biscuit
225 g unsalted butter, room temp
110 g caster sugar
1 tsp vanilla bean paste
175 g plain flour, sifted, plus extra for dusting
50 g cocoa powder, sifted
100 g cornflour, sifted
50 g roasted hazelnuts, blitzed to a crumb

For the Jam
100 g fresh raspberries
110 g jam sugar

For the Marshmallow Fluff
4 gelatin sheets
100 ml water
200 g golden caster sugar
1½ tsp liquid glucose
1 large egg white
1½ tsp vanilla bean paste

To Finish
350 g milk or dark chocolate

8-cm/3-in. cookie cutter
baking tray, lined

Start with the biscuits. Cream together the butter, sugar and vanilla bean paste until light and fluffy – either using a stand mixer machine with the paddle attachment or an electric hand whisk.

In a separate bowl, mix the plain flour, cocoa powder, cornflour and blitzed hazelnuts before adding to the butter. Mix until the ingredients have come together in large clumps.

Press out the dough onto some lightly floured clingfilm, wrap entirely and pop in fridge for 15 minutes. The butter needs to firm up before rolling out. If you don't do this, the dough will be sludge and you will be sad.

Lightly flour your worktop before rolling out the chilled dough to about 3 mm/⅛ in. thick. Use the 8-cm/3-in. cookie cutter to cut out all your biscuits. Try to not overwork it, as it will begin to get tough and bitty. You should get about 24–28 biscuits from this dough in total, if you are savvy with your spacing. My top tip is to roll out the dough directly onto your lined baking tray and then cut out your biscuits, removing the surplus.

Use a fork to prick the tops of each one lightly, transfer to the lined baking tray if they're not already on it, and pop into freezer for 45 minutes until completely frozen through. This is key to prevent shrinkage and butter leaking out.

While we are waiting for them to chill, preheat the oven to 165°C fan/185°C/gas mark 5.

Make sure there's a bit of space between each biscuit before popping in the oven and baking for 12 minutes. Allow to cool on the tray for a few minutes to firm up, then remove using a palette knife and transfer to a cooling rack.

If you are making your own jam, it couldn't be easier. (If you are using store-bought, I won't judge you.) Add the raspberries and jam sugar to a saucepan. Lightly mush together using the back of a wooden spoon and bring to the boil over a low heat until the sugar has dissolved.

Continue to boil the raspberries for another 5 minutes until thickened. Pass through a sieve to remove the bits, and leave to cool completely. Transfer to a large, shallow baking tray to cool – this is much quicker than leaving in a bowl.

This is the fun bit. It's time to make the marshmallow fluff! Bloom the gelatin sheets in a bowl of cold water for 5 minutes. Add the water, sugar and liquid glucose to a pan. Place this over a low heat and gently cook until the sugar has dissolved. Crank the heat up a notch to bring the liquid to the boil at a temperature of 120°C/248°F. Meanwhile, whisk the egg white in a bowl until stiff but not dry.

Remove the sugar syrup pan from the heat once it has reached the right temperature and add the gelatin sheets. Give it a good mix to dissolve.

Back to our whisked egg white. Pop the mixer on full speed and, carefully and slowly, pour in the hot sugar syrup. Once all the syrup has been added, keep whisking on high for about 6–8 minutes until it has turned glossy, smooth and thick. Add the vanilla bean paste and mix.

Scoop out the fluff and transfer it to a piping bag with a small round nozzle attached. Leave to cool and let the marshmallow relax at room temperature for about 30 minutes until set.

Pipe the fluff onto the biscuit, leaving a gap around the outside – we are anticipating overspill! Add 1 tsp of jam to another biscuit and use the back of a spoon to spread evenly. Press the two biscuits together gently. Repeat with the remaining biscuits, marshmallow fluff and jam.

Chill the filled biscuits in the fridge while you melt the chocolate for coating. Do this either in the microwave in short bursts or in a heatproof bowl set over a pan of simmering water. You can dip the sandwiched biscuits into the chocolate or pour the chocolate on top and leave to set on a wire rack. Transfer to the fridge to set hard before serving. Enjoy the *snap*.

Plant-Based Chocolate Wagon Wheels with Raspberry Jam and Hazelnut Biscuit

Makes: 12–14

For the Biscuit
225 g unsalted plant-based butter, room temp
110 g caster sugar
1 tsp vanilla bean paste
175 g plain flour, sifted, plus extra for dusting
50 g cocoa powder, sifted
100 g cornflour, sifted
50 g roasted hazelnuts, blitzed to a crumb

For the Jam
100 g fresh raspberries
110 g jam sugar

For the Marshmallow Fluff
400-g tin chickpeas, drained, liquid only
½ tsp cream of tartar
¾ tsp xanthan gum
110 g caster sugar
1½ tsp vanilla bean paste

To Finish
350 g plant-based milk or dark chocolate

8-cm/3-in. cookie cutter
baking tray, lined

Start with the biscuits. Cream together the butter, sugar, and vanilla bean paste until light and fluffy – either using a stand mixer machine with the paddle attachment or an electric hand whisk.

In a separate bowl, mix the plain flour, cocoa powder, cornflour and blitzed hazelnuts before adding to the butter. Mix until the ingredients have come together in large clumps.

Press out the dough onto some lightly floured clingfilm, wrap entirely and pop in fridge for 15 minutes. The butter needs to firm up before rolling out. If you don't do this, the dough will be sludge and you will be sad.

Lightly flour your worktop before rolling out the chilled dough to about 3 mm/⅛ in. thick. Use the 8-cm/3-in. cookie cutter to cut out all your biscuits. Try to not overwork it, as it will begin to get tough and bitty. You should get about 24–28 biscuits from this dough in total, if you are savvy with your spacing. My top tip is to roll out the dough directly onto your lined baking tray and then cut out your biscuits, removing the surplus.

Use a fork to prick the tops of each one lightly, transfer to the lined baking tray if they're not already on it, and pop into freezer for 45 minutes until completely frozen through. This is key to prevent shrinkage and butter leaking out.

While we are waiting for them to chill, preheat the oven to 165°C fan/185°C/gas mark 5.

Make sure there's a bit of space between each biscuit before popping in the oven and baking for 12 minutes. Allow to cool on the tray for a few minutes to firm up, then remove using a palette knife and transfer to a cooling rack.

If you are making your own jam, it couldn't be easier. (If you are using store-bought, I won't judge you.) Add the raspberries and jam sugar to a saucepan. Lightly mush together using the back of a wooden spoon and bring to the boil over a low heat until the sugar has dissolved.

Continue to boil the raspberries for another 5 minutes until thickened. Pass through a sieve to remove the bits, and leave to cool completely. Transfer to a large, shallow baking tray to cool – this is much quicker than leaving in a bowl.

This is the fun bit. It's time to make the marshmallow fluff! Add the drained chickpea water to the bowl of a stand mixer. Use the whisk attachment to whisk until stiff – fyi, this will take a long time, up to 10–15 minutes. Don't even try to do this by hand (although an electric hand whisk is fine, it just will take that bit longer). Once stiff, add the cream of tartar and xanthan gum. Mix for a few rotations until combined.

Next, we go in with the caster sugar, 1 tbsp at a time, making sure you are mixing well between each addition. We want the sugar to have dissolved before adding in the next lot, otherwise you will get grainy fluff. And no one wants grainy fluff. Once all the sugar has been added, finish by mixing on high for 5 minutes. Add the vanilla bean paste and mix.

Scoop out the fluff and transfer to a piping bag with a small round nozzle attached. Pipe onto one biscuit, leaving a gap around the outside – we are anticipating overspill! Add 1 tsp of jam to another biscuit and use the back of a spoon to spread it evenly. Press the two biscuits together gently. Repeat with the remaining biscuits, marshmallow fluff and jam.

Set aside while you melt the chocolate for coating. Do this either in the microwave in short bursts or in a heatproof bowl set over a pan of simmering water.

You can dip the sandwiched biscuits into the chocolate or pour the chocolate on top (super-messy either way) and leave to set on a wire rack. Transfer to the fridge to set hard before tucking in.

Shortest Shortbread You'll Ever Eat

The recipe below is yours to tweak and make your own. Zests of citrus fruits are a great way of lifting buttery bakes – swiftly taking them from sickly to moreish. Adding a teaspoon of a spice makes the biscuits feel festive. Adding a sprinkling of fresh herbs to the dough or pressed into the top of each biscuit makes it a great carrier for heavier, more savoury accompaniments. Try not to add any more dried ingredients to the mix (e.g., ground almonds) or too much additional liquid (e.g., fresh fruit juice). The biscuit dough is incredibly soft and short, so tampering with the balance of ingredients is a risky business.

Makes: 24 individual 5-cm/2-in. rounds

---

225 g unsalted butter or plant-based unsalted butter, room temp
110 g caster sugar, plus extra for dusting
1 tsp vanilla bean paste
grated zest of 1 citrus fruit (lemon, lime or orange)

225 g '00' or plain flour, sifted, plus extra for dusting
100 g cornflour, sifted
pinch of salt

cookie cutter (optional)

This recipe really couldn't be easier. First up, let's add the room temp butter and sugar into the bowl of a stand mixer and cream together using the paddle attachment. You want to let this do its thing on medium speed for at least 5 minutes until light and fluffy – the more aerated the mixture, the more melt-in-the-mouth the end result will be.

Scrape down the sides of the bowl with a rubber spatula before going in with the vanilla bean paste and citrus zest of your choice. Adding the zest is entirely optional, but it's a great way to add a little oomph to the bake. Mix on medium speed until everything is combined.

Add the sifted flour and cornflour to the bowl, sprinkle in the salt and mix together on low speed until JUST combined. Yes the capital letters is totally needed, because we really don't want to overwork this dough. We are after crumbly, not clunky.

Lightly dust your worktop with flour, tip the bowl out and gently bring the dough together. Lay out a sheet of clingfilm, lightly dust again and place the dough on top. Press down to flatten (this will help for when you roll it out later) and wrap tightly, before placing onto a baking tray and popping in the fridge for about 30 minutes. This is a key step, because if you try to roll this straight after mixing, the dough will be too pliable and soft. Let it chill in the fridge to allow the butter to harden slightly before using. Don't defy me on this, okay!

Remove the chilled dough from the fridge and place a sheet of greaseproof paper on the worktop.

Lightly flour and place the dough on top. Place another piece of greaseproof paper on top and roll the dough to about 3 mm/⅛ in. thick. I like my biscuits nice and thin, but you can go traditional and keep 'em chunkier.

Use your cookie cutter or a knife to cut out your biscuits. Remove the surplus dough from the sheet and gently prick the tops of the biscuits with a fork. Don't get rid of the scrap dough, you can re-roll it twice, but any more than this and the biscuits will be tough AF.

Place the sheet onto a baking tray and pop into the freezer for at least 30 minutes to freeze. This is a golden rule for basically anything when you want to prevent shrinkage or butter leaking – same applies for any prepared biscuit or pastry.

In this time, cut out the rest of your biscuits or save the dough for another time. This will keep well in the freezer for up to 3 months, providing it is tightly wrapped or stored in a sealed container.

When you are ready to bake, preheat the oven to 160°C fan/180°C/gas mark 4.

Bake the shortbread biscuits for 13–15 minutes until the edges are lightly golden brown. Leave the biscuits to sit on the tray for a few minutes, before transferring to a cooling rack. Dust the tops with some caster sugar to finish.

My advice would be to chomp one of these while warm because they are buttery soft fresh out the oven and save the rest to cool... IF you have any willpower.

Chai Custard Creams

Biscuits can be the most rewarding bake as they are the easiest to double up on. And I would always recommend doing so, cause if you're already baking, you might as well bake bigger – always think of the freezer stash. For most of these recipes, the biscuit dough freezes well, meaning a sneaky stash for whenever the time calls for it. I love past me for caring about future me's happiness.

This version of the famous biscuit is a prime candidate for tea dunking. The myriad spices, the complexity and depth of the chai, the subtle warmth from the heady combination teamed with a classic custard filling, is the only way you should be eating custard creams from here on.

I've done you all a solid and given a recipe for a homemade chai spice mix in case you struggle to find it in the shops – keep this stored in a sealed container or jar and this will keep you going for a few months. Add it to cakes, add it to tea, add it to your lattes, add it to your biscuits. CHAI IS LIFE.

Chai Custard Creams

Makes: 24

For the Chai Spice Mix
3 tbsp ground ginger
2 tbsp ground sweetened cinnamon
1½ tbsp ground cardamom
½ tbsp ground cloves
½ tbsp ground nutmeg
¼ tsp ground star anise

For the Biscuit
275 g unsalted butter, room temp
115 g icing sugar
1 tsp vanilla bean paste
200 g plain flour, plus extra for dusting

100 g custard powder
¾ tbsp chai spice mix (see opposite or
    use store-bought)

For the Custard Buttercream
70 g unsalted butter, room temp
115 g icing sugar, sifted
40 g custard powder
1 tsp vanilla bean paste
1 tbsp milk

2 baking trays, lined

If you are making the chai spice mix, add all the ingredients to a bowl and mix well. I like to add this to a mini blender and whizz for 10 seconds just to make sure all the spices have mixed well with each other. Pop this into a jar and set aside.

For the biscuit dough, add the butter and sugar to a bowl and cream together for 5 minutes until light and fluffy. Add the vanilla bean paste and mix to combine.

In a separate bowl, mix together the flour, custard powder and chai spice mix using a balloon whisk. Add the spiced flour to the butter and mix until just combined.

Lightly flour your worktop and turn out the dough. Use your hands to work the dough and bring it all together once it is soft and smooth. Roughly mould the dough into a disc and press down gently to flatten before wrapping tightly in clingfilm. Pop it in the fridge to chill for 15 minutes.

Remove the chilled dough from the fridge and roll out on a lightly floured silicone mat or sheet of greaseproof paper to about 4 mm/⅛ in. thick. Using the cutter of your choice, stamp out the biscuits, and add to the prepared baking trays. Any surplus dough is good to be re-rolled twice, but after this, the dough will begin to toughen, so be savvy with your dough cutting!

Place the trays in the freezer to set for 45 minutes.

Preheat oven to 165°C fan/185°C/gas mark 5.

While you are waiting for the biscuits to set, make the custard buttercream. Add all the ingredients, except the milk, to a bowl. Use an electric hand whisk or a balloon whisk to combine until smooth. Add the splash of milk at the end to loosen the buttercream before transferring to a piping bag.

Once the biscuits have set, pop one tray into the oven and bake for 13 minutes until lightly golden. Repeat with the second tray. Baking them separately just ensures an even bake across both batches.

Leave the biscuits to set and harden on the trays for 5 minutes before transferring to a cooling rack to cool completely.

When they are completely cool, pipe the custard buttercream onto one biscuit, leaving a slight border around the sides, before sandwiching with another biscuit. Gently press together so the filling comes to the edges. Repeat with all the remaining biscuits and buttercream.

I like these once they have firmed up a little, so I pop my finished biscuits in the fridge for about 30 minutes before dunking and demolishing. Keep these stored with no lid on, to keep that biscuit snap and freshness at its peak.

Plant-Based Chai Custard Creams

For me, these biscuits taste better the plant-based way. The texture, the finish and the snap are incomparable, so this recipe for me would always be my go-to, out of the two.

Makes: 24

For the Biscuit
275 g plant-based unsalted butter, room temp
115 g icing sugar
1 tsp vanilla bean paste
200 g plain flour, plus extra for dusting
100 g custard powder
¾ tbsp chai spice mix (see pages 196–7
  or use store-bought)

For the Custard Buttercream
75 g plant-based unsalted butter, room temp
110 g icing sugar, sifted
40 g custard powder
1 tsp vanilla bean paste
1 tbsp soy milk

2 baking trays, lined

For the biscuit dough, add the butter and sugar to a bowl and cream together for 5 minutes until light and fluffy. Add the vanilla bean paste and mix to combine.

In a separate bowl, mix together the flour, custard powder and chai spice mix using a balloon whisk. Add the spiced flour to the butter and mix until just combined.

Lightly flour your worktop and turn out the dough. Use your hands to work the dough and bring it all together once it is soft and smooth. Roughly mould the dough into a disc and press down gently to flatten before wrapping tightly in clingfilm. Pop it in the fridge to chill for 15 minutes.

Remove the chilled dough from the fridge and roll out on a lightly floured silicone mat or sheet of greaseproof paper to about 4 mm/⅛ in. thick. Using the cutter of your choice, stamp out the biscuits, and add to the prepared baking trays. Any surplus dough is good to be re-rolled twice, but after this, the dough will begin to toughen, so be savvy with your dough cutting!

Place the trays in the freezer to set for 45 minutes.

Preheat oven to 165°C fan/185°C/gas mark 5.

While you are waiting for the biscuits to set, make the custard buttercream. Add all the ingredients, except the soy milk, to a bowl. Use an electric hand whisk or a balloon whisk to combine until smooth. Add the splash of milk at the end to loosen the buttercream, then transfer it to a piping bag.

Once the biscuits have set, pop one tray into the oven and bake for 13 minutes until lightly golden. Repeat with the second tray. Baking them separately just ensures an even bake across both batches.

Leave the biscuits to set and harden on the trays for 5 minutes before transferring to a cooling rack to cool completely.

When they are completely cool, pipe the custard buttercream onto one biscuit, leaving a slight border around the sides, before sandwiching with another biscuit. Gently press together so the filling comes to the edges. Repeat for all remaining biscuits and filling.

I like these once they have firmed up a little, so I pop my finished biscuits in the fridge for about 30 minutes before dunking and demolishing. Keep these stored with no lid on, to keep that biscuit snap and freshness at its peak.

Spiced Linzer Cookies with Blueberry Jam

Okay, sure, these just look exactly like our jammy dodger friends. But I promise you, despite looking the same, they are infinitely better.

Linzer cookies are the handsome, overachieving offspring of the Linzertorte – which is an Austrian almond-crusted tart filled with berry preserves and occasionally a few roasted nuts, and topped with an intricate lattice crust. These cookies on the other hand are a much quicker way of getting to eat that torte – the biscuit has a super almondy, marzipan-esque sort of flavour, which I have spiked with a hint of clove – which is then topped with blueberry jam and a good dusting of icing sugar.

You've got a whole section dedicated to homemade curds and jams in this book, so mix it up every time you make these. This is also a great recipe to double up if you are making as an edible gift.

Spiced Linzer Cookies with Blueberry Jam

Makes: 32 individual or 16 sandwiched

For the Biscuit
115 g unsalted butter, room temp
70 g caster sugar
1 large egg yolk
grated zest of 1 lemon
20 ml freshly squeezed lemon juice
⅛ tsp ground cloves
155 g plain flour, sifted, plus extra for dusting
65 g ground almonds
½ tsp vanilla bean paste
1 tsp almond extract
pinch of salt

To Fill and Finish
150 g blueberry jam (see page 297 or
    use store-bought)
icing sugar, for dusting

6-cm/2½-in. cookie cutter
2 baking sheets, lined

Add the butter and sugar to the bowl of a stand mixer and cream together using the paddle attachment for 5 minutes until light and fluffy. Add the egg yolk and mix again. Next in is the lemon zest and juice. Mix well and don't fret if the biscuit mixture looks a little curdled at first, keep on mixing through that worrying stage and it will all start to emulsify together.

In a separate bowl, add the flour, ground almonds and ground clove. Use a balloon whisk to combine all the ingredients together. The aim of this step is just to intersperse the clove amongst all the flour for an even distribution. It's not about eating a clump of clove, trust me. Add this spiced flour mix to the mixer with the vanilla bean paste, almond extract and salt.

Mix with the paddle attachment until just combined. The magic of these lies in the short crumb, so less is definitely more when it comes to working the dough. Alternatively, use a mixing bowl and eletric hand whisk.

Transfer the dough to a lightly floured worktop, bring it together in a disc shape, and gently press down. Wrap the dough in clingfilm and pop in the fridge for 1 hour to firm up.

Once the biscuit dough has firmed up, flour your worktop before rolling the biscuit dough out to about 3 mm/⅛ in. thick. You may find it easier to cut the dough in half and work in two batches. Use the cookie cutter to cut out the rounds. Transfer half of the cookies to one prepared baking sheet, leaving some space between them all, and then use a smaller cutter to cut out the middle of the remaining cookies. Transfer these to the other baking sheet – these will be the top-layer cookies.

Pop both sheets into the freezer to chill for at least 45 minutes.

Preheat the oven to 150°C fan/170°C/gas mark 3.

I like to bake the trays separately to ensure an even bake across both, so pop one tray into the oven and bake for 14 minutes until dry. These won't look golden, so don't be tempted to overbake. Repeat with the remaining tray.

Leave to sit on the baking tray for 5 minutes to harden before transferring to a cooling rack to cool completely.

Once completely cool, add 1 tsp of blueberry jam to each whole cookie, then sandwich with a cut-out top-layer biscuit. Gently press down to seal. When all the cookies have been sandwiched, lightly dust with icing sugar to finish.

Plant-Based Spiced Linzer Cookies with Blueberry Jam

Makes: 24 individual or 12 sandwiched biscuits

For the Biscuit
115 g plant-based unsalted butter, room temp
70 g caster sugar
grated zest of 1 lemon
20 ml freshly squeezed lemon juice
⅛ tsp ground cloves
140 g plain flour, sifted, plus extra for dusting
65 g ground almonds
½ tsp vanilla bean paste
1 tsp almond extract
pinch of salt

To Fill and Finish
150 g blueberry jam (see page 297 or
    use store-bought)
icing sugar, for dusting

6-cm/2½-in. cookie cutter
2 baking sheets, lined

Add the butter and sugar to the bowl of a stand mixer and cream together using the paddle attachment for 5 minutes until light and fluffy. Next in is the lemon zest and juice. Mix well and don't fret if the biscuit mixture looks a little curdled at first, keep on mixing through that worrying stage and it will all start to emulsify together.

In a separate bowl, add the flour, ground almonds and ground clove. Use a balloon whisk to combine all the ingredients together. The aim of this step is just to intersperse the clove amongst all the flour for an even distribution. It's not about eating a clump of clove, trust me. Add this spiced flour mix to the mixer with the vanilla bean paste, almond extract and salt.

Mix with the paddle attachment until just combined. The magic of these lies in the short crumb, so less is definitely more when it comes to working the dough. Alternatively, use a mixing bowl and electric hand whisk.

Transfer the dough to a lightly floured worktop, bring it together in a disc shape, and gently press down. Wrap the dough in clingfilm and pop in the fridge for 1 hour to firm up.

Once the biscuit dough has firmed up, flour your worktop before rolling the biscuit dough out to about 3 mm/⅛ in. thick. You may find it easier to cut the dough in half and work in two batches. Use the 6-cm/2½-in. cookie cutter to cut out the rounds. Transfer half of the cookies to one baking sheet, leaving some space between them all, and then use a smaller cutter to cut out the middle of the remaining cookies. Transfer these to the other baking sheet – these will be the top-layer cookies.

Pop both sheets into the freezer to chill for at least 45 minutes.

Preheat the oven to 150°C fan/170°C/gas mark 3.

I like to bake the trays separately to ensure an even bake across both, so pop one tray into the oven and bake for 14 minutes until dry. These won't look golden, so don't be tempted to overbake. Repeat with the remaining tray.

Leave to sit on the baking tray for 5 minutes to harden before transferring to a cooling rack to cool completely.

Once completely cool, add 1 tsp of blueberry jam to each whole cookie, then sandwich with a cut-out top-layer biscuit. Gently press down to seal. When all cookies have been sandwiched, lightly dust with icing sugar to finish.

Passion Fruit Viennese Fingers with White Chocolate and Coconut Ganache

The lightest of biscuits paired with the jammy, creamy filling is a dangerous combo, and one that tests my willpower every time (I fail, naturally). The tropical pairing of passion fruit and coconut give these Viennese fingers the glow up of their life. The velvety tang from the passion fruit against the cooling, creamy white chocolate and coconut whipped ganache filling gives these biscuits a real summery twist.

A steady and light hand is needed when making these — the biscuit is super short and soft once baked. Allow them to cool fully before handling, otherwise your biscuity dreams will become a crumbly mess right in front of your eyes. And speaking as someone whose cake fell over on national TV, the trauma from this is real.

Passion Fruit Viennese Fingers with White Chocolate and Coconut Ganache

I like to finish these biscuits off with a sprinkling of coconut flakes just for that extra touch of decadence. But other nice touches would be chopped almonds, chopped macadamia nuts or blitzed freeze-dried raspberries.

Makes: 15

For the Biscuit
175 g unsalted butter, room temp
65 g icing sugar, sifted
1½ tsp vanilla bean paste
145 g plain flour, sifted, plus extra for dusting
65 g cornflour, sifted
½ tsp baking powder, sifted
50 ml passion fruit juice (approx. 6 passion fruits)
35 ml full-fat milk

For the Coconut Filling
60 ml coconut cream
65 ml double cream
130 g white chocolate, chopped
15 g desiccated coconut

To Finish
50 g coconut flakes
icing sugar, for dusting

baking tray, lined

The biscuit dough is super simple to come together. Pop the butter, icing sugar and vanilla bean paste into the bowl of a stand mixer and cream together using the paddle attachment for about 5 minutes until light and fluffy.

In the meantime, add the sifted flour, cornflour and baking powder to a separate bowl and mix together to combine.

Once the butter is fluffy, scrape down the sides of the bowl. Add the flour mix, followed by the passion fruit juice and milk. (A top tip to extracting as much juice from a passion fruit as possible: Place all the fleshy seeds into a sieve and smush this around with a rubber spatula to get all of that glorious golden juice.)

Gently mix on low speed for a few rotations before working the rest of the mixture by hand. You want this to be just combined and not overworked (like us on a Friday, am I right?). The dough will be a little sticky, but don't panic, this is totally normal. Pop this into a piping bag fitted with a star nozzle and pipe either biscuit rounds or fingers onto the prepared baking tray.

Place the tray into the freezer for about 1 hour to freeze through. We really want the biscuit dough to keep all that buttery goodness within and not leak out, so make sure you don't skip this step.

Meanwhile, preheat the oven to 160°C fan/ 180°C/gas mark 4.

To make the coconut filling, pop the coconut cream and double cream into a saucepan. Place the pan over a medium heat and bring to a near boil, then remove from the heat and add the chopped white chocolate. Swirl around the cream to coat and leave to sit for 2 minutes, then use a rubber spatula or a balloon whisk to mix until smooth. Transfer the coconut ganache to a shallow tray to help cool it down quickly. Leave the tray for 15 minutes at room temperature before placing into the fridge to cool completely.

Once the biscuits are frozen, bake them for 20–22 minutes. Keep an eye on these because you want these to be lightly golden around the sides, not completely tanned all over. Leave to sit on the tray for 5 minutes before transferring to a cooling rack to cool completely.

Meanwhile, remove the cooled white chocolate and coconut ganache from the fridge and sprinkle the desiccated coconut on top. Use an electric hand whisk to whisk until thickened and pale, then transfer to a piping bag.

Pipe a generous layer of coconut ganache on one biscuit and sandwich with another, gently pressing down. Repeat with all the biscuits and filling. Roll the sides in the coconut flakes and lightly dust the biscuit tops with icing sugar.

These are great freshly baked, but also keep well for a few days (if you have the willpower) stored, uncovered, in the fridge.

Plant-Based Passion Fruit Viennese Fingers with White Chocolate and Coconut Ganache

Makes: 15

For the Biscuit
175 g plant-based unsalted butter, room temp
65 g icing sugar, sifted
1½ tsp vanilla bean paste
145 g plain flour, sifted, plus extra for dusting
65 g cornflour, sifted
½ tsp baking powder, sifted
50 ml passion fruit juice (approx. 6 passion fruits)
35 ml coconut milk

For the Coconut Filling
60 ml coconut cream
65 ml plant-based double cream
130 g plant-based white chocolate, chopped
15 g desiccated coconut

To Finish
50 g coconut flakes
icing sugar, for dusting

baking tray, lined

The biscuit dough is super simple to come together. Pop the butter, icing sugar and vanilla bean paste into the bowl of a stand mixer and cream together using the paddle attachment for about 5 minutes until light and fluffy.

Meanwhile, add the sifted flour, cornflour and baking powder to a separate bowl and mix together to combine.

Once the butter is fluffy, scrape down the sides of the bowl. Add the flour mix, followed by the passion fruit juice and coconut milk. (A top tip to extracting as much juice from a passion fruit as possible: Place all the fleshy seeds into a sieve and smush this around with a rubber spatula to get all of that glorious golden juice.)

Gently mix on low speed for a few rotations before working the rest of the mixture by hand. You want this to be just combined and not overworked (like us on a Friday, am I right?). The dough will be a little sticky, but don't panic, this is totally normal. Pop this into a piping bag fitted with a star nozzle and pipe either biscuit rounds or fingers onto the prepared baking tray.

Place the tray into the freezer for about 1 hour to freeze through. We really want the biscuit dough to keep all that buttery goodness within and not leak out, so make sure you don't skip this step.

Preheat the oven to 160°C fan/180°C/gas mark 4.

While we are waiting for the biscuits to freeze, let's make the coconut filling. Pop the coconut cream and double cream into a saucepan. Place the pan over a medium heat and bring to a near boil, then remove from the heat and add the chopped white chocolate. Swirl around the cream to coat and leave to sit for 2 minutes, then use a rubber spatula or a balloon whisk to mix until smooth. Transfer the coconut ganache to a shallow tray to help cool it down quickly. Leave to cool for 15 minutes at room temperature before placing into the fridge to cool completely.

Once the biscuits are frozen, bake them for 20–22 minutes. Keep an eye on these because you want these to be lightly golden around the sides, not completely tanned all over. Leave to sit on the tray for 5 minutes before transferring to a cooling rack to cool completely.

Meanwhile, remove the cooled white chocolate and coconut ganache from the fridge and sprinkle the desiccated coconut on top. Use an electric hand whisk to whisk until thickened and pale, then transfer to a piping bag.

Pipe a generous layer of coconut ganache on one biscuit and sandwich with another, gently pressing down. Repeat with all the biscuits and filling. Roll the sides in the coconut flakes and lightly dust the biscuit tops with icing sugar.

These are great freshly baked, but also keep well for a few days (if you have the willpower) stored, uncovered, in the fridge.

Chocolate Alfajores with Dulce de Leche

Alfajores are these incredible South American melt-in-your-mouth biscuits, which have a decadent dulce de leche filling and are rolled in desiccated coconut to top it all off. I've added a naughty little addition of cocoa powder to the biscuit dough to really guarantee that these will be some of the best biscuits you've ever eaten. Guaranteed to rival any you think are your ultimate faves.

These aren't hugely popular or found in the UK, and golly, we are a bunch of losers missing out. These are good to be eaten for breakfast, brunch, a lunchtime snack, and basically every breathing moment – the depth of flavour alongside the buttery biscuit and coconut finish is nothing short of addictive. You. Are. Welcome.

Chocolate Alfajores with Dulce de Leche

Makes: 28 sandwiched biscuits

For the Biscuit
115 g salted butter, room temp
110 g icing sugar
1 tsp vanilla bean paste
2 large egg yolks
2 tbsp milk
145 g plain flour, sifted, plus extra for dusting
55 g cocoa powder, sifted
40 g cornflour, sifted
1 tsp baking powder, sifted

For the Filling
397-g tin of caramel (or see pages 160–1 to make dulce de leche from scratch)

To Finish
75 g desiccated coconut
icing sugar, sifted (optional)

5-cm/2-in. cookie cutter
2 baking trays, lined

In a bowl, cream together the butter and icing sugar for a few minutes until paler in colour and airy in texture. Add the vanilla bean paste and egg yolks, and mix until emulsified. Pour in the milk and combine.

In a separate bowl, use a balloon whisk to mix the plain flour, cocoa powder, cornflour and baking powder.

Add the flour to the butter mixture, and whisk until just mixed. The magic of these biscuits is the short, crumbly texture, so the less you work them, the better they will be when baked.

Lightly flour the worktop and bring the dough together with your hands until soft and smooth. If the dough feels too wet, dust the dough with some more flour. Form a disc, lightly press down and wrap in clingfilm before popping in the fridge to chill for 1 hour.

Once the dough has chilled, lightly flour your worktop before rolling the dough out to about 5 mm/¼ in. thick.

Use the cookie cutter to cut out the biscuit rounds before transferring them to the prepared baking trays, leaving some space between them all. Place the trays in the freezer for 45 minutes to freeze through – this will just help prevent the biscuits from spreading when baking and make sure all that buttery goodness doesn't leak out.

Preheat the oven to 180°C fan/200°C/gas mark 6.

It's gonna be a little tricky to gauge if the biscuits are done as there'll be no golden brown edges to give the game away, so you'll have to be a little brave with your timings and trust that they are baked. Once the biscuits are frozen, I like to take two biscuits to test out timings. These are normally good being baked for 11 minutes, but depending on your oven, there may be some slight variation. Once you're happy with your timings, bake one tray at a time for 11 minutes (or however long your experiment told you). This just ensures an even bake across both trays. Leave to cool on the tray for 5 minutes before transferring to a cooling rack to cool completely.

Transfer the contents of the caramel tin to a piping bag fitted with a 1-cm/½-in. nozzle. Once the biscuits are completely cool, pipe a 4-cm/1½-in. circle of caramel onto one biscuit and fill the circle with caramel. Sandwich another biscuit on top and gently press the two biscuits together so the filling jussst comes to the edges (but does not overflow). Repeat with all the biscuits.

When all the biscuits have been sandwiched, pour the desiccated coconut onto a baking tray. Roll the edge of the sandwiched biscuit across the desiccated coconut, allowing the caramel to act as a glue. Finally, finish the biscuits with a light dusting of icing sugar and get ready to gobble the lot.

Plant-Based Chocolate Alfajores with Dulce de Leche

Makes: 28 sandwiched biscuits

For the Filling
397-g tin coconut condensed milk
2 tsp cornflour, sifted (optional)

For the Biscuit
115 g plant-based salted butter, room temp
110 g icing sugar
1 tsp vanilla bean paste
35 g unsweetened apple sauce (see page 302)
2 tbsp coconut milk
145 g plain flour, sifted, plus extra for dusting

55 g cocoa powder, sifted
40 g cornflour, sifted
1 tsp baking powder, sifted

To Finish
75 g desiccated coconut
icing sugar, sifted (optional)

5-cm/2-in. cookie cutter
baking tray, lined

216

First up we have to get our filling sorted, as this will take a few hours. Take the tin of condensed milk and place it into a large saucepan. Completely cover with water and bring to the boil. Reduce the heat to a simmer and let it do its thing for 4 hours – you want to make sure the water level in the pan never goes below the tin height, so keep an eye on it and keep topping that baby up. Once done, remove from the water and open the tin. If the mixture has thickened to a piping consistency, GLORIOUS. Well done you. (If not, no worries. Just empty the tin contents into a saucepan, sprinkle the cornflour on top, and mix well before placing over a medium heat. Bring to the boil, then reduce the heat to a simmer and let it reduce to a thick consistency, about 15–20 minutes.) Transfer the caramel to a bowl and leave to cool at room temperature for 1 hour before popping in the fridge. This will thicken significantly once chilled, so give this a little time before moving on to the next step.

Into a bowl, cream together the butter and icing sugar for a few minutes until paler in colour and airy in texture. Add the vanilla bean paste and apple sauce, and mix until emulsified. Pour in the coconut milk and combine.

In a separate bowl, use a balloon whisk to mix the flour, cocoa powder, cornflour and baking powder.

Add the flour to the butter mixture and whisk until just mixed. The magic of these biscuits is the short, crumbly texture, so the less you work them, the better they will be when baked.

Lightly flour the worktop and bring the dough together with your hands. If the dough feels too wet, dust the dough with some more flour. Form a disc, lightly press down and wrap in clingfilm before popping in the fridge to chill for 1 hour.

Once the dough has chilled, lightly flour your worktop before rolling the dough out to about 5 mm/¼ in. thick.

Use the cookie cutter to cut out the biscuit rounds before transferring them to the prepared baking trays, leaving some space between them all. Place the trays into the freezer for 45 minutes to freeze through – this will just help prevent the biscuits from spreading when baking and make sure all that buttery goodness doesn't leak out.

Preheat the oven to 180°C fan/200°C/gas mark 6.

It's gonna be a little tricky to gauge if the biscuits are done as there'll be no golden brown edges to give the game away, so you'll have to be a little brave with your timings and trust that they are baked. Once the biscuits are frozen, I like to take two biscuits to test out timings. These are normally good being baked for 11 minutes, but depending on your oven, there may be some slight variation. Once you're happy with your timings, bake one tray at a time for 11 minutes (or however long your experiment told you). This just ensures an even bake across both trays. Leave to cool on the tray for 5 minutes before transferring to a cooling rack to cool completely.

Transfer the thickened condensed milk to a piping bag fitted with a 1-cm/½-in. nozzle. Once the biscuits are completely cool, pipe a 4-cm/1½-in. circle of caramel onto one biscuit and fill the circle with caramel. Sandwich another biscuit on top and gently press the two biscuits together so the filling jussst comes to the edges (but does not overflow). Repeat with all the biscuits.

When all the biscuits have been sandwiched, pour the desiccated coconut onto a baking tray. Roll the edge of the sandwiched biscuit across the desiccated coconut, allowing the dulce de leche to act as a glue. Finally, finish the biscuits with a light dusting of icing sugar and get ready to demolish them.

She's the Cookie Queen

Literally no one calls me this. I call me this. I get my partner to call me this and that's about it. Saying that, I DO make bloody damn good cookies, and a good cookie recipe is one thing I think everyone needs in their locker.

The base for these cookies is solid – don't you even dare think about changing that because you're playing with the best. Think like Messi or Rihanna levels. But base aside, these are your babies. Go wild with the toppings and fillings. I've given you some suggestions to help along the way, with the method the same each time, but my advice to you would be to raid your kitchen cupboards.

There's nothing better after a long day than popping some frozen cookie dough into the oven and tucking into a slightly warm, slightly gooey, and slightly under-baked cookie on the sofa. The key to these is freezing them before you bake. This way, you will get that slightly chunky cookie and they won't all splodge out in a mess. Freezing them also means you can hoard a secret stash whenever the cookie cravings call.

Soft, gooey middle, crisp crunchy edges. *This* is how you do cookies, just the way they should be.

She's the Cookie Queen

Makes: 15

Classic Chocolate Chip
225 g unsalted butter, room temp
115 g light soft brown sugar
110 g caster sugar
1 large egg
100 g condensed milk (it makes sense, trust me)
1½ tsp vanilla bean paste
360 g self-raising flour
pinch of salt
275 g milk or dark chocolate chunks

Raspberry, White Chocolate and Macadamia
225 g unsalted butter, room temp
115 g light soft brown sugar
110 g caster sugar
1 large egg
100 g condensed milk
1½ tsp vanilla bean paste
360 g self-raising flour
pinch of salt
250 g white chocolate
90 g macadamia nuts, roughly chopped
275 g fresh raspberries
Note: When using fresh fruit in cookies, don't
   mix them into the dough as this will create a
super-wet, sticky dough, which will alter
the final texture of the cookie. Instead,
press them in on top of the scooped
cookie dough before freezing.

Nutella-Stuffed Cookies
225 g unsalted butter, room temp
115 g light soft brown sugar
110 g caster sugar
1 large egg
100 g condensed milk
grated zest of 2 large oranges
1½ tsp vanilla bean paste
360 g self-raising flour
pinch of salt
75 g blanched almonds, roughly chopped
225 g milk chocolate chunks
300 g Nutella or homemade Nutella
   (see page 288)
Note: For this recipe you will need to pipe out
   Nutella rounds onto a baking tray and freeze
   fully before using in the dough.

ice-cream scoop
baking tray, lined

In the bowl of a stand mixer, cream the butter and both sugars with the paddle attachment for a minute or two until combined. We aren't after this to be light or fluffy, we just want this mixed well. Next in are the egg and condensed milk. Just trust me on the latter, it will forever change your cookie game. Mix until everything is emulsified.

Now is when you put in your flavourings, e.g., vanilla bean paste, orange zest, lemon zest, almond extract, etc. Add whatever tickles your pickle and give it all another quick mix.

Add the sifted flour, salt and the remaining ingredients or your chosen extras, e.g. milk/dark/white chocolate chunks, chopped nuts, dried fruits, crushed salted pretzels, etc. Mix this until everything has combined and no visible streaks of flour are left. By this point, it should very much look like a dough.

Use the ice-cream scoop to scoop out dough balls and place on your lined baking tray. You don't need to worry about spacing them out at this point, plonk them all together to save space.

For a melty filling: If you are including a Nutella or other filling, press one of the frozen rounds into the dough ball and cover completely.

For a fruity topping: If you are using fresh fruit in your cookies, add them now. I know it looks like one raspberry covers the entire top of the dough ball but trust me, just stick them on around the sides and push them all together. They will spread out once baked, so it will all make sense then.

Place the baking tray into the freezer and leave for at least 4–6 hours but preferably overnight.

Once they have frozen through, preheat the oven to 160°C fan/180°C/gas mark 4.

Place a few of the dough balls onto a lined baking tray, leaving plenty of space around each one, and bake for 14 minutes.

While the cookies are still hot, use either a large round glass or large cookie cutter to scoot around the edges of each cookie to round it off. Let the cookies sit on the tray for at least 30–45 minutes before moving them onto a cooling rack. If you try and move these before, they'll probably crumble into a pile of mush in front of your eyes, which is worse than heartbreak, I promise you.

After that, do with the cookies what you may. Eat them cold, eat them slightly warm, share them, gobble them yourself, add a scoop of ice cream on top, add a scoop of ice cream between two for a sandwich cookie, eat them all, eat the crumbs and be delighted that you've just found the best cookie recipe there is. Hopefully now, Cookie Queen makes sense.

Plant-Based
She's the Cookie Queen Ⓔ🇫

The one thing I will say about these cookies, they always taste better the day after they have baked. They've chilled, they've relaxed, the gooey insides are still lovely and soft while holding their shape.

The below recipes all use unsweetened apple sauce as the egg replacer, but the below also works with using an oil substitute or even mashed bananas. Just be aware that bananas will, of course, impart quite a heavy taste, so if that doesn't tickle your pickle, steer clear. Make sure you check out page 310 for more info on egg replacers and what you can use. I know, I'm pretty nifty, aren't I?

Makes: 15

Classic Chocolate Chip
225 g plant-based unsalted butter, room temp
120 g light soft brown sugar
110 g caster sugar
175 g unsweetened apple sauce (see page 302)
1½ tsp vanilla bean paste
360 g self-raising flour
pinch of salt
275 g plant-based milk or dark chocolate chunks

Raspberry, White Choc and Macadamia
225 g plant-based unsalted butter, room temp
115 g light soft brown sugar
110 g caster sugar
175 g unsweetened apple sauce (see page 302)
1½ tsp vanilla bean paste
360 g self-raising flour
pinch of salt
250 g plant-based white chocolate chunks
90 g macadamia nuts, roughly chopped
275 g fresh raspberries

Biscoff Stuffed Cookies
225 g unsalted butter, room temp
115 g light soft brown sugar
110 g caster sugar
175 g unsweetened apple sauce (see page 302)
1½ tsp vanilla bean paste
360 g self-raising flour
pinch of salt
75 g blanched almonds, roughly chopped
225 g plant-based milk chocolate chunks
300 g Biscoff spread
Note: For this recipe you will need to pipe out Biscoff rounds onto a baking tray and freeze.

ice-cream scoop
baking tray, lined

Into the bowl of a stand mixer, add the butter and both sugars. Cream together using the paddle attachment for a minute or two until combined. We aren't after this to be light or fluffy, we just want this mixed well. Next in is the apple sauce. Mix these until everything is emulsified.

Now is when you put in your flavourings, e.g., vanilla bean paste, orange zest, lemon zest, almond extract, etc. Add whatever tickles your pickle and give it all another quick mix.

Add the sifted flour, salt and the remaining ingredients or your chosen extras, e.g. plant-based chocolate chunks, chopped nuts, dried fruits, etc. Mix this until everything has combined and no visible streaks of flour are left. By this point, it should very much look like a dough.

Use the ice-cream scoop to scoop out dough balls and place on your lined baking tray. You don't need to worry about spacing them out at this point, plonk them all together to save space.

For a melty filling: If you are including a Biscoff filling, press one of the frozen rounds into the dough ball and cover completely.

For a fruity topping: If you are using fresh fruit in your cookies, add them now. I know it looks like one raspberry covers the entire top of the dough ball but trust me, just stick them on around the sides and push them all together. They will spread out once baked, so it will all make sense then.

Place the baking tray into the freezer and leave for at least 4–6 hours but preferably overnight.

Once they have frozen through, preheat the oven to 160°C fan/180°C/gas mark 4.

Place a few of the dough balls onto a lined baking tray, leaving plenty of space around each one, and bake for 14 minutes.

While the cookies are still hot, use either a large round glass or large cookie cutter to scoot around the edges of each cookie to round it off. Let the cookies sit on the tray for at least 30–45 minutes before moving them onto a cooling rack. If you try and move these before, they'll probably crumble into a pile of mush in front of your eyes, which is worse than heartbreak I promise you.

After that, do with the cookies what you may. You can add a scoop of plant-based ice cream between two cookies for a sandwich cookie or just gobble them all up. Cookie Queen, I told ya!

Sweeter Things

Treats that don't fit into boxes – The Inbetweeners

Lemon Meringue Traybake with Coconut and Cardamom

You can have this as a tart, as squares, as slices, or, if you are anything like me, just as a slab ready to be attacked with a fork, an empty belly, and a cup of ginger tea to wash it down (I was going to say a G&T, but if you are making this at early o'clock in the morning, I want no judgements thrown my way).

This originally started off as a vegan, dairy-free and gluten-free masterpiece, which I then happened to work back into a dairy version, to give everyone a bit of both. The flavours in this are a real dream combo. The coconut and cardamom are a match made in buttery, biscuit heaven, while the tart lemon filling will make the backs of your cheeks squeal in delight.

If you are low on time or are a little eager beaver, the biscuit base can be made the day before, while the lemon curd filling will sit pretty in a sterilised jar or container for up to a week stored in the fridge. The only bit I will stand firm on you making fresh on the day of serving is the meringue – both plant-based and non-plant-based – as we want this to be a fluffy cloud sitting on top of that tart curd, so do the deliciousness justice and do it on the day.

Lemon Meringue Traybake with Coconut and Cardamom

Serves: 18

For the Biscuit Base
220 g unsalted butter, room temp and diced
125 g caster sugar
150 g coconut flour, plus extra for dusting
50 g desiccated coconut
¾ tsp ground cardamom or 10 cardamom
  pods, crushed and ground
1 tsp vanilla bean paste

For the Speedy Lemon Curd Filling
75 g cornflour, sifted
300 g caster sugar
275 ml freshly squeezed lemon juice
  (approx. 6 medium lemons)

grated zest of 4 lemons
550 ml coconut milk, fridge temp
yellow food colouring (optional)

For the Meringue
4 large egg whites
½ tsp cream of tartar
1 tsp vanilla bean paste
115 g caster sugar

20 x 30-cm/8 x 12-in. tin, greased and lined
  (allow the paper to come up over the sides)
cook's blowtorch (optional)

230

Put the butter and sugar into the bowl of a stand mixer and cream together with the paddle attachment for a few minutes. Next, add the coconut flour, desiccated coconut, cardamom and vanilla bean paste. Mix on medium speed until the mixture comes together and forms a rough dough – this should take a minute or so. Alternatively, if you don't have one of these fancy machines, you can use an electric hand whisk for the same results.

Turn out the dough directly into your prepared tin and lightly dust your fingertips with some coconut flour before pressing the dough into the tin. I like to use a flour-dusted glass tumbler to roll on top of the dough or the base of a flat-bottomed glass to even out the dough. A cake scraper also does the trick. This is not necessary, but does ensure an even layer all the way through, meaning an even bake. Lightly prick the top with a fork before popping the tin into the freezer for 30 minutes.

Preheat the oven to 160°C fan/180°C/gas mark 4.

When the biscuit base is frozen, place the tin into the oven and bake for 16–18 minutes until the top is lightly golden. Set aside to cool.

Put all the speedy lemon curd filling ingredients into a medium saucepan, and use a balloon whisk to mix well, ensuring there are no lumps from the cornflour. Place over a medium heat for a few minutes until the sugar dissolves, and then give the mixture another few minutes to begin to bubble and thicken. You're looking for a curd consistency here, so something that will coat the back of a wooden spoon when dipped in.

Once thickened, pour on top of the cooled biscuit base and shake the tin a little to level it out. Leave to cool at room temperature for 1 hour before transferring to the fridge to cool completely.

Once the curd is set and cooled, let's move on to making the meringue. Pour the egg whites into the bowl of a stand mixer fitted with the whisk attachment. Again, an electric hand whisk will do the job, but I would highly recommend not doing this by hand, unless you're super bored and have biceps like Arnie. Set the speed to medium and mix until the whites are stiff but not dry. Add the cream of tartar and mix for a few more rotations to disperse.

In a small bowl, combine the vanilla bean paste and sugar. Add the sugar mixture to the stand mixer, 1 tbsp at a time, keeping the mixer running on medium speed and ensuring each addition of sugar has dissolved before going in with the next lot. This step takes a bit of time and patience, but is worth it – no one wants a grainy meringue. You can judge this by taking a little bit of the mix and smushing it between two fingers; if you can feel grains, go low and slow on speed and additions.

Once all the sugar has been added, leave to mix on high speed for 5 minutes. The meringue should now be thick, glossy and firm enough for you to be able to hold the bowl upside down over your head. Go onnnnn, give it a go, you know you wanna!

You can transfer the meringue to a piping bag with nozzle attached, if you want to be fancy, and pipe the meringue on. Alternatively, just grab your spatula to spread the meringue on top of the cooled curd. Use the back of a spoon to swirl around or an offset palette knife to level out.

When you're happy with how it looks, use a blowtorch (if you have one) to lightly toast the top or place under a hot grill (be careful and watch this like a hawk if you go for this option; it will go from golden brown to incinerated in the blink of an eye).

Let the meringue sit for about 10 minutes before slicing it with a hot knife.

Plant-Based Lemon Meringue Traybake with Coconut and Cardamom

Serves: 18

For the Biscuit Base
200 g plant-based butter, room temp and diced
125 g caster sugar
150 g coconut flour
50 g desiccated coconut
¾ tsp ground cardamom or 10 cardamom
   pods, crushed and ground
1 tsp vanilla bean paste

For the Lemon Curd Filling
75 g cornflour, sifted
300 g caster sugar
275 ml freshly squeezed lemon juice
   (approx. 6 medium lemons)

grated zest of 4 lemons
550 ml coconut milk, fridge temp
yellow food colouring (optional)

For the Meringue
400-g tin chickpeas
½ tsp cream of tartar
1 tsp vanilla bean paste
115 g caster sugar

20 x 30-cm/8 x 12-in. tin, greased with
   coconut oil and lined (allow the paper
   to come up over the sides)
cook's blowtorch (optional)

Put the butter and sugar into the bowl of a stand mixer and cream together with the paddle attachment for a few minutes. Next, add the coconut flour, desiccated coconut, cardamom and vanilla bean paste. Mix on medium speed until the mixture comes together and forms a rough dough – this should take a minute or so. Alternatively, if you don't have one of these fancy machines, you can use an electric hand whisk for the same results.

Turn out the dough directly into your prepared tin and lightly dust your fingertips with some coconut flour before pressing the dough into the tin. I like to use a flour-dusted glass tumbler to roll on top of the dough or the base of a flat-bottomed glass to even out the dough. A cake scraper also does the trick. This is not necessary, but does ensure an even layer all the way through, meaning an even bake. Lightly prick the top with a fork before popping the tin into the freezer for 30 minutes.

Preheat the oven to 160°C fan/180°C/gas mark 4.

When the biscuit base is frozen, place the tin into the oven and bake for 16–18 minutes until the top is lightly golden. Set aside to cool.

Put all the ingredients for the lemon curd filling into a medium saucepan, and use a balloon whisk to mix well, ensuring there are no lumps from the cornflour. Place over a medium heat for a few minutes until the sugar dissolves, and then give the mixture another few minutes to begin to bubble and thicken. You're looking for a curd consistency here, so something that will coat the back of a wooden spoon when dipped in.

Once thickened, pour on top of the cooled biscuit base and shake the tin a little to level it out. Leave to cool at room temperature for 1 hour before transferring to the fridge to cool completely.

Once the curd is set and cooled, let's move on to making the meringue. Place a sieve on the bowl of a stand mixer bowl and empty out the chickpea tin into it. Let the chickpeas sit in the sieve for 5 minutes to drain all the aquafaba. Using the whisk attachment, mix the aquafaba on medium–high speed until it becomes stiff but not dry (this will take time, even if it's been mixing for 10 minutes and it's still basically water, just keep on persisting, it will eventually get there). Add the cream of tartar and mix for a few more rotations to disperse.

In a small bowl, combine the vanilla bean paste and sugar. Add the sugar mixture to the stand mixer, 1 tbsp at a time, keeping the mixer running on medium speed and ensuring each addition of sugar has dissolved before going in with the next lot. This step takes a bit of time and patience, but is worth it – no one wants a grainy meringue. You can judge this by taking a little bit of the mix and smushing it between two fingers; if you can feel grains, go low and slow on speed and additions.

Once all the sugar has been added, leave to mix on high speed for 5 minutes. The meringue should now be thick, glossy and firm enough for you to be able to hold the bowl upside down over your head. Go on, give it a go, you know you wanna!

You can transfer the meringue to a piping bag with nozzle attached, if you want to be fancy, and pipe the meringue on. Alternatively, just grab your spatula to spread the meringue on top of the cooled curd. Use the back of a spoon to swirl around or an offset palette knife to level it out.

When you're happy with how it looks, use a blowtorch (if you have one) to lightly toast the top or place under a hot grill (be careful and watch this like a hawk if you go for this option; it will go from golden brown to incinerated in the blink of an eye).

Let the meringue sit for about 10 minutes before slicing it with a hot knife.

Tropical Trifle with Ginger Sponge, Mango Custard and Pomegranate Jelly

The classic trifle reminds me of Christmas, so I wanted to make this version the complete opposite. This is a summer holiday in your mouth. She's a little sweet, a little sour, a bit sticky, a bit smooth, very yummy, and very scrummy. Yes, those last two words are basically the same but I just wanted to double-down on how good this is.

Serves: 8

For the Ginger Sponge
130 g unsalted butter, room temp
110 g dark soft brown sugar
50 g golden syrup
40 g black treacle
2 large eggs
120 g self-raising flour, sifted
¾ tbsp ground cinnamon
1¼ tbsp ground ginger
1 tsp vanilla bean paste
20 g soured cream
3 preserved stem ginger pieces, finely diced
4 tbsp stem ginger syrup, from the jar

For the Pomegranate Jelly
250 g pomegranate seeds
   (approx. 2 whole pomegranates)
500 ml water
1–2 tbsp caster sugar, to taste
5 sheets of gelatin

For the Mango Custard
3 large egg yolks
50 g caster sugar
15 g cornflour, sifted
10 g plain flour, sifted
150 ml full-fat milk
1 tsp vanilla bean paste
175 ml mango purée

For the Coconut Cream
135 g mascarpone cheese
135 g coconut cream
50 g icing sugar, sifted
1½ tsp vanilla bean paste
350 ml double cream

To Finish
tropical fruit of your choice (optional)
toasted flaked coconut

2 x 18-cm/7-in. cake tins, greased and lined

Preheat the oven to 150°C fan/170°C/gas mark 3.

Add the butter, sugar, golden syrup and treacle to the bowl of a stand mixer and mix on medium speed until light and fluffy – this should take a few minutes. Next, add the eggs. These go in one by one as you want each egg to emulsify fully before adding the next.

In a separate bowl, combine the flour, cinnamon and ground ginger with a fork or balloon whisk. Add one-third to the stand mixer bowl. Mix well.

Use a rubber spatula or large metal spoon to fold in another one-third of the flour, along with the vanilla bean paste, before adding the remaining flour alongside the soured cream and finely diced stem ginger. Keep the folding light to make sure you keep as much air in the batter.

Divide the cake batter evenly between the two lined tins, then bake them for 24–26 minutes until the sides of the sponge come away from the tin edge and the sponge tops are bouncy and firm when gently pressed – just watch those fingertips please!

Allow to cool in the tins for 5 minutes, then turn out onto a wire rack for 30 minutes. Brush the stem ginger syrup over the sponges before wrapping in clingfilm and leaving to cool completely.

Make the jelly by adding the pomegranate seeds to a pan, along with the water and sugar. Place over a medium heat and bring to the boil, then turn down the heat to a simmer and let it do its thing for about 15 minutes – we want to break the seeds down slightly, extracting the juice, which in turn gives you that gorgeous colour.

While the water is simmering, bloom the gelatin sheets in cold water for 5 minutes. Once bloomed, squeeze out the excess water from the sheets and add to the pan. For the mixture to set, you want the temperature to be over 35°C/95°F – so give this a check with a thermometer probe, if you have one (if you don't, if the water has been simmering, there's a good chance it is well over that anyway). When the sheets have dissolved into the water, remove from the heat and pour into your serving bowl. Leave to cool at room temperature for 30 minutes, then pop in the fridge to set.

Once the jelly has set firm, make the custard. Put the egg yolks in a bowl with the sugar, cornflour and flour, and whisk with a balloon whisk until pale in colour.

Add the milk to a saucepan with the vanilla bean paste and mango purée, and place over a medium heat. Once it is near-boiling, pour one-third of the milk into the egg yolk mixture and whisk immediately until smooth. Pour the mixture back into saucepan and mix. Reduce the heat and continue to stir the custard. Keep stirring until it thickens – we want this quite thick, a good sign to stop is when it begins to bubble in the middle. You want a thick, smooth, spreadable consistency. Leave to cool.

While we are waiting for the custard to cool, make the coconut cream by adding all the ingredients, except the double cream, to a bowl. Mix well until smooth. Add the double cream and mix until it reaches medium peaks. Keep in the fridge until needed.

When the custard is cooled, add half to the top of the set jelly. Next is one of the sponges – I like to crumble these slightly to break down the sponge (this makes it easier to scoop out on serving), but you do you. You could keep it whole, cut it into chunks, crumble it, whatever floats your boat. Either pipe or use a spoon to spread one-quarter of the coconut cream on top of the sponge, before adding the remaining custard on top. Level out and add the second sponge on top.

Finish off this tropical extravaganza by dolloping on the remaining coconut cream. Smush this around with the back of a spoon or offset palette knife, and top it all off with a mountain of fresh fruit and a good sprinkling of toasted flaked coconut.

Plant-Based Tropical Trifle with Ginger Sponge, Mango Custard and Pomegranate Jelly

Serves: 8

For the Ginger Sponge
135 ml soy milk
¾ tbsp apple cider vinegar
175 g plant-based unsalted butter
140 g dark soft brown sugar
65 g golden syrup
65 g black treacle
2½ preserved stem ginger pieces, finely diced
4 tbsp syrup from jar
265 g self-raising flour, sifted
⅛ tsp bicarbonate of soda
1¼ tbsp ground ginger
1 tbsp ground cinnamon
1 tsp vanilla bean paste

Pomegranate Jelly
225 g pomegranate seeds
  (approx. 2 whole pomegrantes)
500 ml water
1–2 tbsp caster sugar (depending on seed
  sweetness)
1¼ tsp agar agar

For the Mango Custard
75 g caster sugar
18 g cornflour, sifted
15 g plain flour, sifted
110 ml coconut milk
1½ tsp vanilla bean paste
250 ml mango purée

For the Coconut Cream
100 g plant-based cream cheese
175 g coconut cream
50 g icing sugar, sifted
1½ tsp vanilla bean paste
350 ml plant-based double cream

To Finish
tropical fruit of your choice (optional)
toasted flaked coconut

2 x 18-cm/7-in. cake tins, greased with
  coconut oil and lined

Preheat the oven to 150°C fan/170°C/gas mark 3.

Add the soy milk and cider vinegar to a bowl and leave to sit for 10 minutes to curdle lightly.

In the meantime, add the butter, sugar, golden syrup and treacle to a saucepan and gently heat until the butter has melted and the sugar has dissolved. We don't want this boiled, so take it low and slow. Remove the pan from the heat and add the chopped stem ginger. Give it all a good mix and set aside to cool.

In a large bowl, add the remaining dry ingredients and use a balloon whisk to combine. Pour in the cooled butter mix, the curdled soy milk and the vanilla bean paste, and mix until smooth.

Divide the cake batter evenly amongst the three lined tins, and bake for 26–28 minutes until the sponge comes away from the sides of the tin and a cocktail stick inserted into the sponge comes out clean.

Allow to cool in the tins for 5 minutes, then turn out onto a wire rack for 20 minutes. Brush the stem ginger syrup over the sponge tops using a pastry brush before wrapping in clingfilm and leaving to completely cool.

Make the jelly by adding the pomegranate seeds to a pan, along with the water and sugar. Place over a medium heat and bring to the boil, then turn down the heat to a simmer and let it do its thing for about 15 minutes – we want to break the seeds down slightly, extracting the juice, which in turn gives you that gorgeous pinky red colour.

Once you've managed to extract that colour, remove the pan from the heat and add the agar agar. Whisk well before placing back on the heat and bringing back to the boil. For the mixture to set, you want the temperature to be over 35°C/95°F – so give this a check with a thermometer probe, if you have one (if you don't, if the water has been simmering, there's a good chance it is well over that anyway).

Remove from the heat and pour into your serving bowl. Leave to cool at room temperature for 30 minutes before popping into the fridge to set.

Once the jelly has set firm, make the custard by mixing together the sugar and both flours in a small bowl.

Add the coconut milk to a saucepan with the vanilla bean paste and mango purée and place over a medium heat. Once it is near-boiling, pour one-third of the milk into the sugar-flour mix and whisk immediately until smooth. Pour the mixture back into saucepan and mix. Reduce the heat and continue to stir the custard until it thickens – we want this quite thick, a good sign to stop is when it begins to bubble in the middle. You want a thick, smooth, spreadable consistency.

While we are waiting for the custard to cool, make the coconut cream by adding all the ingredients, except the double cream, to a bowl. Mix well until smooth. Add the double cream and mix until it reaches medium peaks. Keep in the fridge until needed.

When the custard is cooled, add half to the top of the set jelly. Next is one of the sponges – I like to crumble these slightly to break down the sponge (this makes it easier to scoop out on serving), but you do you. You could keep it whole, cut it into chunks, crumble it, whatever floats your boat. Either pipe or use a spoon to spread one-quarter of the coconut cream on top of the sponge, before adding the remaining custard on top. Level out and add the second sponge on top.

Finish off this tropical extravaganza by dolloping on the remaining coconut cream. Smush this around with the back of a spoon or offset palette knife, and top it all off with a mountain of fresh fruit and a good sprinkling of toasted flaked coconut.

Time to dive in HEAD FIRST into creamy, dreamy, fruity paradise.

Any Berry Crumble Bars with Almond Shortbread and Vanilla Custard

If you haven't guessed it yet, I love custard. Like bloody adore it. I know for a fact that I get this from my dad. He stockpiles tinned custard under the stairs like a world shortage is upon us. One time, I came walking down the stairs and caught him red-handed, eating custard straight out of the tin with a spoon. I asked him what on earth he was doing, because a) it was 8 a.m. and b) most importantly, he's diabetic. And he replied 'you only live once' and continued to eat away. I mean, you gotta give it to the guy. He knows what he wants and he's doing it at whatever cost. I admire his tenacity and his commitment to his love for custard.

So, these teeny tiny slices of buttery, custardy, berry goodness are for Bill. And now for you. YOLO.

Any Berry Crumble Bars with Almond Shortbread and Vanilla Custard

Makes: 16

For the Almond Shortbread
225 g unsalted butter, room temp
110 g caster sugar
1½ tsp almond extract
225 g plain flour, sifted
100 g cornflour, sifted

For the Berry Filling
450 g blueberries, raspberries or strawberries
20 g caster sugar
1 tsp cornflour, sifted

For the Vanilla Custard
½ sheet of gelatin
6 egg yolks

100 g caster sugar
25 g cornflour, sifted
20 g plain flour, sifted
500 ml full-fat milk
2 tsp vanilla bean paste

For the Ginger Crumble
135 g unsalted butter, fridge temp and diced
100 g Demerara sugar
200 g plain flour, sifted
½ tsp ground ginger
40 g flaked almonds
1 preserved stem ginger piece, finely chopped

20 x 30-cm/8 x 12-in. tin, greased and lined

Let's get cracking with the shortbread base by placing the butter, sugar and almond extract into a bowl and beating until light and fluffy. You can use a stand mixer or an electric hand whisk for this, but I would advise against a wooden spoon BECAUSE THIS ISN'T HELL. Scrape down the sides of the bowl. Mix the flour and cornflour in a separate bowl, then add to the butter. Mix until just combined.

Press the shortbread dough into the base of the prepared tin and level it out by using the base of a flat-bottomed glass or a cake scraper. Prick the base gently with a fork before popping it in the freezer for 30 minutes, or until frozen through.

Preheat the oven to 160°C fan/180°C/gas mark 4.

Bake the set shortbread for 30 minutes, then remove from the oven and gently press down on any bits that have raised – again a flat-bottomed glass works well here. Set aside to cool.

While the shortbread is cooling, pop three-quarters of the berries and the sugar into a saucepan and gently cook over a medium heat until the berries soften slightly and start to release some juice. Sift in the cornflour, mix, and take the pan off the heat. Add the remaining berries, mix, and set aside to cool.

Once the shortbread is cool to touch, begin to make the custard. Add the gelatin sheet to a bowl of cold water to bloom for 5 minutes.

Put the egg yolks in a bowl with the sugar, cornflour and flour. Mix with a balloon whisk until pale in colour.

Add the milk to a saucepan along with the vanilla bean paste and heat over a low–medium heat until near boiling. When near boiling, pour one-third of the milk into the egg yolk mixture and whisk immediately until smooth. Pour the egg

yolk and milk mixture back into saucepan and mix. Reduce the heat to low and continue to stir the custard. Don't rest on this bit, as no one wants lumpy, scrambled custard! Keep stirring until it is quite thick; a good sign to stop is when it bubbles in the middle.

Take the pan off the heat, add the softened gelatin sheet, and mix well to dissolve. Place back over a gentle heat for a further minute.

Pour the hot custard on top of the cooled shortbread before adding the berries on top. Don't let the custard cool first, as it will start to set in the pan.

Whack the temperature of the oven up a notch to 175°C fan/195°C/gas mark 5.

To complete, let's quickly make the crumble. Add the butter, sugar, flour and ground ginger to a bowl. Use your fingers to rub in the butter until it resembles breadcrumbs, or pop this all into a food processor and pulse.

Add the flaked almonds and chopped stem ginger, and mix through with a fork. Pile the crumble mix on top of the berries, then pop the tin in the oven for 30 minutes until golden.

If you have zero willpower, scoop this into bowls fresh from the oven for a heartwarming pud. Or, for that fresh, clean slice, let it cool at room temperature for 1 hour, then transfer to the fridge for 4 fours or overnight to set firm. Use a hot knife to slice and enjoy this simple stack of joy.

Plant-Based Any Berry Crumble Bars with Almond Shortbread and Vanilla Custard

Makes: 16

For the Almond Shortbread
225 g plant-based unsalted butter, room temp
110 g caster sugar
1½ tsp almond extract
225 g plain flour, sifted
100 g cornflour, sifted

For the Berry Filling
450 g blueberries, raspberries or strawberries
20 g caster sugar
1 tsp cornflour, sifted

For the Vanilla Custard
100 g caster sugar
25 g cornflour, sifted
20 g plain flour, sifted

500 ml coconut milk
2 tsp vanilla bean paste
¼ tsp agar agar
yellow food colouring (optional)

For the Ginger Crumble
135 g plant-based unsalted butter, fridge temp and diced
100 g Demerara sugar
200 g plain flour, sifted
1 tsp ground ginger
50 g flaked almonds
1 preserved stem ginger piece, finely chopped

20 x 30-cm/8 x 12-in. tin, greased with coconut oil and lined

Let's get cracking with the shortbread base by placing the butter, sugar and almond extract into a bowl and beating until light and fluffy. You can use a stand mixer or an electric hand whisk for this, but I would advise against a wooden spoon BECAUSE THIS ISN'T HELL. Scrape down the sides of the bowl. Mix the flour and cornflour in a separate bowl, then add to the butter. Mix until just combined.

Press the shortbread dough into the base of the prepared tin and level it out by using the base of a flat-bottomed glass or a cake scraper. Prick the base gently with a fork before popping it in the freezer for 30 minutes, or until frozen through.

Preheat the oven to 160°C fan/180°C/gas mark 4.

Bake the set shortbread for 30 minutes, then remove from the oven and gently press down on any bits that have raised – again a flat-bottomed glass works well here. Set aside to cool.

While the shortbread is cooling, pop three-quarters of the berries and the sugar into a saucepan and gently cook over a medium heat until the berries soften slightly and start to release some juice. Sift in the cornflour, mix, and take the pan off the heat. Add the remaining berries, mix, and set aside to cool.

Once the shortbread is cool to touch, begin to make the custard. Use a balloon whisk to mix the sugar, cornflour and flour together in a bowl.

Add the coconut milk to a saucepan along with the vanilla bean paste and heat over a low–medium heat until near boiling. When near boiling, pour one-third of the milk into the sugar-flour mix, and whisk immediately until smooth. Pour the mixture back into saucepan and mix. Reduce the heat and continue to stir the custard.

Don't rest on this bit as no one wants lumpy custard! Keep stirring until it is quite thick; a good sign to stop is when it bubbles in the middle. Take the pan off the heat, add the agar agar, and mix well to dissolve. Place back over a gentle heat for a further minute. If you want the custard to have more of a custardy vibe looks-wise, add a touch of yellow food colouring. This way you can go as yellow as you want but my advice is to go chill on it, as it will brighten in colour once heated and set.

Pour the hot custard on top of the cooled shortbread, then add the berries on top. Don't let the custard cool first, as it will start to set in the pan.

Whack the temperature of the oven up a notch to 175°C fan/195°C/gas mark 5.

To complete, let's quickly make the crumble. Add the butter, sugar, flour and ground ginger to a bowl. Use your fingers to rub in the butter until it resembles breadcrumbs or pop this all into a food processor and pulse. Add the flaked almonds and chopped stem ginger, and mix through with a fork. Pile the crumble mix on top of the berries, then pop the tin in the oven for 30 minutes until golden.

You can scoop this into bowls fresh from the oven for a heartwarming pud, if you like. If you have the willpower, let it cool at room temperature for 1 hour, then let it set in the fridge for at least 4 hours or overnight. Use a hot knife to slice this into clean slices.

Nectarine and Blackberry Pavlova with Basil Crème Diplomat

We are keeping this one simple, yet effective. Your chances of burning down the kitchen are relatively low, but the chance of you devouring every last bit is high. The best bit about this is it's incredibly light, meaning a second and third helping of this pud is on the cards.

This is a great summery dessert. It is showstopping enough for a celebration, but also chill enough to make just as a pud to round off your dinner. I love a bake that looks killer, but in reality has been low-key to make, and this one is no different. You can make pretty much every component of this ahead of time, so break it up for yourself and just construct before you serve. This is also a great dessert to make into individual portions.

We've got pillowy, soft and chewy pavlova with a white chocolate base, topped with lashings of a basil crème diplomat and dollops of rich and fruity nectarine curd. It is finished with slices of fresh nectarine and booze-soaked blackberries. The perfect dessert to treat the Queen in your life. (If in any doubt, you = Queen.)

Nectarine and Blackberry Pavlova with Basil Crème Diplomat

Serves: 12

For the Pavlova
4 medium egg whites
230 g golden caster sugar
½ tsp apple cider vinegar
1 tsp cornflour, sifted

For the Crème Diplomat
250 ml full-fat milk
1 tsp vanilla bean paste
3 large egg yolks
50 g golden caster sugar
10 g cornflour, sifted
10 g plain flour, sifted
300 ml double cream
4–5 fresh basil leaves, finely chopped,
  or to taste

For the Nectarine Curd
225 g roughly chopped nectarines
freshly squeezed juice of ½ lemon
150 g caster sugar
1 large egg
2 large egg yolks
75 g unsalted butter

To Finish
200 g fresh blackberries
crème de cassis, for soaking
80 g white chocolate, melted and cooled
2 nectarines, stoned and sliced
fresh basil leaves, to decorate

Let's get the pavlova out the way as this will take up majority of the cooking time. Preheat the oven to 90°C fan/110°C /gas mark ¼.

Place the egg whites into the bowl of the stand mixer fitted with the whisk attachment (or a large mixing bowl if you are using an electric hand whisk). Whisk the egg whites until they are stiff, and slowly begin adding the sugar, 1 tbsp at a time. Make sure you give each addition plenty of time to dissolve into the whites before adding more – pavlova is great, but not when it is grainy. Once all the sugar has been incorporated, add the vinegar and cornflour, and whisk well. We are after stiff peaks, so mix it for a further 5 minutes once everything has been added.

Transfer to a piping bag and pipe the mixture onto greaseproof paper – we need two circles, 20 cm/8 in. in diameter. I like to trace over some dinner plates before turning the greaseproof paper over as a stencil. Alternatively, go rogue and just use a spoon to form the circles. Bake for 1½ hours. Do not be tempted to oven the oven while it is baking!

Meanwhile, let's cook the custard base for the crème diplomat. Add the milk and vanilla bean paste to a saucepan and place over a medium heat.

In a bowl, whisk together the egg yolks, sugar, and both flours with a balloon whisk until fully combined.

When the milk is warm, pour half onto the whisked egg yolks and stir quickly to avoid curdling. When mixed, pour the mixture back into the saucepan and continue to cook, stirring constantly, otherwise this baby is going to get thick and lumpy real quick, until thickened. Set aside to cool.

Add the nectarines to a food processor with the lemon juice and blitz until smooth, then add the sugar, egg and egg yolks.

Into another pan, melt the butter. When melted, add the blitzed nectarines and cook over a low–medium heat for about 20 minutes, stirring often to stop it from sticking, until it has thickened enough to coat the back of a spoon. Remove from the heat and pass through a sieve to remove any lumps and skin. Leave to cool.

Put the blackberries in a small bowl and pour over enough crème de cassis to cover. Set aside to macerate (this is just a fancy word for soak).

To finish off the crème diplomat, whip the double cream and chopped basil in a large mixing bowl until thickened. Pour in the cooled custard from earlier, and fold in. The custard will loosen the cream, so be gentle when mixing. Taste and add more chopped basil, if needed. Cover and pop into the fridge for later.

Your pavlovas should be done by now, so turn your oven off, crack open the door slightly and allow to cool in the oven for 30 minutes, then remove from the oven and carefully transfer to a wire rack to cool.

Use a pastry brush or a spoon to coat the flat bottoms of the pavs with the melted white chocolate. When set, place one of the pavlova discs onto your serving plate. Don't worry if they break or crack, you're gonna load these babies up with a ton of cream and fruit, so no one will know.

Top with half the basil crème diplomat, dollops of the nectarine curd, and a few of the fresh sliced nectarines and boozy blackberries. Sandwich the other pavlova disc on top and pour over the remaining crème diplomat and more dollops of curd, then pile on the remaining nectarine slices and boozy blackberries. To finish it off, add a few small basil leaves of on top. All that's left is to tuck in and enjoy.

Plant-Based Nectarine and Blackberry Pavlova with Basil Crème Diplomat

Serves: 12

For the Pavlova
300 ml aquafaba (liquid from approx.
  2½ x 400-g tins chickpeas)
¾ tsp cream of tartar
350 g golden caster sugar
1 tsp xanthan gum
1 tsp vanilla bean paste

For the Crème Diplomat
250 ml coconut milk
1 tsp vanilla bean paste
50 g golden caster sugar
10 g cornflour, sifted
20 g plain flour, sifted
300 ml plant-based double cream
4–5 fresh basil leaves, finely chopped,
  or to taste

For the Nectarine Curd
225 g roughly chopped nectarines
freshly squeezed juice of ½ lemon
150 g caster sugar
25 g cornflour, sifted
275 ml coconut milk solids (from tinned
  coconut milk)
1 tsp vanilla bean paste
10 g plant-based unsalted butter

To Finish
200 g fresh blackberries
crème de cassis, for soaking
80 g plant-based white chocolate, melted
  and cooled
2 nectarines, stoned and sliced
fresh basil leaves, to decorate

Let's get the pavlova out the way as this will take up majority of the cooking time. Preheat the oven to 100°C fan/120°C/gas mark ½.

Drain the chickpeas into a large sieve sitting on top of a stand mixer bowl to drain the aquafaba. Using the whisk attachment, mix the aquafaba on medium–high speed until it becomes stiff but not dry (this will take time, even if it's been mixing for 10 minutes and is still watery, keep on persisting, it will eventually get there). Add the cream of tartar and mix to disperse.

Add the sugar mixture to the stand mixer, 1 tbsp at a time, keeping the mixer running on medium speed and ensuring each addition of sugar has dissolved before going in with the next lot. This step takes a bit of time and patience, but is worth it – no one wants a grainy meringue. You can judge this by taking a little bit of the mix and smushing it between two fingers; if you can feel grains, go low and slow on speed and additions.

Once all the sugar has been added, leave to mix on high speed for 5 minutes. The meringue should be thick, glossy and firm enough for you to be able to hold the bowl upside down over your head. Finally, add the xanthan gum and vanilla bean paste and mix for a further minute before transferring the mix to a piping bag.

Pipe the mixture onto greaseproof paper – two circles, 20 cm/8 in. in diameter. I like to trace over some dinner plates as a stencil. Alternatively, go rogue and just use a spoon to form the circles. Bake for 1½ hours. Do not be tempted to open the oven while it is baking!

Meanwhile, cook the custard base for the crème diplomat. Add the coconut milk and vanilla bean paste to a saucepan and place over a medium heat. In a separate bowl, whisk the sugar and both flours with a balloon whisk until combined.

Once the milk is warm, pour half onto the sugar-flour mixture and stir quickly to avoid any lumps. When mixed, pour back into the saucepan and cook, stirring constantly until the custard has thickened. Allow to cool.

Add the nectarines to a food processor with the lemon juice and blitz until smooth, then add the remaining ingredients, except the butter. Blitz again until smooth.

In a pan, melt the butter. When melted, add the blitzed nectarines and place over a low-medium heat for 15 minutes, stirring regularly to stop from sticking, until the curd is thick enough to coat the back of a spoon. Remove from the heat and pass through a sieve to remove any lumps and skin. Leave to cool.

Put the blackberries in a small bowl and pour over enough crème de cassis to cover. Set aside to macerate (this is just a fancy word for soak).

To finish off the crème diplomat, whip the double cream and chopped basil in a large mixing bowl until thickened and near stiff peak stage. Fold in the cooled custard from earlier. Taste and add more chopped basil, if needed. Cover and pop into the fridge for later.

Your pavlovas should be done by now, so turn your oven off, crack open the door slightly and allow to cool in the oven for 1 hour, then transfer carefully to a wire rack to cool completely.

Use a pastry brush or a spoon to coat the flat bottoms of the pavs with the melted white chocolate. When set, place one of the pavlova discs onto your serving plate. Don't worry if they break or crack, you're gonna load these up with a ton of cream and fruit, so no one will know.

Top with half the basil crème diplomat, dollops of the nectarine curd, and a few of the fresh sliced nectarines and boozy blackberries. Sandwich the other pavlova disc on top and pour over the remaining crème diplomat and more dollops of curd, then pile on the remaining nectarine slices and boozy blackberries. To finish it off, top with a few small basil leaves.

Salted Caramel Basque Cheesecake with Raspberries and Pistachios

I hate sheep mentality, but it's that very thing that led me to developing this recipe. For yonks, all I saw on social media was a slice of cheesecake and people taking a slow, dramatic scoop out of it. I resisted the urge to fall foul of the trend for months. Then one day I tasted a Basque cheesecake in a restaurant and realised I had played myself all this time by denying myself the joy of making one of these.

This dessert is painfully easy to make. Yet it looks worthy of being the centrepiece dessert for any dinner party. My take on the normal Basque cheesecake has bundles of salted caramel – in and on top. It is finished with a mountain of tart raspberries to cut through the sweetness and some much-needed texture from the pistachios. This versatile dessert will be one you'll run back to more times than you did your ex.

Salted Caramel Basque Cheesecake with Raspberries and Pistachios

Serves: 9

For the Cheesecake
700 g full-fat cream cheese, room temp
285 g golden caster sugar
5 medium eggs
1½ tsp vanilla bean paste
115 g soured cream, room temp
250 g double cream, room temp
50 g salted caramel sauce (see page 290),
   plus extra for drizzling
40 g cornflour, sifted

To Finish
handful of fresh raspberries
handful of pistachios, roughly chopped

23-cm/9-in. springform cake tin, greased and
   lined with 2 layers of greaseproof paper,
   pressed into the tin and coming up around
   the sides (it will look rustic!)

254

Preheat the oven to 200°C/gas mark 6. Do not use the fan setting here; we want a slow, steady bake.

Put the cream cheese in the bowl of a stand mixer and use the paddle attachment to beat until smooth. Once smooth, add the sugar and mix again until fully incorporated. Add the eggs, one by one, mixing well between each addition, then add the vanilla bean paste, soured cream, double cream and salted caramel. Mix well.

Sift in one-third of the cornflour, mix until combined, the repeat with the remaining two-thirds. Going slow and steady just helps to ensure the cornflour doesn't become lumpy.

Pour the cream mix into the prepared tin, scraping down the sides and making sure there are no clumps of cornflour or cream cheese. If there are, pass the mixture through a fine sieve to remove.

Place the tin onto a baking tray (this will just help you remove it from the oven when the tin is hot) and pop onto the middle shelf of the oven. Bake for 45 minutes and then turn down the temperature to 180°C/gas mark 4 for another 5 minutes until the top is darkened. It may look burnt, slightly cracked around the sides, and still wobbly in the middle, but fear not, this is exactly what we are after.

Leave to cool completely at room temperature before popping into the fridge overnight to set perfectly.

Before serving, add a few spoons of salted caramel sauce to the top, and use the back of a spoon to coat and swirl it around. Pile on fresh raspberries and a generous scattering of chopped pistachios to finish.

Use a hot knife (run under hot water or hold over a steaming kettle and wipe) for that *perfect* velvety, caramel-drowning slice.

Plant-Based Salted Caramel Basque Cheesecake with Raspberries and Pistachios

Baking can be tricky. Vegan baking is on another level. But the joy in this bake is how stripped back, simple and uncomplicated it all is. There's no addition of salted caramel to the cheesecake base, so instead we are pouring all that golden goodness on top.

Serves: 9

For the Cheesecake
600 g silken tofu
400 ml coconut cream
65 g cornflour, sifted
225 g golden caster sugar
2 tsp vanilla bean paste

To Finish
1 quantity salted caramel sauce
  (see page 290)
handful of fresh raspberries
handful of pistachios, roughly chopped

20-cm/8-in. springform cake tin, greased
  with coconut oil and lined with 2 layers of
  greaseproof paper, pressed into the tin and
  coming up around the sides

Preheat the oven to 210°C/gas mark 6. Do not use the fan setting here, we want a slow, steady bake.

In the bowl of a stand mixer, add the silken tofu and mix well. Go in with all the remaining ingredients and mix on medium speed to incorporate – you want this velvety smooth without overmixing.

Pour the mixture into the prepared tin, scraping down the sides and making sure there are no clumps of tofu. If there are, pass the mixture through a fine sieve to remove.

Place the tin onto a baking tray (this will just help you remove it from the oven when the tin is hot) and pop it onto the middle shelf of the oven. Bake for 40 minutes and then turn down the temperature to 200°C/gas mark 6 for another 10 minutes until the top is golden. It may look slightly cracked around the sides and still wobbly in the middle, but fear not, this is exactly what we are after.

Leave to cool completely at room temperature, before popping into the fridge overnight to set perfectly.

Before serving, add a few generous spoons of salted caramel sauce to the top, and use the back of a spoon to swirl it on. Pile on fresh raspberries and a generous scattering of chopped pistachios to finish.

Use a hot knife (run under hot water or hold over a steaming kettle and wipe) for that *perfect* slice.

Peach and Amaretto Cheesecake with Pistachio Kataifi

Everyone needs a good cheesecake recipe in their life, and congrats; you have found it. The flavours in this one are a major win. We are talking roasted peaches with an amaretto glaze, an almond cheesecake filling with a crushed shortbread biscuit base, all sitting below a flaky, crispy, golden kataifi crown, bejewelled with pistachios.

Impress your friends, impress your family, and, most importantly, impress your damn self. It looks special as hell, but great news for us all, it's easy to make. Long gone are the days of the store-bought cheesecakes – you deserve better than that. You deserve *this*.

Serves: 8

For the Base
280 g shortbread biscuits, blitzed to a crumb
   (FYI ginger biscuits also work fab)
90 g unsalted butter, melted

For the Cheesecake
500 g peaches, stoned and halved
50 ml amaretto (optional)
5 g caster sugar
700 g full-fat cream cheese, room temp
260 g golden caster sugar
5 medium eggs
1½ tsp vanilla bean paste

2 tsp almond extract
200 g double cream
110 g soured cream
20 g cornflour, sifted

To Finish
100 g kataifi/kadaif or shredded filo
30 g unsalted butter, melted
handful of salted pistachios, roughly chopped

23-cm/9-in. springform cake tin, greased
   and lined (base and sides)
2 baking trays, lined

Preheat the oven to 180°C fan/200°C/gas mark 6.

In a large bowl, mix together the crushed shortbread biscuits and half the melted butter with a wooden spoon. Add the rest of the melted butter and make sure all the biscuit crumb is coated before transferring to the prepared tin. Press the crumb into the base of the tin, tightly packing it in. Use the base of a flat-bottomed glass to really make it all compact and smushed together. Place the tin into the fridge to set.

Onto a lined baking tray, place the halved peaches, cut-side up. Use a pastry brush to glaze the tops with the amaretto, if using. Place the tray into the oven and roast the peaches for 20–25 minutes.

Remove from the oven and sprinkle the caster sugar on top. Place back into the oven and bake for a further 5–10 minutes until they are lightly charred on top, but still holding their shape.

Set aside the peaches to cool, but make sure you keep hold of any leftover syrup as this stuff is liquid GOLD.

Turn the oven up to 200°C/gas mark 6. Do not use the fan setting on this, we want the cheesecake to bake gently.

For the cheesecake filling, add the cream cheese to a bowl and beat until smooth. Once smooth, add the sugar and mix again until fully incorporated. Add the eggs, one by one, mixing well between each addition, followed by the vanilla bean paste and almond extract. Add the double cream, soured cream, and any remaining amaretto to the bowl and mix well.

Sift in one-third of the cornflour and mix until combined, then repeat with the remaining two-thirds. Going slow and steady just helps to ensure the cornflour doesn't become lumpy.

Arrange one-third of the roasted peaches on top of the biscuit base. I like to give these a little squish to break them up slightly. Pour the cream mix into the tin, scraping down the sides and making sure there are no clumps of cornflour or cream cheese. (If there are lumps, pass the mixture through a fine sieve to remove.)

Place the tin onto a baking tray (this will just help you remove from the oven when the tin is hot) and pop onto the middle shelf. Bake for 45 minutes and then turn down the temperature to 180°C/gas mark 4 for another 5 minutes until the top has turned golden brown. We are after a wobbly middle, so do not over-bake this (it will set once cool). Turn off the oven and prop open the door with a wooden spoon. Allow the cheesecake to cool in the oven for 1 hour, then transfer to the fridge to set for at least 4 hours, but preferably overnight.

Once set, release the cheesecake from the springform tin and transfer to your serving plate.

Preheat the oven to 180°C fan/200°C/gas mark 6.

Grab the other lined baking tray and use your tin to help you shape the kataifi into a perfect circle to sit on top of the cheesecake once baked. Drizzle over the melted butter to coat the pastry liberally, and use a pastry brush to really coat all the nooks and crannies. Pop the tray into the oven to bake the kataifi until golden brown; about 15 minutes. Allow to cool.

Once the kataifi is cool enough to handle, carefully place the pastry crown on top of the cheesecake, then layer on the remaining roasted peaches.

Drizzle over any reserved peach syrup and a good handful of chopped pistachios. Serve this baby up and serve it PROUD. Isn't she a beauty?

Plant-Based Peach and Amaretto Cheesecake with Pistachio Kataifi

Serves: 8

For the Base
280 g plant-based shortbread or ginger
  biscuits, blitzed to a crumb
75 g plant-based unsalted butter, melted

For the Cheesecake
500 g peaches, stoned and halved
50 ml amaretto (optional)
5 g caster sugar
800 g plant-based cream cheese
450 ml coconut cream
260 g golden caster sugar
1½ tsp vanilla bean paste

1½ tsp almond extract
squeeze of fresh lemon juice
40 g cornflour, sifted

To finish
100 g kataifi/kadaif or shredded filo
30 g plant-based unsalted butter, melted
handful of salted pistachios, roughly chopped

23-cm/9-in. springform cake tin, greased
  and lined (base and sides)
2 baking trays, lined

Preheat the oven to 180°C fan/200°C/gas mark 6.

Wrap the outside of your lined tin with foil. This will a) help an even cook, and b) prevent any water from getting into your cheesecake mix when placed in a water bath.

Put the crushed biscuits and half the melted butter into a large bowl. Mix well with a wooden spoon, then add the rest of the melted butter. Make sure all the biscuit crumb is coated before transferring to the lined tin. Press the crumb into the base of the tin, tightly packing it in. Use the base of a flat-bottomed glass to really make it all compact and smushed together. Place the tin into the fridge to set.

Onto a lined baking tray, place the halved peaches, cut-side up. Use a pastry brush to glaze the tops with the amaretto, if using. Place the tray into the oven and roast the peaches for 20–25 minutes.

Remove from the oven and sprinkle the caster sugar on top. Place back into the oven and bake for a further 5–10 minutes until they are lightly charred on top, but still holding their shape.

Set aside the peaches to cool, but make sure you keep hold of any leftover syrup as this stuff is liquid GOLD.

Reduce the oven to 170°C/gas mark 3. Do not use the fan setting on this, we want the cheesecake to bake gently.

For the cheesecake filling, add the cream cheese to a bowl and beat until smooth. Once smooth, add all the remaining ingredients, except the cornflour, and mix again until everything is fully incorporated.

Sift in one-third of the cornflour and mix until combined, then repeat with the remaining two-thirds. Going in slow and steady just helps to ensure the cornflour doesn't become lumpy.

Give it a quick taste because you are the chef and you bloody well deserve a sneaky treat.

Arrange half of the peaches on top of the set biscuit base – I like to give some of these a little squish to break them up gently. Pour the cream mix into the tin, scraping down the sides and making sure there are no clumps of cornflour or cream cheese. (If there are lumps, pass the mixture through a fine sieve to remove.)

Place the tin into a large, deep baking tray. Fill the tray with hot water, making sure at least half of the cake tin is submerged in the water. Pop the baking tray onto the middle shelf and bake for 1 hour, then turn down the temperature to 150°C/gas mark 2 for another 10–15 minutes until the top is golden brown. We are after a wobbly middle so do not over-bake; it will set once cool.

Turn off the oven and prop open the door with a wooden spoon. Allow the cheesecake to cool in the oven for 1 hour, then transfer to the fridge to set overnight. Trust me, the wait is well worth it.

Once set, release the cheesecake from the springform tin and transfer to your serving plate.

Preheat the oven to 180°C fan/200°C/gas mark 6.

Grab the other lined baking tray and use your tin to help you shape the kataifi into a perfect circle to sit on top of the cheesecake once baked. Drizzle over the melted butter to coat the pastry liberally, and use a pastry brush to really coat all the nooks and crannies. Pop the tray into the oven to bake the kataifi until golden brown; about 15 minutes. Allow to cool.

Once the kataifi is cool enough to handle, carefully place the pastry crown on top of the cheesecake, then layer on the remaining roasted peaches. Drizzle over any reserved peach syrup and a good handful of chopped pistachios. Serve this baby up and serve it PROUD. Isn't she a beauty?

Piña Colada Meringue Roulade with Roasted Pineapple

The joy of a meringue roulade, as opposed to a sponge number, is the delicate lightness you get with it. The lighter something is, the more you can eat... or at least that's the logic I live by.

The roasted pineapple against the creamy, cooling (and very boozy, if you wish) coconut is heaven. This dessert, albeit simple in its components, has flavour by the bucketful. Nailing that crackly meringue and tight swirl is easier than you think – just follow the instructions, do not deviate (especially when it comes to the baking of the meringue and rolling) and you won't be getting caught in the rain with this one. Was that cheesy? Sorry.

Piña Colada Meringue Roulade with Roasted Pineapple

Serves: 8

For the Filling
3 x 435-g tins pineapple rings
300 ml double cream
150 g mascarpone cheese
3 tbsp coconut rum (optional, but a very good idea)
20–25 g icing sugar, to taste
50 g coconut cream
1 tsp vanilla bean paste

For the Syrup
25 g caster sugar

For the Meringue
4 large egg whites
225 g caster sugar
50 g sweetened desiccated coconut
1 tsp white wine vinegar

To Finish
icing sugar, for dusting

baking tray, lined
Swiss roll tin, greased with coconut oil and lined

Preheat the oven to 180°C fan/200°C/gas mark 6.

Begin by roasting the pineapple for the filling. Drain the tinned pineapple, reserving the juice. Slice the pineapple rings into small chunks and arrange on the prepared baking tray. To really intensify the flavour, pour some of the reserved juice from the tin over the pineapple to coat. Place the pineapple into the oven for about 15–20 minutes until reduced in size and the tops are partially golden. Transfer to a bowl to cool.

For the syrup, pour the remaining juice from the tins into a saucepan and add the sugar. Place over a medium heat and cook until it reaches a syrup consistency. Set aside to cool.

Before we start on the meringue, ensure the bowl is completely clean – any trace of grease and your whites won't whisk and meringue will be unstable. I use half a lemon to wipe the inside of the bowl, before wiping it down with a cloth.

Place the egg whites into the bowl. Attach the whisk attachment and place on medium speed until the egg whites begin to stiffen. Once the egg whites are stiff, but not dry (I know this sounds confusing, but this means when the egg white structure is holding its shape and hasn't broken down), gradually add the sugar, 1 tbsp at a time, mixing well between each addition. Go low and slow here, as you want the meringue to be smooth and not grainy, so give each spoonful time to dissolve into the egg whites. Continue to mix until thick, firm and glossy – you should be able to turn the bowl upside down over your head with no meringue falling out.

Remove the bowl from the stand and add the desiccated coconut and vinegar. Using a spatula, gently fold in until incorporated. You want to keep in as much air as possible. The best way to fold is scrape all the way round the outside once before cutting through the middle, turn the bowl 90 degrees and repeat. Do this a further three times, or at least until evenly mixed.

Use the spatula to scoop the meringue into the prepared tin. Using a palette knife, ensure the mixture is evenly distributed, then tap the tin on the worktop a few times to remove any air pockets. Place the tin into the oven and bake for 8 minutes until the top is lightly golden. Turn down the oven temperature to 160°C fan/180°C/gas mark 4 and bake for another 10 minutes.

While the meringue is baking, get cracking with the filling by adding the double cream, mascarpone, rum (if using), icing sugar, coconut cream and vanilla bean paste to a bowl. Using a handheld whisk, whip until the cream is at medium peak – this will firm up as you smush it around on the meringue, so try not to overwork. Give it a taste to check you're happy with the rum and coconut quantities. Transfer to a piping bag and chill in the fridge.

Remove the meringue from the oven and place the tray on a cooling rack. Cover the meringue top with baking paper and leave to cool.

Place a large piece of baking paper on the worktop and generously dust with icing sugar. Carefully turn out the meringue onto the icing sugar. Pipe the coconut cream filling on top before using a palette knife to spread it evenly. You will have extra, but leave this to one side for the topping. Scatter the chopped roasted pineapple evenly over the cream, leaving a handful for the topping.

With a knife, gently score a line along the short edge nearest you, about 1 cm/½ in. from the edge. Using the baking paper, gently roll the meringue roulade tightly, but carefully. If you are serving this later, keep the roulade rolled in the baking paper in the fridge until needed.

Before serving, remove the roulade from fridge, unwrap, and place on a serving plate. Pipe the remaining coconut cream on top and drizzle the pineapple syrup over. Decorate with the reserved roasted pineapple. Slice and enjoy.

Plant-Based Piña Colada Roulade with Roasted Pineapple

Let's just call this one a like-for-like-ish recipe? So sure, the below isn't a meringue roulade, but it is a roulade... just of a different kind.

Serves: 8

For the Filling
3 x 435-g tins pineapple rings
100 g plant-based cream cheese
150 ml plant-based double cream
2 tbsp coconut rum (optional, but a very good idea)
1 tsp vanilla bean paste
15 g icing sugar, or to to taste
25 g coconut cream
20 g desiccated coconut

For the Sponge
260 ml coconut milk
1¼ tsp apple cider vinegar
185 g self-raising flour

35 g cornflour, sifted
¼ tsp xanthan gum
15 g coconut flour or desiccated coconut
110 g golden caster sugar
50 ml coconut oil, melted
1½ tsp vanilla bean paste

For the Syrup
25 g caster sugar

To Finish
icing sugar, for dusting

baking tray, lined
Swiss roll tin, greased with coconut oil and lined

Preheat the oven to 180°C fan/200°C/gas mark 6.

Let's begin by roasting the pineapple for our filling. Drain the tinned pineapple, reserving the juice. Set the juice aside. Slice the pineapple rings into small chunks and arrange on the prepared baking tray. To really intensify the flavour, pour some of the reserved juice from the tin over the pineapple to coat. Place the pineapple into the oven for about 15–20 minutes to roast – you are looking for the pineapple to have reduced in size slightly and the tops to become partially golden. Transfer to a bowl to cool.

For the syrup, pour the remaining juice from the tins into a saucepan and add the sugar. Place over a medium heat and cook until it reaches a syrup consistency. Set aside to cool.

Turn down the oven temperature to 160°C fan/180°C/gas mark 4.

For the sponge, pour the coconut milk and cider vinegar into a bowl and leave to curdle for 10 minutes.

Meanwhile, add all the dry ingredients to a bowl and give it all a mix to combine. Once the milk has lightly curdled, add the coconut oil and vanilla bean paste, and use a balloon whisk to mix. Pour straight into the dry mix and fold all the ingredients through to combine. You don't want to overmix here; stop as soon as there are no visible streaks of flour remaining.

Pour the batter into the prepared tin and use a palette knife to ensure the mixture is evenly distributed. Tap the tin on the worktop a few times to remove any air pockets. Pop the tray into the oven and bake for 15–18 minutes. Keep an eye on this as it bakes quicker than you think!

While the sponge is baking, get cracking with the cream filling by adding the cream cheese, double cream, rum (if using), vanilla bean paste, icing sugar and coconut cream to a bowl. Using a handheld whisk, whisk for a few minutes and give it a taste to check you're happy with the rum and coconut quantities.

Continue to whip until the cream is at stiff peaks – this will firm up as you smush it around on the meringue so try not to overwork. Pop into a piping bag and leave to chill.

Remove the sponge from the oven and place the tray on a cooling rack. Let it chill there for a minute while you place a tea towel onto the worktop and generously dust with icing sugar.

Carefully turn out the sponge onto the icing sugar. Dust the back of the sponge generously once again, and use the tea towel to roll the sponge from the short side, as you would with a Swiss roll. You want to do this while the sponge is warm and pliable, otherwise it will crack and you'll be sad – so don't say you haven't been warned.

Let the sponge cool until lukewarm and then carefully unroll. Note, the sponge may crack slightly or stick to the tea towel if you didn't dust with enough icing sugar. We will ice over all the cracks, so don't fret.

Pipe the coconut cream filling on top before using a palette knife to spread evenly. You will have extra, but keep to one side for the topping. Scatter the chopped roasted pineapple evenly over the cream, leaving a handful for the topping.

With a knife, gently score a line along the short edge nearest you, about 1 cm/½ in. from the edge. Using the baking paper, gently roll the sponge roulade tightly, but carefully. Leave to set in the fridge for at least 1 hour.

Before serving, remove the roulade from fridge, unwrap and place on serving plate. Pipe the remaining coconut cream on top and lightly drizzle the pineapple syrup over. Decorate with the reserved roasted pineapple. Share or don't, it's up to you.

Plum, Pistachio and Cardamom Crumble with Almond Crème Anglaise

This is a real crowd-winning pud – another low-effort, max-return sort of vibe, which can be adapted and mixed up as the seasons change and the year goes on. Swap out the plums for rhubarb at the start of the year, summer berries and stone fruits from spring to summer, and end the year on a sweet, sweet high with apples and pears. The all-rounder recipe you'll keep coming back to.

Serves: 9

For the Fruit Filling
900 g plums, stoned and thickly sliced
300 g blackberries
2 tbsp lemon juice
30 g cornflour, sifted
100 g light soft brown sugar
pinch of sea salt
1 tsp vanilla bean paste
¼ tsp ground cardamom

For the Crumble
200 g plain flour, sifted
½ tsp ground cardamom
100 g Demerara sugar

140 g unsalted butter, fridge temp and diced
70 g pistachios, roughly chopped
30 g flaked almonds

For the Almond Crème Anglaise
125 ml full-fat milk
125 ml double cream
1½ tsp almond extract
1 tsp vanilla bean paste
3 large egg yolks
40 g caster sugar
20 g cornflour, sifted

large, deep baking dish

Preheat the oven to 160°C fan/180°C/gas mark 4.

In a large bowl, mix all the fruit filling ingredients and let sit for about 5–10 minutes.

The next step is to make the crumble topping – two options here:

Option 1: In a food processor, lightly pulse together the flour, cardamom and sugar to mix through. Add the butter and pulse until the mixture resembles breadcrumbs. This is by far the easiest and quickest way.

Option 2: Do it by hand, by chucking all the ingredients together into a large bowl. Mix through with your hands before rubbing the butter into the flour until you get 'breadcrumbs'. A longer way to get the same results.

Either way, pour this crumble mix into a large bowl and lightly stir through the chopped pistachios and almonds.

Transfer the fruit and liquid to the baking dish. Generously load the crumble topping on top, then bake for 40–45 minutes until the crumble top is gorgeously golden brown and the fruit juice is bubbling up on the sides. Remove from the oven and set aside to cool slightly while you make the crème Anglaise.

Add the milk, double cream, almond extract, and vanilla bean paste to a saucepan and bring to a near simmer.

In another bowl, mix together the egg yolks, sugar and cornflour with a balloon whisk.

Once the milk is simmering, pour one-third into the egg yolk mixture. Mix well with the whisk and pour the mixture back into the saucepan. Keep stirring over the heat until thickened slightly and the cream coats the back of a spoon. Take off heat and pour into a pouring jug.

Now all that's left to do is serve up generous portions of your slightly cooled crumble, then pour over the piping hot crème Anglaise until it's drowning.

Plant-Based Plum, Pistachio and Cardamom Crumble with Almond Crème Anglaise

Serves: 9

For the Fruit Filling
900 g plums, stoned and thickly sliced
300 g blackberries
2 tbsp lemon juice
30 g cornflour, sifted
100 g light soft brown sugar
pinch of sea salt
1 tsp vanilla bean paste
¼ tsp ground cardamom

For the Crumble
200 g plain flour, sifted
½ tsp ground cardamom
100 g Demerara sugar

140 g plant-based unsalted butter, fridge temp and diced
70 g pistachios, roughly chopped
30 g flaked almonds

For the Almond Crème Anglaise
150 ml almond milk
100 ml plant-based double cream
1½ tsp almond extract
1 tsp vanilla bean paste
50 g caster sugar
20 g cornflour, sifted

large, deep baking dish

Preheat the oven to 160°C fan/180°C/gas mark 4.

In a large bowl, mix all the fruit filling ingredients and let sit for about 5–10 minutes.

The next step is to make the crumble topping – two options here:

Option 1: In a food processor, lightly pulse together the flour, cardamom and sugar to mix through. Add the butter and pulse until the mixture resembles breadcrumbs. This is by far the easiest and quickest way.

Option 2: Do it by hand, by chucking all the ingredients together into a large bowl. Mix through with your hands before rubbing the butter into the flour until you get 'breadcrumbs'. A longer way to get the same results.

Either way, pour this crumble mix into a large bowl and lightly stir through the chopped pistachios and almonds.

Transfer the fruit and liquid to the baking dish. Generously load the crumble topping on top,

then bake for 40–45 minutes until the crumble top is gorgeously golden brown and the fruit juice is bubbling up on the sides. Remove from the oven and set aside to cool slightly while you make the crème Anglaise.

Add the almond milk, double cream, almond extract and vanilla bean paste to a saucepan and bring to a near simmer.

In another bowl, add in the sugar and cornflour before using a balloon whisk to mix well.

Once the milk is simmering, pour one-third into the sugared flour, mix well with the whisk and pour back into the saucepan. Keep stirring over the heat until thickened slightly and the cream coats the back of a spoon. Take off the heat and pour into a pouring jug.

Serve generous portions of your slightly-cooled crumble with plenty of piping hot crème Anglaise – and enjoy!

Malt Tiramisu
with Milk Chocolate

Now, I know I say this a lot but this time, I truly mean it. This is my favourite bake. It's like when you ask a mother who her favourite child is and she'll say all of them, but really, deep down, we all know there is secretly one who comes out on the top tier. Well, this malt and milk chocolate tiramisu is the baking equivalent of my favourite child.

Now here comes the controversy. I do not like normal tiramisu. You know the sort where the lady fingers are drenched in coffee and that is all you can taste? I honestly think it is one of the worst desserts known to mankind, which is why I was desperate to make a version for myself. Malty, chocolatey goodness. It isn't sickly sweet, but instead leaves you craving more. This is the dessert I would implore you to make. Simple, straight-up delicious flavours, with minimal fuss but maximum enjoyment.

Malt Tiramisu with Milk Chocolate

Serves: 10

For the Soaked Lady Fingers
400 ml water
25 g caster sugar
75 g chocolate Ovaltine or hot chocolate
   powder
400 g lady fingers

For the Ganache Layer
175 g milk chocolate, chunks or callets
200 ml double cream, plus extra if needed

For the Malt Cream
4 large egg yolks
175 g caster sugar
500 g mascarpone cheese, room temp
400 ml double cream
1½ tsp vanilla bean paste
75 g malt powder or Horlicks

To Finish
cocoa powder, sifted

deep 18 x 24-cm/7 x 9½-in. dish

To begin, let's make the malt chocolate lady finger soak. Add the water, caster sugar and Ovaltine (or hot chocolate powder, if that's what you are using) to a small saucepan and place over a medium heat. Allow to simmer for about 10–15 minutes. We are after a slightly reduced consistency, so the colour will have deepened slightly and the flavour intensified. When done, remove from the heat and leave to cool.

Next up is the chocolate ganache. Add the milk chocolate to a large bowl. Pour the cream into a saucepan and gently warm over a medium heat. You want this near boiling, so remove just before it comes to the boil and immediately pour it over the chocolate. Cover the bowl with a plate for a minute or two before removing and mixing with a balloon whisk or rubber spatula until smooth and glossy. Set aside to cool.

For the malt cream, add the egg yolks and 150 g caster sugar to a heatproof bowl. Mix well using an electric hand whisk until smooth; it will take a good couple of minutes to really start working some volume into the mixture. Sit the bowl on top of a pan of simmering water to cook the yolks gently for about 10 minutes and continue whisking the yolks with the electric hand whisk to increase the volume of the egg yolks and to ensure the bottom of the bowl doesn't catch. By the time the yolks are cooked, the mixture should be pale and thick. Carefully remove the bowl from the heat and allow to cool for 15 minutes, then add the mascarpone and mix well. Set aside.

Put the remaining 25 g caster sugar into the bowl of a stand mixer with the cream, vanilla bean paste and malt powder (aka Horlicks) and use the whisk attachment (or use an electric hand whisk) to bring it to just near stiff peaks. Gently fold into the mascarpone mixture, making sure it is well combined. Give it taste for no other reason than it being bloody delicious. Did you try it? See, I was right, wasn't I?

The good news is, it is time to assemble. Spread one-third of the cream over the bottom of the dish and level it out evenly. Dollop spoonfuls of the cooled chocolate ganache on top and use the back of a spoon to swirl. Dip the sponge fingers into the cooled malt chocolate soak, letting them sit for a minute or so (I prefer less for more bite, but go as soggy as you wish) and layer them on top of the cream.

Repeat the cream, ganache, and sponge finger process one more time, then finish with a smooth layer of cream and pour the remaining chocolate ganache on top. (If your ganache isn't pourable, or is a little too thick, add an additional 50 ml of double cream to your ganache and heat it gently to loosen. Allow to cool before using, because we don't want to end up with melty mush.)

Use an offset palette knife or the back of a spoon to spread the ganache out, before dusting the entire top with cocoa powder.

You can serve this straight away for a softer serve, or pop it in the fridge for a couple of hours (or overnight if your willpower allows you) for a cleaner, sturdier slice. Go ahead. Savour this life-changing moment. Doesn't it feel good?

Plant-Based Malt Tiramisu with Milk Chocolate

Serves: 10

For the Plant-based Lady Fingers
500 g plain flour, sifted
40 g cornflour, sifted
2 tsp baking powder, sifted
pinch of sea salt
400-g tin chickpeas
½ tsp cream of tartar
290 g caster sugar
70 ml vegetable oil
1½ tsp vanilla bean paste
icing sugar, for dusting

For the Soaked Lady Fingers
400 ml water
25 g caster sugar
75 g plant-based hot chocolate powder
400 g plant-based lady fingers (see above or use store-bought)

For the Ganache Layer
175 g plant-based milk chocolate, chunks or callets
200 ml plant-based double cream or coconut cream, plus extra if needed

For the Malt Cream
340 g plant-based unsalted butter, melted
700 g silken tofu
100 g vanilla plant-based yoghurt, plus extra if needed
2 tsp vanilla bean paste
175 g caster sugar
120 g plant-based malt powder or Horlicks

To Finish
cocoa powder, sifted

silicone lady finger moulds, lightly greased, or 2–3 baking trays, lined

If you aren't using store-bought lady fingers, let's get these made first. Preheat the oven to 150°C fan/170°C/gas mark 3.

In a large bowl, add the flour, cornflour, baking powder and salt and mix to combine.

Place a sieve on the bowl of a stand mixer bowl and empty out the chickpea tin to drain the aquafaba. Using the whisk attachment, mix the aquafaba on medium–high speed until it becomes stiff but not dry (this will take time, even if it's been mixing for 10 minutes and it's still watery, just keep on persisting, it will eventually get there). Add the cream of tartar and mix for a few more rotations to disperse.

Add the sugar mixture to the stand mixer, 1 tbsp at a time, keeping the mixer running on medium speed and ensuring each addition of sugar has dissolved before going in with the next lot. You can judge this by taking a little bit of the mix and smushing it between two fingers; if you can feel grains, go low and slow on speed and additions. We are after a medium–stiff peak here.

Pour the vegetable oil into the flour mix and stir. The flour will get a little clumpy, but use your fingers to break these down until you get a smooth-ish consistency. Fold the flour mixture and vanilla bean paste into the whipped aquafaba until combined. It will get quite stiff, but work through it and make sure everything is mixed well. Let the mixture sit for 5 minutes, then transfer the batter to a piping bag. Don't worry if you can see small clumps of flour, these will bake out in the oven.

Either pipe the mix into the prepared silicone moulds or pipe lines onto the lined baking tray, 1.5 cm/⅝ in. wide lines and roughly 8 cm/3¼ in. in length. Spread these out with space to rise. Dust over a sprinkling of icing sugar across the lady fingers, then bake in the oven for 22–25 minutes until lightly browned and firm. If the tops are still soft, bake for a further 5 minutes. Once they are baked, remove from the oven and allow them to sit on the trays for 10 minutes before

gently removing using a palette knife. Transfer to a cooling rack to harden and cool completely.

Now, let's make the malt chocolate lady finger soak. Add the water, sugar and hot chocolate powder to a small saucepan over a medium heat and mix. Simmer for 10–15 minutes until reduced and deepened in colour.

Next up is the chocolate ganache. Add the milk chocolate to a large bowl. Pour the cream into a saucepan and gently warm over a medium heat. Remove just before it comes to the boil and immediately pour over the chocolate. Cover the bowl with a plate for a minute before removing and mixing with a balloon whisk or rubber spatula until smooth and glossy. Set aside to cool.

For the malt cream, add all the malt cream ingredients to a food processor or blender. Mix until super smooth. If the cream looks curdled or split, add a little more yoghurt, 1 tbsp at a time, to bring back to a smooth consistency. Taste the malt cream and adjust the sweetness levels.

It is time to assemble. Evenly spread one-third of the cream over the bottom of the dish. Dollop spoonfuls of the cooled chocolate ganache on top and use the back of a spoon to swirl. Dip the sponge fingers into the cooled malt chocolate soak, letting them sit for a minute or so (as soggy as you wish) and layer them on top of the cream.

Repeat the cream, ganache, and sponge finger process one more time, then finish with a smooth layer of cream and pour the remaining chocolate ganache on top. (If your ganache isn't pourable, or is a little too thick, add an additional 50 ml of double cream to your ganache and heat it gently to loosen. Allow to cool before using.)

Use an offset palette knife or the back of a spoon to spread the ganache, before dusting the top with cocoa powder. Pop the tray in the fridge for at least 4 hours to set, but preferably overnight. This will give you a cleaner, sturdier slice.

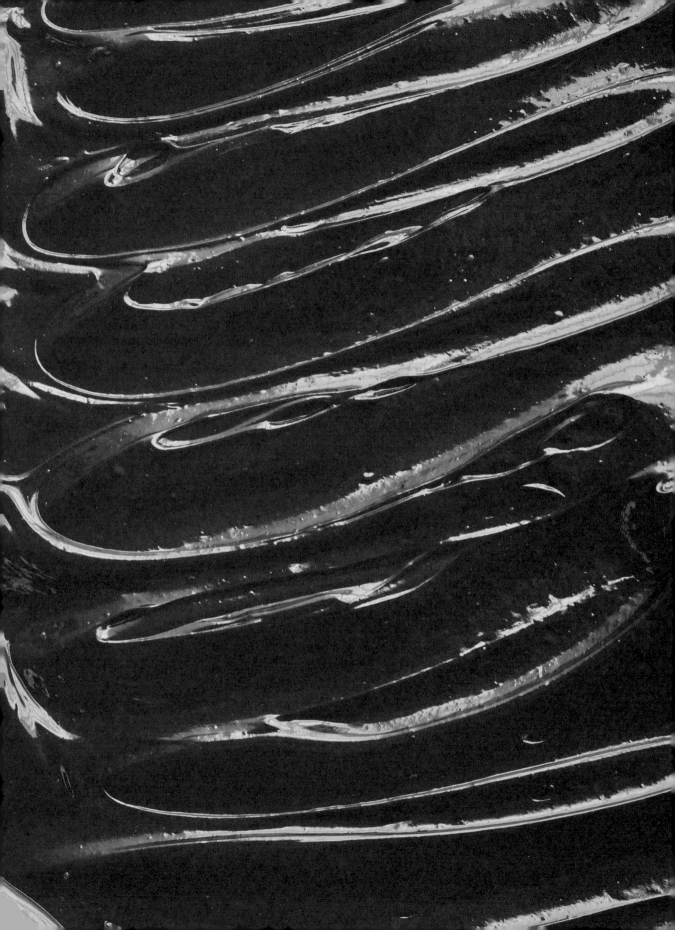

Keeping it Saucy

Total game-changer additions to be pick 'n' mixed

Butterscotch Sauce

Just think of this like caramel's better, more delicious sibling. It has all the traits of caramel, but more buttery, more velvety, and more glorious than it could ever be. Butterscotch sauce is one of those things that once you make it, you will want to use it with everything. Drizzling it a little here, pouring it on over there, adding it to cake fillings, smothering it all over proved dough, filling a baked tart case with it, scooping a dollop straight into your mouth — all are viable options as to how to use butterscotch sauce.

Butterscotch Sauce

Makes: 250 ml

150 ml double cream
75 g light soft brown sugar
45 g unsalted butter, diced
1 tsp vanilla bean paste
pinch of sea salt (optional)

In a saucepan, add the cream, sugar and butter. Cook over a low–medium heat until the sugar has dissolved, the butter has melted, and the liquid begins to bubble. Take off the heat, stir in the vanilla bean paste, and add the salt, if you like (just a tiny pinch). Give it a mix before transferring to a bowl.

Use straight away as a hot drizzle over ice cream and sponges, or leave to cool in the fridge to firm up as the perfect filling for stacked cakes or filled sweet buns and doughnuts.

Plant Based Butterscotch Sauce

Makes: 250 ml

150 ml plant-based double cream or
   coconut cream
75 g light soft brown sugar
45 g plant-based unsalted butter, diced
½ tsp cornflour, sifted
1 tsp vanilla bean paste
pinch of sea salt (optional)

In a saucepan, add the cream, sugar and butter. Cook over a low–medium heat until the sugar has dissolved, the butter has melted, and the liquid begins to bubble. Add the cornflour, and mix well until dissolved.

Take off the heat, stir in the vanilla bean paste, and add the salt, if using (just a tiny pinch). Give it a mix before transferring to a bowl.

Use straight away as a hot drizzle over ice cream and sponges, or leave to cool in the fridge to firm up as the perfect filling for stacked cakes or filled sweet buns and doughnuts.

Classic Vanilla Crème Anglaise

Must we have this conversation again about how much I love custard? It's like liquid gold to me. If I was Superman, custard would be my kryptonite. There is something super nostalgic about custard. A certain type from a tin takes me straight back to school dinners and being served up one lousy ladleful of custard. It was lumpy and tasted slightly synthetic, but it was vanilla-y and it was god damn delicious. I don't care if it's the looser, crème Anglaise pouring type or the thicker, pipeable crème pâtissière type, whichever one it is, just shove it right in my gob.

Custard is simply glorious, and a necessity in any baker's repertoire. The recipe opposite is my go-to and is a great base for adding your own flavour twists. It works well with zest from citrus fruit, a splash of almond extract, a pod or two of cardamom — basically whatever floats your boat.

Classic Vanilla Crème Anglaise

Serves: 4

125 ml double cream
125 ml full-fat milk
1½ tsp vanilla bean paste
40 g caster sugar
3 egg yolks

Add the cream, milk and vanilla bean paste to a saucepan and place over a medium heat.

Meanwhile, in another bowl, combine the sugar and egg yolks with a balloon whisk to mix well. You will need to work through the gritty, clumpy yolk stage for a minute before it becomes smooth.

Bring the cream and milk to near simmering, then pour one-third into the egg yolk mixture, mixing quickly with a whisk to avoid scrambling the egg. Pour the eggy milk mixture back into the saucepan. Keep stirring until slightly thickened and the custard coats the back of a spoon.

Take off the heat and pour into a serving jug... or your mouth.

Plant-Based Classic Vanilla Crème Anglaise

Serves: 4

150 ml full-fat soy/almond/coconut milk
100 ml plant-based double cream
1½ tsp vanilla bean paste
50 g caster sugar
25 g cornflour, sifted
a drop of yellow food colouring (optional)

Add the milk of your choice, double cream and vanilla bean paste to a saucepan and place over a medium heat.

Meanwhile, in another bowl, combine the sugar and cornflour with a balloon whisk.

Once the milk is near simmering, pour one-third into the sugar mix and whisk well before pouring back into the saucepan. Drop the heat to low before adding the food colouring to look more 'custardy'. Keep stirring until thickened. Take off the heat and pour into a serving jug.

Chocolate Ganache Three Ways: Glazed, Whipped and Piped

(GF) (EF)

Ganache is one of those super-easy, super-versatile things you can use to top bakes and construct cakes. There are three ways I wanna show you, each with their own chocolate to cream ratio, just to demonstrate its willingness to be used for basically everything.

You can have it warm, which is great for sauces, drip cakes, glazes and dips. You can have it cooled, which is great for constructing cakes, as it sets super-sturdy. It also gives that perfectly smooth layer that you want before adding a mirror glaze, works as a base for truffles, is perfect as a decadent filling for tarts, and is also pipeable. Or you can whip it, which is deliciously light and airy, that's great for topping and filling cakes, adding beautiful pipe work for decoration, and as a cheat's version of mousse. Each has their own time to shine.

You can also steep the cream with additional flavourings to jazz up your ganache. Mint, orange zest, sea salt, vanilla pods, peanut butter (yup, you read that right), all work so well in offering up another flavour dimension. You can keep this stored in the fridge for up to 2 weeks once made. Just allow it to come up to room temperature before using.

**For warm (Ratio: 1 part chocolate to
   1.4 parts cream)**
Serves: 6

280 ml double cream or coconut cream solids
   from a tin, chilled overnight and at fridge
   temp
tiny pinch of sea salt
200 g milk/dark chocolate, chunks or callets

**For cooled (Ratio: 2 parts chocolate to
   1 part cream)**
Makes: enough to crumb coat 2 x 20 cm/8-
   inch sponges

100 ml double cream or coconut cream solids
   from a tin, chilled overnight and at fridge
   temp
tiny pinch of sea salt
200 g milk/dark chocolate, chunks or callets

**For whipped (Ratio: 1 part chocolate to
   1 part cream)**
Makes: enough to fill and decorate 2 x 2 x 20
   cm/8-inch sponges

200 ml double cream or coconut cream solids
   from a tin, chilled overnight and at fridge
   temp
tiny pinch of sea salt
200 g milk/dark chocolate, chunks or callets

Pour the cream into a saucepan with the salt and place over a medium heat. If you are using tinned coconut milk, scoop out and use the chilled milk solids at the top of the tin, as this holds all the fat content (which we need). Stir occasionally to ensure the bottom doesn't catch and bring this to a near simmer, then remove from the heat and immediately add the chocolate.

Swirl the cream around to cover all the chocolate and cover the pan with either a cloth or plate. Leave to sit for 2 minutes, then use a balloon whisk or rubber spatula to mix until smooth and glossy. If the chunks haven't melted, transfer the chocolate mix to a heatproof bowl and place on top of a pan of simmering water (making sure the bottom of the bowl doesn't touch the water). Allow the chocolate to gently heat and mix.

For warm: Set aside for 15 minutes.

For cooled: Set aside for 1 hour at room temperature, then transfer to the fridge for 4 hours.

For whipped: Set aside for 1 hour at room temperature, then transfer to the fridge for 2 hours. Whisk until increased in volume and lighter in colour and texture.

Homemade Nutella

Yeah sure, the stuff you get ready-made in the jar is very good. But have you ever tried to make a homemade version? If not, you really gotta. The freshness and depth of flavour of making a batch really just hits new levels of yum. The best bit? It is super-easy to make – whether you make the dairy version or the plant-based version. Store in a jar in the fridge for up to 2 weeks once made, or keep in a sealed jar in your cupboard for up to a month. Spread this stuff over toast, use it as a cake-filler, smush it onto unbaked dough, pipe it into doughnuts, dunk your biscuits into it, fold it through buttercream – whatever you wanna do with it, it is spoon-dippingly good.

Makes: 600 g

250 g blanched hazelnuts
50 g milk chocolate, melted, or plant-based
 dark chocolate, melted
1 tsp vanilla bean paste
25 g cocoa powder, sifted
75 g icing sugar, sifted
good pinch of sea salt
milk of your choice (optional)

Preheat the oven to 180°C fan/200°C/gas mark 6.

Place the blanched hazelnuts onto a baking tray and pop in the oven for 5 minutes. Give the tray a bit of a jiggle to move the hazelnuts around, then roast for another 5 minutes. We want the hazelnuts to be a light golden-brown colour – roasting them will intensify the flavour and just make the hazelnuts even more... hazelnutty. Once the nuts have been roasted, place them into a food processor and blitz until the oils have been released and the hazelnuts have blended to a creamy consistency. You want to really work through the bitty stage so the hazelnuts become velvety smooth, so give it time and patience.

Add the melted chocolate, vanilla bean paste, cocoa powder, icing sugar and salt and blend again until smooth. If you want a looser mix, add in a few tbsp of milk and mix, otherwise transfer the homemade Nutella to a storage jar.

Keep in the fridge for up to 2 weeks. When you want to use it, let it sit at room temperature or warm in the microwave in 5-second bursts to loosen.

Wet and Dry Caramel

The end result for each of these is the same: Delicious, golden, luscious caramel. There are two ways of making it, but the key in both versions is patience. Dry caramel is just sugar in a pan, which is quicker to make, but more prone to burning. Wet caramel is a combination of water, sugar and liquid glucose, which is slower to make, but can be vulnerable to crystallising.

Salted Caramel Sauce

Makes: approx. 275 g

200 g light soft brown sugar
90 g unsalted butter, diced, or plant-based
 unsalted butter, diced
115 ml double cream or plant-based double
 cream/coconut cream
1 tsp vanilla bean paste
1 tsp sea salt

Grab yourself a pan that has a base with a large surface area and pour in the sugar. We are going with a dry caramel base, so you want this over a medium heat. Allow it to melt down into a lovely, golden-brown liquid.

Add the unsalted butter and give it all a really good mix to emulsify.

Once the butter has been mixed in well, slowly go in with the cream, while continuing to mix. Once all the cream has been added, give it all a good mix and let it continue to cook out over a medium heat for a few minutes.

Remove from the heat, add the vanilla and salt, and give it one last mix before transferring to sterilised jars. Cover and pop in the fridge to set, if you are not using straight away.

Note: This will cool to a firm texture. To loosen, pop in the microwave and heat in short, sharp bursts to the desired consistency.

Dry Caramel

Makes: approx. 300 g

300 g caster sugar
a beady eye

Grab yourself a pan that has a base with a large surface area. Pour in the sugar and place over a medium heat. Do not mix with a spoon or touch the sugar – keep a close eye on spots where the sugar has melted and gently swirl the pan. The caramelisation happens pretty quickly, so keep an eye on this. You'll know the caramel is done when it hits 160°C/320°F, or is a deep amber colour. Remove from the heat.

Wet Caramel

Makes: approx. 300 g

225 g caster sugar
60 ml water
45 g liquid glucose
patience

Prepare an ice water bath.

Grab yourself a pan that has a base with a large surface area, and pour in the sugar, water and liquid glucose. Give it all a quick mix with a wooden spoon before placing over a medium heat. Have some patience and let the water evaporate and the sugar gently melt. You can prevent any sugar crystals forming on the sides by gently brushing the edges with a wet pastry brush, but DO NOT STIR. You can swirl the pan gently, but resist the urge to get a spoon involved. Cook until the edges start to get a nice deep-golden colour.

Immediately plunge the pan into the iced water bath to stop the caramel from cooking.

Pralines, Brittles and Nougatine

Okay, so in today's lesson of who, when, where and, importantly, why, we are gonna break down what the hell all three of these are.

So, let's kick things off with a brittle. This delicious hard, sugared confectionery is super-easy to make and equally as easy to eat. Think of a set caramel/butterscotch sauce loaded with peanuts, pecans, or almonds, which is then broken down into pieces ready to be devoured. A great addition to the tops of cakes and pastries, or eaten as they are — they also make for lovely edible gifts at Christmas, if you can bear to part ways with it.

Praline isn't cooked to the same temperature as a brittle, and, more often than not, is blitzed down to form a gorgeously nutty, rich, indulgent paste, which is great for filling cakes, choux buns, Chelsea buns and tarts, and adding to ice creams, flavouring dough, or using as a biscuit filling. Alternatively, you can blitz the set praline to a dust and then use this dust to make sugar tuiles.

And as for nougatine, this is basically a super-thin set praline in disguise, except it uses flaked almonds in a set caramel, which can be rolled to create decorative pieces for cakes and desserts. Despite it looking fancy, it's probably the easiest to make out of the lot.

Lesson over. Now let's make 'em!

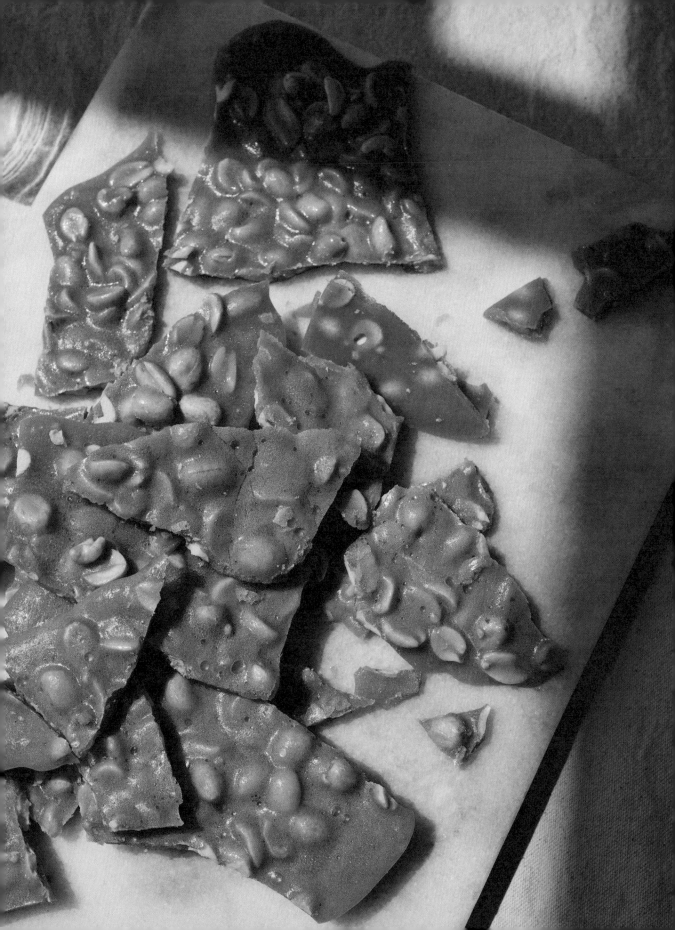

Salted Peanut Brittle ⓖⓕ ⓔⓕ

Makes: approx. 500 g

200 g caster sugar
170 g golden syrup
120 ml water
110 g unsalted butter, diced
225 g blanched peanuts
1 tsp sea salt
1 tsp bicarbonate of soda

2 baking trays, lined with silicone mats
   or greaseproof paper

In a large saucepan, add the sugar, golden syrup and water. Place over a medium heat and stir occasionally until the sugar dissolves. Once the sugar has dissolved, bring it to the boil. As soon as the sugar begins to boil, add the diced butter to the pan, stirring well to mix.

Let the sugar syrup do its thing until it reaches 110°C/230°F (known as the thread stage). If you don't have a thermometer probe, grab a glass of cold water and drip some of the sugar syrup from a spoon into the water. The sugar should form thin threads.

Once it's reached the temperature, stir it occasionally. When it has reached 140°C/284°F, add the peanuts and salt, and give it all another good mix.

As soon as it hits the hard crack stage, which is at 150°C/302°F, remove the pan from the heat, add the bicarbonate of soda and mix well. It will begin to froth up and get bubbly, as it would if you were making honeycomb. Immediately pour it onto the prepared baking trays (silicone mats are best here) and leave to cool completely.

Once set hard, break into smaller pieces and store in an airtight container to retain that snap.

Praline (GF) (EF)

Makes: Enough to fill a /3 x 18-cm/7-in. stacked cake

100 g caster sugar
100 g blanched hazelnuts, almonds or pecans

baking tray, lined with a silicone mat
  or greaseproof paper

Add the sugar to a large, heavy-bottomed pan. Give the pan a shake to spread the sugar evenly and place over a medium heat. The key here is to not touch the sugar at all – just let it do its thing. We are basically making a dry caramel, so we want the sugar to become a nice, deep amber colour before we add the nuts.

Because you don't want to stir the sugar, occasionally swirl the pan to distribute any melted pockets of caramel. Dry caramel is super easy to make, but incredibly easy to burn.

Once the sugar has completely melted to a dark golden-brown colour, add the nuts and give it all a good mix with a wooden spoon or rubber spatula. You want to make sure all the nuts are coated before you scoop out the praline onto the prepared baking tray (I always use a silicone mat here for ease).

Try to press out the praline into an even layer, so it all sets at the same time. Let the praline set at room temperature – do not put it in the fridge.

When the praline is set, use it as you wish. Keep it chunky, blitz it to a dust, or blitz it to a paste.

Tip: Roast your blanched nuts before you use them for an intensified flavour, or add a sprinkling of sea salt when adding the nuts for an added flavour profile.

Nougatine (GF) (EF)

Makes: approx. 400 g

250 g caster sugar
60 ml water
120 g flaked almonds

2 baking trays, lined with silicone mats
  or greaseproof paper

Add the sugar and water to a large saucepan, before placing over a medium heat until the sugar is dissolved. The key is not to touch the liquid, as this has a wet caramel base. Use a wet pastry brush to remove any crystals that form.

Once the liquid has turned syrupy, golden brown and reached 170°C/338°F, add the nuts. Turn down the heat and use a rubber spatula to coat the nuts with the caramel.

Pour the nougatine onto the prepared baking trays and let it sit at room temperature to cool. Place another sheet of greaseproof paper directly on top of the nougatine and use a rolling pin to flatten to a thin, even layer.

Once thin enough, use a knife or biscuit cutter to cut out your nougatine or place the sheet over a bowl to mould – make sure it is cool enough to touch before handling, because this stuff is HOT!

Coulis, Compotes and Jams

By definition, a coulis is a smooth, thickened, pourable fruit sauce strained to remove any lumps. A coulis can be flavoured with alcohol or icing sugar for sweetness, and can be a great for topping meringues or pavlovas, or drizzling over a sponge loaf, ice creams, or sundaes (why do we not sundae as much as we should sundae?).

For a compote, the fruit and sugar are gently cooked to break down into a syrupy, fruity little number. I always like to fold in a bit of uncooked fruit at the end for bite and texture. It's perfect for topping a stack of pancakes, adding to crumble bars, or filling doughnuts, pastries, sandwich cakes, biscuits and everything else in between.

And jam? Well, jam is just jam, isn't it?

Coulis (GF) (EF)

Makes: approx. 400 g

400 g fruit of your choice, e.g., raspberries
2 tbsp icing sugar, sifted

Add the fruit and icing sugar to a saucepan, stirring over a medium heat. We want the fruit to begin to release its juices and begin to break down – this should only take a few minutes.

Using a hand blender, blitz the fruit and released juices in a bowl until mushy.

Pass the fruit through a fine sieve to remove any seeds.

Use straight away or transfer to a jar and keep for up to 2 days in the fridge.

Compote ⒼⒻ ⒺⒻ

Makes: approx. 500 g

500 g fruit of your choice, e.g. stone fruit or
   berries (destoned and roughly chopped)
50 g caster sugar, plus extra if needed
squeeze of lemon juice

In a saucepan, add three-quarters of the fruit.
Add the sugar and lemon juice. Stir and place
over a medium heat until the fruit starts to break
down and become syrupy.

Add the remaining one-quarter of fruit. Cook for
a few minutes before removing from the heat.

Taste the compote. If you need more sweetness,
add more sugar, ½ tsp at a time. Leave to cool
and store in the fridge for up to 3 days or in the
freezer for 3 months.

Note: If you require a looser compote with a
saucier finish, add 2–3 tbsp water when adding
the sugar and lemon juice, and bring to the
boil, before reducing the heat and adding the
remaining fruit.

Jam ⒼⒻ ⒺⒻ

Makes: approx. 500 g

500 g fruit of your choice (destoned and
   roughly chopped)
400–500 g jam sugar (depending on whether
   you want a looser or firmer set)

This really couldn't be any simpler, just add
everything to a pan and mix. The lower quantity
of jam sugar will give a looser set; the higher
quantity will give a firmer set.

Place the pan over a low heat to give the
sugar time to dissolve, before bringing to the
boil. You want to bring this to a temperature
of 105°C/221°F to set. If you don't have a
thermometer probe, you can tell when the fruit
is jammy when the mixture begins to relax into

a slower boil and froth has accumulated on the
sides of the pan. The surface of the fruit should
have a sheen to it and will have thickened
considerably in texture. Once you've reached
this point, remove from the heat and transfer the
jam to sterilised jars while hot.

Jam stored in jars will keep for up to 3 weeks in
the fridge, or, if stored in a sealed jar, can be
kept in the cupboard for 3 months.

Note: My advice is always undercooking the
jam if in doubt. You can always bring it back up
to the boil again if it hasn't set enough, rather
than the other way around. Even if the jam
seems loose, it will thicken once cooled. Once
you've nailed how to make a basic jam, begin to
introduce flavours – spices, herbs, or a variety
of fruits.

Every Type of Curd
You Curd Ever Want

Curd is a little bit magical. The thing I love about curd is a) how damn easy it is to make and b) how you can literally make any fruit a curd. An orange? Curd. Strawberries? Bad boy curd. Raspberries? Little tart curd. Passion fruit? The A-Lister of curds. Lemons? The OG of curds. Mango? The curd you ain't ready for. Cherries? CURD IT UP BABY. Any fruit, curdless possibilities.

On top of that, the ways in which you can use it are endless. Add it to a trifle, cake, tiramisu (I make a mean lemon, white chocolate and basil one), sandwich it between biscuits, add it to bread, spoon it on top of whipped yoghurt.

Both ways of making curd couldn't be simpler, but I'm gonna level with you: While you can get a velvety smooth finish by using egg yolks, my go-to curd recipe is the vegan sort. Why? No egg whites are going to waste, minimal ingredients, and it takes even less time to make it. It is so damn quick and idiot-proof, you could do it with your eyes closed.

For both, I have included recipes for my fave passion fruit curd and also a lemon curd. The ingredients change slightly, while the method is exactly the same. You can use either recipe as a base for any other fruit purée, just adjust the sweetness or tartness as required.

Every Type of Curd You Curd Ever Want

Makes: approx. 350 g

For the Passion Fruit Curd
2 large eggs
2 large egg yolks
12 passion fruit, pulp only, deseeded
75 g caster sugar
1 tsp cornflour, sifted
½ tsp vanilla bean paste
75 g unsalted butter, room temp

For the Lemon Curd
2 large eggs
2 large eggs yolks
grated zest and freshly squeezed juice of
   5 lemons
100 g caster sugar
1 tsp cornflour, sifted
½ tsp vanilla bean paste
75 g unsalted butter, room temp

To start, place the eggs and egg yolks (make sure you save the whites for meringue/pavlova/buttercreams, etc) ino a large heatproof bowl with all the remaining ingredients, except the softened butter. Give it a good old mix with a wooden spoon.

Place the bowl over a saucepan of simmering water and stir until the sugar has dissolved and the butter has melted. Keep over the heat until the mixture has thickened slightly and coats the back of a spoon; this should take about 15 minutes. I always like to give it a good mix with a balloon whisk every now and then to ensure there are no lumps and it remains silky smooth.

Once it has thickened, add the butter and mix well until combined.

Pour into sterilised jars and leave to cool. If you are using it straight away, just leave to cool, but make sure you cover the top with some re-usable parchment to prevent a skin from forming.

Tip: If you're storing for later, this will keep well in the fridge for up to 2–3 weeks or in the freezer for 2 months. Allow to thaw in the fridge overnight the day before you want to use it.

Plant-Based Every Type of Curd You Curd Ever Want

Makes: approx. 350 g

For the Lemon Curd
150 g caster sugar, or to taste
25 g cornflour, sifted
275 ml coconut milk solids, from a tin
175 ml freshly squeezed lemon juice, grated
    zest and pulp (squeeze and scoop it all out!)
1 tsp vanilla bean paste
yellow food colouring (optional)
10 g plant-based unsalted butter

For the Passion Fruit Curd
150 g caster sugar, or to taste
25 g cornflour, sifted
275 ml coconut milk solids, from a tin
12 passion fruit, pulp only, seeded
squeeze of lemon juice, or to taste
1 tsp vanilla bean paste
10 g plant-based unsalted butter

Add all the ingredients, except the butter, to a saucepan. Mix well using a balloon whisk and then place over a medium heat. Stir until the curd has thickened and coats the back of a spoon. Taste and adjust the sweetness or tartness by adding more caster sugar or lemon, as needed.

Add the butter, and mix well until melted and combined, before removing from heat.

Leave to cool for 15 minutes before transferring to a sterilised jar. This will keep in the fridge for up to 2 weeks.

Unsweetened Apple Sauce (GF) (EF)

This sauce is an important element when eliminating eggs from a bake, as it plays a similar role — especially when used in bread baking. When making an enriched bread dough, the eggs don't work as the raising agent — that's what yeast is for. Instead, the eggs make it fluffier and lighter in texture, inhibiting a tight gluten formation. This is similar to any other fat, meaning it has room to expand. Where the non-plant-based recipes use a combination of eggs and butter, the plant-based versions often use a combo of apple sauce and butter. The apple sauce is unsweetened, so as to not affect the overall taste of the bake.

Once you've made it, store in a sterilised jar for up to a week in the fridge, or pop it in the freezer for up to 1 month. For other useful substitutions, check out The Essentials chapter (see pages 310–11). I've got a whole list of egg subs, dairy subs, fat subs, THE LOT.

Makes: 250 ml

500 g Gala or Pink Lady apples (about 6 large), peeled, cored and roughly chopped
40 ml water
freshly squeezed juice of 1 lemon

Add the apples to a large pan with the water and lemon juice. Give it a little stir before placing over a high heat and bringing to the boil.

Once boiling, reduce to a medium heat and cook for a further 10 minutes until the apples have softened. Stir this often to prevent the bottom from catching.

Place the softened apples, plus any liquid from the pan, into a blender or food processor. Blitz to a purée.

Add the puréed apples back to the pan, bring back to the boil, then remove from the heat and transfer to a sterilised jar. Place the lid on and leave to cool completely.

Sugar Syrups (GF) (EF)

When I first started baking, I had no idea that one little nifty tip would make my baking 'handshake worthy' on *Bake Off*. Lemme introduce you to a simple game-changing move – drizzling your sponges in a sugar syrup.

A sugar syrup is another opportunity to add more flavour. Add some lemon zest and juice for a sugar syrup for your lemon drizzle. Add a touch of almond extract for a cherry cake syrup. Add some coconut water and desiccated coconut for a syrup for a mango cake. Go in with a splash of booze, fruit juice, or a dollop of curd. Go wild and get your Willy Wonka on.

Makes: enough to soak 3 x 18-cm/7-in. sponges

For the Simple Vanilla Syrup
125 ml water
110 g caster sugar
1 tsp vanilla extract or vanilla bean paste

For the Almond Sugar Syrup
125 ml water
110 g caster sugar
1½ tsp almond extract

For the Lemon Sugar Syrup
75 ml freshly squeezed lemon juice
grated zest of 1 lemon
50 ml water
110 g caster sugar
1 tbsp lemon curd (see pages 300–1)

For the Coconut Sugar Syrup
75 ml coconut water
75 ml water
100 g caster sugar
25 g desiccated coconut

For the Mint Sugar Syrup
125 ml water
110 g caster sugar
4 fresh mint leaves

Add all the ingredients to a saucepan and mix. Place over a medium heat and simmer for 15 minutes until the sugar has dissolved and the water has thickened to a loose syrup consistency – one you can easily drizzle.

Remove from the heat and leave to cool.

303

Royal and Water Icing

Water icing is basically just that. Water (or your liquid of choice) plus icing sugar equals something akin to a lovely glossy glaze. The amount of liquid added will determine how translucent or opaque the icing is – think of your iced finger bun topping for a thicker glaze or a Krispy Kreme original glazed doughnut for a thinner, silkier glaze.

Royal icing, on the other hand, includes egg whites or egg white powder, resulting in a hard, candy-like texture once fully dried, making it ideal for iced biscuits and cookies, coating Christmas cakes, decorating and constructing gingerbread houses, and intricate wedding cake details.

Water Icing (GF) (EF)

Makes: enough to glaze 12 iced buns/doughnuts

200 g icing sugar, sifted
25–60 ml water, depending on whether you
   want a thick or thin glaze
flavouring of your choice (optional)

Add the icing sugar to a bowl. Pour in the water in stages, so you can monitor the consistency.

Go in with the food flavouring of your choice, if using. Vanilla bean paste, almond extract, citrus juice, GO WILD.

Royal Icing (GF)

Makes: enough to decorate ½ batch of Gingerbread (see pages 184–5)

230 g icing sugar, sifted
45 g egg whites
food colouring (optional)

Add the icing sugar to a bowl with the egg whites. Use an electric hand whisk or balloon whisk to whisk until smooth. Check the consistency: Too thick, add more egg white; too thin, add more icing sugar. You are after a fluid but firm consistency.

Add your chosen food colouring, if using, mix well and transfer to piping bags.

Plant-Based Royal Icing (GF) (EF)

Makes: enough to decorate ½ batch of Gingerbread (see pages 184–5)

50 ml aquafaba (liquid from tinned chickpeas)
1 tsp almond extract (or whatever flavour extract you fancy)
325 g icing sugar, sifted, plus extra if needed
food colouring (optional)

Pour the aquafaba into a large bowl alongside the flavouring of your choice. Use a balloon whisk to whisk until frothy – this will take a few minutes of rigorous whisking.

Sift in the icing sugar and mix until smooth. We are looking for a firm but pipeable consistency, so if your mixture is looking too loose, add another 5 g of icing sugar, mix, and reassess.

Now is when you would add the food colouring of your choice, if using, and transfer to piping bags. Keep the mixture covered when you're not using it as it will form a crust.

The Essentials

'Alexa – what the hell is the equivalent of 100 g in cups?'

Conversions

My google searches are wild. Everything from temperature conversions to what happens if your dog eats XYZ... Here's a few handy little conversion charts that will stop you from losing your damn mind.

As a note, if you are ever in doubt of how to convert a temperature, you need to multiply °C by 9, divide by 5 and then add 32 for its Fahrenheit equivalent. It's some long winded, odd maths but it stacks up, I promise!

Temperature Conversion Chart

Celsius / °C	Fan / °C	Fahrenheit / °F	Gas Mark
130	150	250	½
140	160	275	1
150	170	300	2
160	180	320	3
170	190	338	4
180	200	356	4
190	210	375	5
200	220	400	6
210	230	410	7
220	240	425	7
230	250	450	8
240	260	464	9

Weight

Metric	Imperial
5 g	$^1/_8$ oz
10 g	¼ oz
15 g	½ oz
25/30 g	1 oz
35 g	1¼ oz
40 g	1½ oz
50 g	1¾ oz
55 g	2 oz
60 g	2¼ oz
70 g	2½ oz
85 g	3 oz
90 g	3¼ oz
100 g	3½ oz
115 g	4 oz
125 g	4½ oz
140 g	5 oz
150 g	5½ oz
175 g	6 oz
200 g	7 oz
225 g	8 oz
250 g	9 oz
275 g	9¾ oz
280 g	10 oz
300 g	10½ oz
325 g	11½ oz

Metric	Imperial
350 g	12 oz
375 g	13 oz
400 g	14 oz
425 g	15 oz
450 g	1 lb
500 g	1 lb 2 oz
550 g	1 lb 4 oz
600 g	1 lb 5 oz
650 g	1 lb 7 oz
700 g	1 lb 9 oz
750 g	1 lb 10 oz
800 g	1 lb 12 oz
850 g	1 lb 14 oz
900 g	2 lb
950 g	2 lb 2 oz
1 kg	2 lb 4 oz
1.25 kg	2 lb 12 oz
1.3 kg	3 lb
1.5 kg	3 lb 5 oz
1.6 kg	3 lb 8 oz
1.8 kg	4 lb
2 kg	4 lb 8 oz
2.25 kg	5 lb
2.5 kg	5 lb 8 oz
2.7 kg	6 lb
3 kg	6 lb 8 oz

Liquid Volume

Metric	Imperial
1.25 ml	¼ tsp
2.5 ml	½ tsp
5 ml	1 tsp
10 ml	2 tsp
15 ml	1 tbsp/3 tsp
30 ml	2 tbsp
45 ml	3 tbsp
60 ml	4 tbsp
75 ml	5 tbsp
90 ml	6 tbsp
15 ml	½ fl oz
30 ml	1 fl oz
50 ml	2 fl oz
75 ml	2½ fl oz
100 ml	3½ fl oz
125 ml	4 fl oz
150 ml	5 fl oz
175 ml	6 fl oz
200 ml	7 fl oz
225 ml	8 fl oz

Metric	Imperial
250 ml	9 fl oz
300 ml	10 fl oz
350 ml	12 fl oz
400 ml	14 fl oz
425 ml	15 fl oz
450 ml	16 fl oz
500 ml	18 fl oz
600 ml	1 pint
700 ml	1¼ pints
850 ml	1½ pints
1 litre	1¾ pints
1.2 litres	2 pints
1.3 litres	2¼ pints
1.4 litres	2½ pints
1.5 litres	2¾ pints
1.7 litres	3 pints
2 litres	3½ pints
2.5 litres	4½ pints
2.8 litres	5 pints
3 litres	5¼ pints

This for That

Here's where you'll find little swaps, tricks to convert and handy substitutions for the times where you thought you had your sh*t together, but maybe not as much as you hoped. I get it, sometimes you have this and not that. Especially when you're trying out plant-based baking, it is always good to have a number of options to fall back on.

Egg Substitution

There's pretty much a decent branded substitute or replacement for all dairy items now. That being said, there are other ways of replacing key ingredients. What you have to do is figure out what role the egg is playing in the recipe; for colour, for richness, for texture, for tenderness. They normally play one of two starring roles:

- **As a binding agent:** Meaning they are used to bring all the ingredients together.

- **As a leavening agent:** Meaning they help the ingredients rise.

Everything shown below is the equivalent of 1 whole egg. Increase the quantities according to how many eggs the recipe specifies.

Binding Agent

Flax egg:
1 tbsp ground flaxseed + 3 tbsp water
= *Whisk until gelatinous.*

Chia egg:
1 tbsp chia seeds + 3 tbsp water
= *Stir and rest for 15 minutes before using.*

Unsweetened applesauce: 60 g for a medium egg; 80 g for a large egg (see page 302)

Banana egg: 75 g mashed banana (this will come with a distinct flavour, so be warned)

Aquafaba egg yolk: 15 ml aquafaba

Leavening Agent

Baking oil egg:
2 tbsp water + 2 tsp baking powder +
1 tsp vegetable oil
= *Whisk until mixed and rest for 5 minutes.*

Commercial egg replacer: There are lots of these on the market (check the instructions on how to use)

Aquafaba egg white:
30 ml aquafaba + ⅛ tsp cream of tartar
= *Whisk until stiff but not dry.*

Aquafaba whole egg: 45 ml aquafaba
= *Whisk until foamy.*

Flour Substitution

There are a ton of flour substitutions on the market, but what happens when there is no raising agent involved? As a general rule of thumb, use the below to convert any plain flour into a self-raising version of itself:

150 g plain flour + 2 tsp baking powder = *Mix well to distribute before using.*

The benefit of making self-raising flour this way is ensuring an adequate ratio of leavening agent to flour. Using straight from a bag of self-raising flour leaves you at the mercy of the baking gods. (Saying that, I will always use this if available, because... anything to cut corners, and I am there.)

Dairy Substitution

We are luckily spoilt for choice in this arena. But I will share some quick tips on how to make some of them at home, should you not have any.

For 100 g buttermilk

100 ml full-fat or soy/coconut milk + ½ tbsp lemon juice
= *Mix and leave to sit for 5–10 minutes until lightly curdled.*

100 ml full-fat milk or soy/coconut milk + ¼ tbsp white wine vinegar
= *Mix and leave to sit for 5 minutes until lightly curdled.*

100 ml full-fat milk or soy/coconut milk + ¾ tsp cream of tartar
= *Mix and use straight away.*

100 ml plain natural yoghurt or plant-based yoghurt + ½ tsp lemon juice
= *Mix and use straight away.*

For 100 g soured cream

100 ml double cream or plant-based double cream + ½ tbsp lemon juice
= *Mix and leave to sit at room temperature for 24 hours until thickened.*

100 ml double cream or plant-based double cream + ½ tbsp white wine vinegar
= *Mix and leave to sit at room temperature for 24 hours until thickened.*

100 g plain natural yoghurt or plant-based yoghurt + 5 ml lemon juice
= *Mix and use straight away.*

Index

Acknowledgements

This page has been harder to write than my whole entire book. Not because I am a diva and the only person I want to thank is myself (only partly true) but because I am bound by page limitations and now my complimentary word vomit must be restricted.

While this book technically has my name on it, taking all the glory for my literary first born would be crazily unfair. Not to brag (that's a lie), but I essentially had the Avengers of the literary world working on this baby.

First up, Heather and Sara. I don't know how you deal with my endless daily gripes but you either a) are angels or b) have a voodoo doll of me. Either way, I hope you know my appreciation for you both runs deep. Thanks to the wider Insanity team for feedback on the first proposal (we all know it was a pile of pants), and particularly Kirsty and Neil. You've championed me in different ways (albeit both with the tenacity of a bulldog) – your support from near and far has been invaluable.

To Lucy and Steph at Pavilion, you understood the vision straight from the off. No arm twisting, nor bribery required, which was mind boggling. To Ellen, for your unwavering confidence in me. You are a dream to work with, I couldn't have been blessed with a better editor. To Alice, for turning the gazillion creative ideas in my head into something more beautiful than I could've ever imagined. The way you both just got 'it' made this whole process a complete joy, so thank you for making me feel pride in myself that I didn't know existed.

On to the ultimate book shooting dream team: Matt, you're a wonderfully talented human. It should be illegal how good your hugs and playlists are. You constantly blew my mind with the magic you were able to capture. Joss, you crazy bundle of chaotic, calming happiness. I would have been lost without you (and probably still there baking away). Elle, you were the essential third musketeer. Thank you for never doubting my written rambles. And lastly, Rachel. Your vision is SO inspiring, I hope you understand just how talented you are. You made me feel so proud of my bakes, so thank you for that gift.

Bell Blood, thank you for coming on to this project and sorry for the countless amends. I know you must secretly hate me, but I'm okay with that. I would hate me, too.

To my bonkers family. Eternal thanks to my favourites Son and Nik, BFF Tarv and GBFF Antony for all the advice and for eating everything I've made – from the good, the bad and the ugly. I would be lost in life without you.

To my mum, for helping me without even knowing it. You blessed me with an insatiable hunger for food and have never doubted anything I have chosen to do. Even if it did mean making myself unemployed and miserable. This book, and everything else, truly is for you.

A loving thanks to my two very best friends, James and Milo. Life wouldn't quite be as fun if it wasn't for you both. James, your patience knows no bounds and your faith in me is the greatest comfort. I know I'm not short of cheerleaders in my life (hi bonkers family) but no one sings my praises louder than you. And Milo, my trusty crumb hoover. You truly are the goodest little boy.

Lastly and wholeheartedly, thanks to you. It's because of you that I get to do this.

Luckiest woman, ever.

Desserts are like the BAD BOYS of the baking world. They're only about for a short time, and the *less* you have, the *more* you want. You can *never* get enough, and they are gone before you know it.

Ghosted forever...
or at least until the *next time*.